Sharon Dawn Feingold

He Loves Me, He Loves Me Not, But God Does

A true story about Internet dating and finding God in the midst of it!

A Molding Messengers Publication

He loves Me, He Loves Me Not, But God Does

Copyright © 2023 by Sharon Dawn Feingold

All rights reserved. Printed in the United States of America. No part of this book may be used or reproduced in any manner whatsoever without written permission except in the case of brief quotations embodied in critical articles or reviews.

This book is a work of fiction. Names, characters, businesses, organizations, places, events and incidents either are the product of the author's imagination or are used fictitiously. Any resemblance to actual persons, living or dead, events, or locales is entirely coincidental.

For information about permission to reproduce selections from this book, Write to Molding Messengers, LLC at 1728 NE Miami Gardens Drive, Suite #111, North Miami Beach, FL, 33179 or email Info.Staff@MoldingMessengers.com or visit www.MoldingMessengers.com

Library of Congress Control Number: 2023903048

Print ISBN: 979-8-218-15123-2

eBook ISBN: 979-8-218-15124-9

Unless otherwise indicated, Bible quotations are taken from:

New King James Version (NKJV) of the Holy Bible,
Copyright 1982by Thomas Nelson, Inc.

New International Version (NIV) Holy Bible, New International Version NIV Copyright 1973, 1978, 1984, 2011 by Biblica, Inc.

New Living Translation (NLT) Holy Bible. New Living Translation Copyright 1996, 2004, 2007 by Tyndale House Foundation

King James Version (KJV). By Public Domain

A Molding Messengers Publication

Foreword

Isn't it beyond our wildest imagination to witness God transform our lives? In our nearly 10 years of friendship, I have seen my very fidgety adult friend who had to be told "not to run through the halls at work," pivot that exact intense energy for His good, to those who are called for His purpose. Sounds just like what God can do, right?

It was a privilege to hear the pre-edition of **He Loves Me, He Loves Me Not, But God Does** reading many years ago at a dinner party. Read aloud with passion and drawn by her well-timed emotional emphasis, our minds drifted into her past while engulfed in literally knee-slapping laughter throughout the evening. But that portion of Sharon's journey was not ready to be told abroad, because the rest of the story was still unwritten. What this released edition now captures is the true presence of Divine intervention.

Everyday God is pouring into Sharon, her family, and her countless friends. I am happy to take part in her journey and His plan. I've learned that God puts you in Sharon's path for a reason. She is driven with a purpose, a high calling, and is a profound advocate and bold soldier for the Lord. The twists and turns that grew her character and changed her life throughout the years are riveting.

All her joy, spunk, and social graces are revealed in these chapters. Beyond doubt, at the very least you will be encouraged and entertained. You are inevitably reading this book for a reason, that's also yet to be told, so jump in, get ready for the ride, and be blessed.

Clearly, we all have a story, but this one is funny. Enjoy!

Kim Sullivan

Friend and Sister-in-Christ, September 2022

I met Sharon at work 4½ years ago. I had never imagined how God would use her to help me with a very difficult crisis I was going through during the pandemic. I believe this book will touch many lives. It will not only impact women's hearts, but men's as well. I admire many qualities Sharon has. God gave her several gifts, but what I admire the most, is the LOVE she has for her Savior, Jesus Christ, her Messiah. She doesn't waste a minute talking about Jesus, our Messiah with everyone, and she spreads the Gospel so passionately, whether she is out walking or shopping in a store. I know the real purpose she wrote this book is to give many out there the Good News of Salvation through the ONLY one who saves: Jesus Christ!

With Him, *Amparo Velasco*

I vividly remember seeing my mother's life become unfolded when she lost the love of her life. She was determined to find someone else who would replace him and who would fill her once again with love and happiness. I wanted to help her, so I introduced her to internet dating. I told her she needed to put herself out there and I sat down with her and showed her a website to set up a dating profile and how to use it. I even helped pick out her picture. She was set to find the love of her life on the internet. I don't think anything could have prepared her for internet dating and the journey she embarked on over a course of many years.

When she started her dating journey, I remember asking her about some of the dates she went on whenever she and I went out to eat. Very often she would come home hysterical laughing or crying, maybe even both. I always say one must realize their journey to understand their destination. I never could have imagined the journey she had just embarked on and the person she would become today from this journey. I bet she would say the same about me.

I'm elated she put her stories on paper and I think you'll enjoy them as much as I have over the years. I'm proud of her, and I'm glad she has created an opportunity to share these stories with you.

I love you, Mom.

Adam Feingold

Dedication

This book took me a long time to write, so I want to dedicate it to family and friends who continuously cheered me on to complete it. Thank you to my sons Adam and Jeremy Feingold who always encouraged me to get it done, and to James Gilman who was always there front and center to encourage, help and be a part of it. To my good friend Celeste Chinelly Fisher who offered a hand when I got stuck in places and needed her help. To my friend and mentor Donna Hartley who know matter what burdens she is facing, she is always a phone call away to bring me through whatever crisis I might be struggling with. And most of all, I dedicate this book to Jesus Christ, my Lord and Savior, who without Him, there would be no book, no salvation and no future in heaven that awaits us when we have faith and believe.

Table of Contents

Dedication VI

Introduction 1

Chapter 1 - The Breakup 4

Chapter 2 - The Dating Game Begins 7

Chapter 3 - Scott 10

Chapter 4 - A Few Bad Men 14

Chapter 5 - Henry 26

Chapter 6 - Speed Dating 29

Chapter 7 - A Lock & Key Party 36

Chapter 8 - An Old Fashion Mixer 42

Chapter 9 - Ronald 51

Chapter 10 - Gary 57

Chapter 11 - Back to Ronald 65

Chapter 12 - MelodyofLove.com 75

Chapter 13 - Single Mingle 84

Chapter 14 - Some Really Strange Men 95

Chapter 15 - Marc 106

Chapter 16 - New Jersey Jim 116

Chapter 17 - Match and Catch 131

Chapter 18 - Men Who Fell Off the Face of the Earth 150

Chapter 19 - Good Men Gone Bad 159

Chapter 20 - Run Like the Wind 180

Chapter 21 - Looking for Men in Other States 194

Chapter 22 - Alex 202

Chapter 23 - Steve 213

Chapter 24 - FBI John 230

Chapter 25 - Bruce 250

Chapter 26 - Justin 260

Chapter 27 - A Bucket of Fish 267

Chapter 28 - A Weekend at Sea 274

Chapter 29 - My Happy Ending 298

Epilogue 310

Author Bio 318

Introduction

I never set out to write a book on dating, let alone internet dating. I never thought I would have had to date. I really believed in my heart, someone would have come along and loved me for everything I am and everything I would be for them. I never in a million years dreamed that dating would become a part of my life. A series of ups and down, very few successes and multiple failures would summarize dating for me so far.

Women like me are snatched up in a heartbeat. I am athletic, playful, pretty, petite, and independent, yet sometimes I can be like a whimsical character in a romantic tale. Everyone thinks I am adorable and yet everything about my dating past, present and future to come has gone wrong or maybe we should say unexplainably cloudy.

There are so many common myths about dating, especially internet dating. It can be a great place to meet someone, and then again it can break down your self-esteem and make you see yourself in a way you never had. It can be addicting like a slot machine in a casino, and when you lose in one club, you feel another club or internet site will bring you a win. This book is not a "how to" or a "how not to" on dating. It is my life, my story, my heart. It will not ease anyone's pain or show anyone how to make it work, it will let you know that if you are failing at it, that you are not alone and that maybe we are all looking for love in all the wrong places.

Maybe love needs to find you instead of you looking for it. When I started thinking about my failed dating experiences, I thought maybe this all goes back to my childhood, my infancy, and maybe love would not find me until I worked out all the other things that were not working in my life. I needed answers to questions I just couldn't solve and maybe for once I needed to come face to face with the question: "What was I doing that was scaring everyone away from me? Could it really be me? Could my whole life have surfaced and come to a head in these internet dating years that I was alone." I needed to know. I needed to analyze, and I needed to fix it.

I had become a desperate woman, scared and lonely and afraid that I would end up the rest of my life alone. I would go always from one dating site to the next. Dating had become a job, a career, and a calling. If it killed me, I would find my soul mate!

I couldn't stop, I couldn't slow down. I was driven by fear, rejection, loneliness, and by most, myself. I had reduced myself to feeling that I was not and would never be complete without a man in my life to love me. At this time in my life these feelings and thoughts had taken over my entire body and soul. I couldn't breathe without feeling pain in my heart that there was no one special in my life.

This is my story and my dating journey that I need to share. This is the journey, the road that has led me to some of my own answers and my own self-discovery of who I am. God said, *"To everything there is a season, and a time to every purpose under the heavens" (Ecclesiastes 3:3 KJV).* I think this journey through hell was meant to bring me closer to heaven. It taught me that I will never find my true happiness in man and that the men I kept meeting would continue to disappoint me, hurt me, and break down my self-esteem over and over again. The only way I would ever learn to love myself, and accept myself for everything I am, would be to draw closer to God, my Creator, my Father, my Lord who loved me just the way I was. I learned that without this hard, pathetic path that I was tumbling on, I might have never found the arms of my Savior Jesus. God opened my eyes after many dark years of internet dating and He taught me that my worth would only be found in Him. In this entire universe, God would be the one who would never leave or forsake me for He loves me.

Chapter 1 - The Breakup

In January of 1997, I decided to leave my husband of 12 years. I had two children, boys, ages seven and ten. They were my life. The marriage was nothing more than a marriage, no romance, no love, and no tenderness. I got my fill of love from my kids. They made me happy. I was 37 and always felt lonely. I spent 12 years sad that I didn't have a best friend. Jason, my ex-husband, was hardly home and he never really touched me or kissed me. I felt empty all the time.

Then out of the blue, a man living with his family in my neighborhood, named Mitch called Jason for some carpentry help. I always thought Mitch was cute, and after Jason helped Mitch, he and I became good friends. His wife had taken his kids and left him. For weeks he and I walked together every night.

The first time he kissed me, I knew he was it, the one I was supposed to be with. Two months later I divorced Jason. The kids and I moved in with Mitch. I had a nice life with Mitch. My kids were happy, it was the first time in my life I had no money problems, and we bought a beautiful house with a pool in Boca Raton. I was able to quit my full-time job and he helped me create a startup, running my story-telling business. I thought I had it all. But did I?

I spent the next eight years of my life with a man who was never going to marry me, never noticed what I was wearing and spoke to me in a very disrespectful manner. I remember crying a lot during that time. I always felt like he was cheating on me.

I started losing my sense of self. I spent days, time, and energy trying to be perfect for him. No matter what I tried I could not get him to fall in love with me and I eventually realized no one should have to try that hard to win love. I had no idea what I was doing then. I guess subconsciously I was defending my turf, as it could be called. I had this great lifestyle, wonderful home, my children had a nice life, they were happy, and everything on the surface was perfect. The truth be told, it was all a façade. I was happy with the materialistic aspect of my life but was back to being once again with another man who had nothing to give me emotionally.

I longed to have someone look at me and yearn for me. I wanted to have someone tell me they love me and really mean it. I never dreamed my longing and desires for this world would eventually become my obsessions and lifetime goals that would haunt me and leave me feeling empty.

I tried even harder to make him love me. I exercised harder than I ever had, kept the house clean, and even created some animated characters and wrote eight children's books based on them. I did everything to try to get published; thinking he would stay with me and love me if I became rich and famous.

I tried everything to get these books recognized. Every time I got a rejection notice, Mitch would seem even more disappointed in me. After eight years of living together and building some type of life, Mitch wanted out of the relationship. He just wanted to sell the house and go out on his own. He said I no longer served a purpose in his life anymore, whatever that means. I felt like trash. He was done with me and now I could be put out with the garbage.

The house went from sale to closing in two weeks. I didn't fight, I didn't beg. I had a new neighbor next door. Her name was Janet. She gave me advice not to fight for this relationship. She told me God would bring the right one into my life when the timing was right and holding onto this relationship would just bring more heartache. Janet gave me a Bible to read and told me it will help me get through the pain and heartache I was having. She prayed with me and told me to talk to God. "He so wants a relationship with you and is waiting for you to come to him," she told me one day. I thought about what she said and agreed there was no use holding onto someone that didn't want me. I had to let it go. It was really over. I turned to the Bible, Janet gave me, but couldn't understand anything I read and felt there would be time later on in my life to have a relationship with God. Right now, I had to find a way to get through this and heal my broken heart.

After we had separated, he later told me he had been with others and that he loved me as a person, but he was never in love with me. The first year had been great, but once I truly opened my eyes to what I was trying to hold onto, I was able to see the demise of the relationship year after year no matter how hard I tried to keep it afloat.

Chapter 2 - The Dating Game Begins

I moved into an apartment with my two sons, after Mitch and I separated. Since I was feeling so alone and depressed, my older son suggested I try a dating site. I had never seen one but had heard about them. He thought Date that Mate would be a great site for me. I told him the men do not have to be of the same background as me. He said some of his friend's moms were on that site and they seemed satisfied with it.

Soon after, he began the process of setting me up on the internet dating site. He was unbelievable. He picked out my screen name, helped me create my profile, and for the first time in a long time I was actually excited about something. I paid the fee to start, and I was ready to begin. I looked over my profile and picture and was quite pleased. My son taught me how to search through the members. I was impressed at how many good-looking professionals there were in my age group. It was like a big candy store. I clicked off because I had to leave and hoped when I came home in a few hours I would have an email or two.

When I got home hours later and clicked on the dating site, I couldn't believe my eyes. I had about 50 emails! Wow! My dating journey had begun. I went through most of the emails and responded to one in particular, that tickled my fancy. His name was Steve. He owned a few dry-cleaning stores, and he had a son that meant the world to him. He was looking for a woman that was family oriented, loved children, and was ready to build a life with him. "Just what I was looking for," I told myself. I responded with hope and joy, and we made plans to meet at a coffee house that evening.

I dressed carefully, making sure I looked perfect. With hope, will, and positive power as I drove to meet Steve. When I got out of my car, he was already standing in front of the store waiting for me. He said hello and asked me if I would like a cup of coffee. He was very good looking, just like his picture. I ordered a vanilla latte, my favorite, and he made a snide comment about my latte being almost $4.00. That was a strange comment and made me extremely uncomfortable.

We sat down and talked about 20 minutes of small talk. He was not warm and fuzzy. He never talked about his son. I wondered if he really had one or if that was just a ploy to win over the hearts of women. After twenty more minutes of more small talk, he asked me if I was ready to do it. I said in a real naïve manner, "Do what?"

He responded, "You know what." I really had no idea what he was talking about.

Then he said, "We met tonight to have sex."

I responded, "You're kidding."

He said, "No I'm not. That's why I am on this site." I told him I was on this site to find love and he got up, walked out and wished me good luck and said all the men were just like him. He just left me standing alone in a daze.

I was shocked. I felt so let down. What a waste of time and energy. Could this be true? Was he right? He had to be wrong, and I was going to prove that he was wrong. I would go back to the dating site and find Mr. Right.

Chapter 3 - Scott

I went back on the internet and emailed a man that seemed like a family man. He lived about on hour away, but I liked him. He asked me really nice questions and we had great phone conversations. I liked his voice. We emailed for a week and a half then we made plans to meet at a Cuban restaurant near my home that was in a beautiful shopping center. I was excited to meet him. We had the same age children and a lot in common. When Saturday night came, I tried to look as perfect as I could; not too overdone, just right.

When I showed up at the restaurant, Scott was sitting there waiting for me with a bouquet of flowers. He kissed me on the cheek, told me I looked beautiful, and we talked for about thirty minutes before we were seated. I liked him! He was cute, charming, and a true gentleman. He encouraged me to try his food and vice-a-versa. I was having a great time! He asked me if I wanted dessert and I told him I wasn't interested, but suggested we get some later.

After we left the restaurant, we walked around the plaza. We talked about everything. I really liked him. We went and got some ice cream and sat on a bench and ate the ice cream and wound up talking until midnight. We both didn't want the night to end.

Afterwards he walked me to my car and gently kissed me and asked me out for the following weekend. I accepted. I was so excited that I met a really nice man who liked me. I couldn't wait until Friday.

We talked a few times that week and I did not go back on the internet. I was content.

Friday night came and he was having a bit of car trouble and asked me to drive to where he lived. I didn't mind. When I got there, he was excited to see me. He was waiting for me outside and kissed me hello. He took my hand and took me into his apartment. He showed me around, we kissed a bit, and asked me if I was hungry. We went out for Chinese food, and he was such a gentleman to be with. We talked for what seemed like forever. We were so comfortable, together and after we left the restaurant we went back to his apartment. He put on some soft music, and we cuddled on the couch for a while. It started getting late and he asked me to stay over. He offered to put me up in his guest room. He was such a gentleman, but I thought it would be best if I went home at this point in the relationship. So, he walked me to my car, kissed me goodbye and told me to call when I got home. I asked what he was doing tomorrow, and he said he was spending some time with his children.

I thought it was a little odd that a 16 and 18 year old would want to spend Saturday night with their Dad, but I decided not to analyze and read into anything. I just wanted to enjoy the fact that I found a great guy.

A few weeks went by, and I was still seeing Scott, but the relationship was standing still. I only saw him either Friday or Saturday night and never during the week. As time went on, he seemed a bit obsessed with his kids, especially his 18 year old daughter. He talked about his daughter nonstop to the point where I felt like I couldn't measure up. He talked about her beautiful body, and when I met her and he introduced me to her he asked, "Isn't she the most beautiful girl you have ever seen. Doesn't she have a great body?"

I felt sick. I saw her the same way I saw my 18 year old son. As a teenager and nothing more. I thought his feelings for his daughter were a little bizarre.

The following week was Memorial Day weekend. Scott and I only talked once that week and it was at that point, I felt like this relationship was going nowhere. We went out to dinner Saturday night, and he seemed quiet and reserved. He said he had to leave early when he dropped me off. I asked if we could get together on Memorial Day. He said he would spend the day with me unless his children needed him. He said he would let me know Monday morning. This was so strange. His kids were his complete life and even though they were 16 and 18 he was going to check with them first before he could make plans with me.

When Monday came, he called and said his kids had plans and he would be able to spend the day with me. He didn't sound that thrilled but he said we could have a picnic at the beach and came over around noon.

When he came in, he seemed depressed. I asked him if anything was wrong, and he told me he was disappointed that his kids had made plans with their friends instead of him. I explained that my children had plans with their friends as well and that this was normal and the way it was supposed to be.

Just as we were leaving to go to the beach it began to rain. I asked if he wanted to get lunch or a movie. He said he wasn't interested in either. My younger son came home around this time and began playing on the computer. Scott went over to him and was hanging with him. Scott appeared to be really happy. He seemed to only be happy when he was talking about or interacting with children.

After two hours of watching them talk about and play this war game his phone rang, and it was his son. After a conversation with his son, he told me his son wanted to have dinner with him and he had to leave.

I said, "We were supposed to have dinner together tonight."

He replied, "I'm sorry but my son comes first," and then he just left.

I tried to sit and analyze the total demise of this relationship as I often do. I blamed myself as I often did for things not working out instead of realizing how unbalanced and seriously depressed, he appeared to be from his divorce.

Scott never called again, and I was okay with that. I never dreamed at this time that this would be one of many dysfunctional relationships that would begin and end with me feeling like a failure at love, romance, and relationship.

Chapter 4 - A Few Bad Men

It was over with Scott. I went back to the drawing board, *"The Internet",* going through the Jewish dating site. I clicked through many profiles. It was like designing a dress. I could pick the color of their eyes, hair, height, career, and salary – how cool was that? Almost like being in a candy store.

Even though I was 45 I kept in shape and looked pretty good for my age, so I got a lot of emails. There was Seth in Boca Raton who kept writing me. He owned a commercial real estate planning corporation and lived in a large home. He had teenage children, was 53, and there were pictures of him skiing, boating, and hiking. He looked sexy and exciting.

We had plans to meet for dessert at a restaurant on Sunday night. I got dressed, put my make-up on and got in my car. I was excited to meet him. We met at the restaurant, and he hugged me hello. He looked much older than his picture and had less hair. I was disappointed but didn't show it. The both of us went into the restaurant and sat at a booth.

He insisted on sitting next to me which was a turn off. We ordered a dessert and coffee, and he kept putting his hand on my leg and I kept pushing it away. I was trying to talk seriously to him, but he kept touching my leg and arm while saying inappropriate things. I ate some cake; told him I had to leave and ran out. He threw money down on the table and ran out after me.

Seth grabbed me in the parking lot by my car. I wasn't scared because there were people everywhere. He asked me why I ran away when I know that we would be great physically together. I told him I am not that type of woman, and he tried putting his hands where they did not belong and told me he knows I want it.

I stayed calm and told him how disgusting he was and kicked him between his legs. He groaned and then released me. I dashed into my car and took off furiously. I was in a state of shock, amazed that a 50 year old professional man with children could act that way. Was it me? I didn't do anything provocative, and I was dressed properly.

I came home very discouraged and went right back to the computer. I was becoming obsessed, like my whole life was dependent on finding someone. I sat down and looked at my emails. I opened one from Dan.

Dan and I had been corresponding all week long and he lived locally. He left his number on the last email he had sent so I picked up my phone and dialed away. I felt possessed.

He answered the phone pretty quickly and we talked for a while. He had a calming voice and there was a cute picture of him on his profile. He was 50, divorced, and had one grown child in college. After a nice conversation we agreed to meet Friday night at a Japanese restaurant for dinner in Boca Raton. In the meantime, I was emailing other men here and there just in case this one didn't work out.

The emails just kept flooding my inbox. It was like the "Flight of the Bumblebee", it never stopped! I checked my emails multiple times every day. I couldn't just let time pass. I was on a mission, and I had to get there. What was happening to me?

There was one man by the name of Dale who emailed me a few times a day. He sold boat parts and participated in various boat shows country wide. He was cute but traveled a lot and was not around very often.

Friday night came and I met Dan at the restaurant. He looked younger and cuter in his pictures, but it didn't faze me as this seemed to be the trend. We sat down in the restaurant and when the waiter came, he ordered an appetizer for us to share. He didn't even ask me if I wanted anything, or if what he ordered was *"okay"*. I was really hungry. We shared the appetizer over some idle conversation but all I could focus on was how hungry I was. When the waiter came back, he asked for the check, and I was in shock…or was I?

Was I just in the twilight zone? We walked out to our cars together and I just kept thinking maybe he doesn't have a lot of money, so I should cut him some slack until he showed me his brand new Silver Jaguar, fully stocked and loaded. All I could think about was that if he sold his car then maybe I could get a real meal. He kissed me good night on the lips and gave me a hug.

"Not bad", I thought to myself. He asked me about going out on Sunday night and figuring maybe he was just cautious on first dates I accepted. Maybe he was just cheap on first dates, and we would go out the proper way on Sunday. He offered to pick me up in his Jaguar, and I needed something positive to hang on to, so I agreed to try going out with him a second time.

I got home and engorged myself in an entire bowl of soup which seemed to disappear in a minute. And then of course went right to my computer to work on my second career, "my dating game".

Dale was still emailing me steadily. He sounded great but he wouldn't be back for at least another 3 weeks. I was also emailing two other men. This was becoming exhausting.

Sunday night rolled around, and sure enough, Dan called and asked if I would meet him at his house. I asked, "Why?"

Dan said, "We could have a little wine and some appetizers that I prepared here before we went out." I agreed, but I couldn't help but thinking this was so he could spend less money at the restaurant. I tried to put that thought out of my head and focused on the positive things. At least I made it to a second date and this time he was good looking.

I had directions to his house and when I passed through the guard gate, I couldn't believe what a beautiful place this man lived in. I pulled up to his driveway and felt assured that the insufficient meal on our first date was strictly a "first meal date thing".

When I rang the doorbell, he answered the door. He was dressed very nicely; he had on a black tight shirt and a pair of khakis with loafers. I felt lucky. His home was beautiful. It had three bedrooms, with a 2 car garage and a beautiful kitchen with a large island in the center of it. On the table, he had 2 glasses of wine, crackers, cheese and fruit. I thought this was so romantic. We made a toast and talked for about an hour over the wine and cheese, this was the type of man I was looking for!

We finished talking and he cleaned up, then led me outside and opened the door of his beautiful new car and helped to put me in ever so gently. We drove to the restaurant. He took me to this really nice Greek restaurant I had never been to. We were seated outside at a table overlooking the lake. Everything seemed perfect and for the first time in a while I felt happy and content.

The waiter came over to take our drink orders and Dan told him to bring two waters. Dan then turned to me and mentioned that we had just had wine and appetizers at his home so it would be crazy to order that here. It was at that moment I started to feel that strange feeling that comes over me when I feel something is not right. I kept reassuring myself to stop imagining things and just be positive.

The waiter came back with our waters and asked if we were ready to order. I decided to play it cool and ordered just a simple piece of salmon with a side of vegetables. When the waiter turned to Dan, he told the waiter he would share the salmon with me.

I couldn't believe it. I felt sick to my stomach and couldn't even look at him. He explained he was full from the wine and cheese at his house. I wanted to run out of this restaurant, how embarrassing!

I hadn't even had his tongue in my mouth yet and I was now going to experience his fork.

The food arrived and the waiter brought two dishes. He split the small piece of salmon with the few vegetables onto the plates and walked away. These "expensive" type of restaurants was not set up for sharing. They gave you small portions. We ate quickly. Maybe it was because my portion consisted of a total of five bites, including the vegetables. Like last time, I was hungry afterwards.

The waiter came back when we were finished and inquired about our desire for desserts or coffee. Dan said we were both really full and we would like the check. I was wondering if he was going to have to forfeit a half tank of gas for his car to pay this bill.

I just wanted to go home. *Another dud date for the record*, I thought. What kind of rocks were these men lurking out of? When we got back to his house, he asked me to come in and offered to make us some coffee. I was not surprised. I had more than my share of Dan for a night and told him I had to get home. He tried to talk me into staying but I left.

Driving home, tears started rolling down my eyes. I felt like I would never find what I longed so much for. I then started to think about Mitch. I missed him so much. How could I not? I felt like I would never be able to move beyond my loss as I continued to fall deeper down the rabbit hole.

I dried my eyes as I walked into my house and ate a snack while my computer turned on. Obsessed with finding the one, I opened my emails to see who was waiting.

I sat down at my computer and found another email from Dale. He was asking if I would call him because he would be in town for a few days next week and would love to meet me. I was excited. I emailed him back with my number. I was enthusiastic to hear his voice for the first time.

The next day at work my phone rang. It was a strange number I didn't recognize, and I hesitantly answered it. It was Dale. I dashed out of the office and went outside to speak with him. He had a beautiful voice, and I was very attracted to it. We talked for about 30 minutes. We definitely could have kept on talking but I needed to get back to work. We were going to meet later that night at a coffeehouse in Boca Raton. I was so excited; I had a good feeling about this one.

The rest of the day felt like it was dragging, and it seemed like forever before my day ended. Finally, I got home, showered, and put on my make-up. I tried to dress nice but remain casual. This was the first time since I could remember that the first thing I didn't do when I got home was race to my computer to check my emails. I was excited about Dale and really wanted him to be the one.

I drove to the coffee house. The bright sky had given way to a dark clear night. It was late October, and you can feel the Florida weather beginning to change in the evenings. I was so nervous. I parked my car and stepped into the coffeehouse. No one here looked familiar, so I tried to wait patiently. I looked "perfect"! The right jeans, a sexy top, my hair came out just the way I wanted it to.

I hope he likes me, I thought to myself. A man walked in that I immediately recognized. He was gorgeous with beautiful hair and a great smile. I wondered if this was Dale. He was a little heavier than his picture but had a dazzling smile. We looked at each other and he came up to me and hugged me. We had instant chemistry. I wasn't going to let the extra weight he had not told me about raining on my parade. Nothing was perfect and I felt chemistry. It was amazing.

We went to the counter, and he got our coffees. We sat down together, and we talked, and talked, and the conversation just seemed to flow. It was great, I was in heaven! After what felt like forever, he asked me if I wanted to take a ride to the beach. Even though I knew I shouldn't get into someone's car on a first date, I went against my better judgment and did so anyway. We went down to the beach and got out of his car, making our way to the boardwalk.

It was very windy, but Dale held me warm and safe in his arms. He was a really big guy, but I kept telling myself this was perfect, and I shouldn't focus on that. We kissed each other for a long time. It's amazing how great this date was in comparison to what I had just been through. It began to rain, and we jumped back into his car, and he drove back to the coffeehouse. He pulled into the parking lot, and we kissed like two 17-year-olds. It was great.

He asked me out for tomorrow night and walked me to my car. I agreed and then he told me to call him when I was safely home. I knew this was it. I had found me a treasure. Driving home from this date was different than all of the others. I felt fulfilled, happy, and content. When I got home, I didn't go to my computer at all. How about that? I gave him a quick phone call, got into bed and drifted off gratifyingly to sleep with thoughts of Dale.

I awoke the next morning as happy as a lark. I got dressed and went to work. The day was moving at a snail's pace. During my lunch break I spoke to Dale, and he asked me to drive over to his house since he lived up the road from where I worked. I couldn't wait to see him.

Eight hours seemed like an eternity, but as soon as I got done, I hurried to my car at 5 pm and proceeded to drive to Dale's home. When I pulled up in front of his house I was impressed. He had a really nice house. I shyly got out of my car and knocked on the door. He answered the door and immediately grabbed me into his arms hugging me tightly.

Wow. He really seemed to like me. Dale gave me a tour of his home. It was a really nice house. I asked him where we were going, and he said he was going to make me pizza. I told him that he didn't have to go through all the trouble, but he insisted.

I wasn't that comfortable with being alone all night with him and really wasn't in a pizza mood. I didn't want to rock the boat with him, so I put on a happy face and didn't let him know I was bothered.

Dale spent some time putting this enormous pizza together. He had bought a giant square of pizza and had a slew of extra cheese, sausage, pepperoni, peppers, and even more extra cheese. I told him I don't eat like that, but he insisted I learn to eat the right way. He was overweight. I didn't understand what would cause him to believe that this could be the right way especially when everything on it was wrong to me.

When the pizza was ready, he served it at the counter instead of the table. He handed me a can of soda and didn't have a napkin in sight. He stood up and must have slobbered down three quarters of the pie while I sat down and spent the time dissecting my slice. I was trying to separate the greasy meat items from the dough, attempting to take bites between the removable items. He didn't seem to notice, or care, that I was struggling with my meal.

This was my first red flag. It never seems to take that long. Afterwards he wanted to just lie in bed and watch television. He left all the food and dirty dishes laying all over the sink and counter. I couldn't help but think of what a slob he was.

He did not want to do anything but lay around and I was feeling bored. I looked at my watch and knew I needed to get home. I still had to work tomorrow. I told Dale that I had to leave, and he got up. We hugged and kissed then walked me to my car.

There were so many things about him I didn't like but so many things about him I did like. Driving home I felt a little indifferent. I really enjoyed him; I just wasn't sure if he was my type. He asked me out for tomorrow.

The same pattern went on for a few weeks between him being away selling boats. He would come home and complain that he missed being home and saying he just wanted to hang with me in his house. We never went out anywhere and when I was hungry, he made me pizza.

I got invited to a pimp and prostitute party for Halloween and my friend Mary who worked at the gym I went to was having the party at her home. Everyone had to get dressed up as a prostitute or a pimp. I went ahead and bought the cutest little sexy witch outfit. I asked Dale to accompany me there. He said he would.

The day of the party Dale was selling boats locally at a show here in Ft. Lauderdale. I was excited about the party, and it would be the first time in three weeks that we went somewhere together.

When Dale came home, I was dressed in my sexy witch costume. I thought I looked adorable. Dale didn't even notice. He lay down on the bed and told me he was exhausted and just wanted to lay down and watch TV. I got upset and told him I wanted to go. It turned into an argument which ended up with him telling me if I went it was over.

I began crying and in an angry tone he agreed to go but said we're only staying for an hour, and I wasn't to wear my costume because I looked like a prostitute in it. I tried to explain to him that was the whole idea of the party, and he flipped out and demanded I change. I should have broken up with him right there but the thought of going back on the internet and going to the party alone was more than I could bear. I swallowed my pride, and like a little girl changed my dress.

We made it to the party, and I walked in with Dale. He just wore a shirt and trousers. Everyone else was dressed in a costume. All of my friends from the gym were there. I tried to shift away from Dale for a few moments, but he hung on me like super glue.

A couple of my friends were amazed at how heavy he was since they knew I liked athletically built men. I ignored everyone's comments. There were all kinds of activities going on, but he wouldn't let me participate in anything. I was having a bad time and it was Dale's fault. I was so unhappy, and nobody liked Dale. He had a bad attitude, and he wore it well.

After about an hour of eating through the buffet, Dale turned to me and demanded we leave. I told him I wanted to stay. He growled at me and told me if I stayed, he was going to leave me here and I wouldn't be able to get back home. Reluctantly, I said goodbye to everyone and left.

We got back to his house, and I immediately left. I never saw Dale again after that. I didn't pick up his calls or answer his emails. He eventually got the hint and stopped trying to reach me.

Chapter 5 - Henry

I woke up in the morning and before doing anything else, I ran to my computer to see what new emails I had received from Date that Mate (of course). There was one from a guy that looked very familiar. It said, "If your name is Sharon and you used to live in Howard Beach, call me. If you're not Sharon, call me anyway because I think you're very cute."

I then realized that this message was from my boyfriend from high school through college that I steadily dated. We were together all the time, and I really liked him, but I never felt that real chemistry you're supposed to feel if that person is "the one". I dated Henry for five years. In the last year he asked me to move to Texas with him where he landed a job promotion. I was in my sophomore year of college enjoying school and turned him down. The truth was while he was a great guy, he didn't light my flame and I didn't want to spend my life with him. He left for Texas, and I went on with my life and had not heard from him until I saw this message today.

I was excited to hear from him. Especially after all the crazy and strange dates I had been on these past months. I emailed him back my phone number and within minutes he called. We talked about everything for hours. Our lives, our kids, everything! It was great and he came over to see me. When he arrived, he looked the way I remembered him. He gave me a big hug and had a gift for me. I felt special. This was great, and the way dating should be.

We went out to a restaurant on the ocean, and I was able to order anything I wanted. We had a beautiful ocean view seat, a great meal, and a great conversation. We then took a walk on the beach and went back to his apartment. He kissed me good night and the chemistry I was looking for still wasn't there.

I had a new mission, to make things work with Henry. I just couldn't go back on the internet where hell waited for me. I would force myself to fall in love with him and find happiness there.

In the weeks that followed Henry and I were in a committed relationship, we even looked at houses together. He was in love with me just the way he was years ago back in college. I just didn't feel much. I wasn't sure if my heart was still aching for Mitch or if it was the aftermath of bad serial dating on the internet. I wasn't sure, but something was off, and I was determined to make this relationship work and kept my feelings to myself.

A few weeks later I was feeling a little depressed and hopeless and Henry told me he bought me an engagement ring. He said when the timing was right, he was going to propose to me.

I felt like all my dreams were coming true and yet I felt like I was trapped in a nightmare. I just didn't love him. For all the reasons that it didn't work back in college, twenty five years later it still wasn't working either. I walked around like a zombie for days and then one Saturday morning while Henry was still sleeping, I was lying in bed with my head spinning and feelings of despair in my heart. I had to tell him, but how?

I went downstairs and started to cry. Why couldn't I love him? What was wrong with me? He could give me the life I lost and desired, but when you do not love someone back, it shows. You feel unfulfilled and lonely. Henry was perfect, but not perfect for me.

Henry came downstairs and saw my face. He told me he had a feeling that I didn't share the same feelings he did and was hesitant to give me the ring. He said he understood, and then we hugged it out. Henry and I remained friends for the next few years until he met someone and got married. We lost touch after that.

Chapter 6 - Speed Dating

After Henry, I was devastated and the thought of going on the internet frightened me. It was addicting like a casino, and I didn't want to get trapped in it again. I decided to try other methods of dating, so I signed up for a speed dating event in a bar and grill in Davie.

I had heard about these events, and they sounded like they were a lot of fun. On the night of the speed dating event, I made sure to look my very best. I bought a brand new outfit and carefully did my hair and makeup until it looked perfect. I got in my car and was excited like a child going to a toy store. When I got to the restaurant hosting this event, the hostess put all the women including myself at different tables that were reserved for this event. These were tiny tables that only sat two people. There were twenty six people signed up. Approximately thirteen women and thirteen men.

When everyone was present, the event host explained all the rules for this event. The women would stay at the first table they were placed at all night and the men would rotate tables every six minutes until they had sat with each of the thirteen women. We were all given a card that had each of our assigned numbers on it with a rating system and comment section. It also stated whether you wanted to receive a contact from any of the people you met. At the end of the evening, the host tallies up the cards and pairs the women and men they each want a contact from. It had to be compatible on both ends. So, for example, if I wanted #7 to call me, he had to also choose me, or the host could not disclose any names or phone numbers. I was sizing up the room to see what the other women looked like, and I felt I looked much younger and cuter than most of them. I also noticed there were also some good looking distinguished men among the group. I was extremely excited and felt deep down in my heart that this would definitely work in my favor that night, and I would actually and finally meet the man of my dreams.

At 8:00 pm, a bell rang, and the men went to the first table on their list. A man sat down at my table and was staring at me. I said hello and he mumbled back something to me. I actually wasn't even sure if he was talking to me or to himself. He was very strange and appeared to be very uncomfortable at my table. I tried to talk to him, but he would just mumble something back and would continually be looking at the other tables instead of me. I believe he had his eye fixed on someone else and just wanted to painfully get through these six minutes of what he felt was hell. We didn't talk much. It was an uncomfortable silence and when the bell rang, it was a feeling of relief, like recess when I was back in grade school.

A second man showed up and while he was very nice, he was not very good looking. His clothes were disheveled and his hair uncombed. He actually looked like he came in for a beer and by accident wound up at my table instead of the bar. We talked some nonchalant small talk and finally the bell rang. Guy #3 came next, he was very good looking, but extremely smug; and trust me, he was no charm. He actually had the nerve to tell me he was hoping the women here would have been a little younger and more built. He was a doctor who thought he was all that and a bag of chips. In my opinion he was a stale bag of chips that has been on the shelf too long. The bell had finally rung after what felt like hours and thank goodness it did before my thoughts became words. I was not having fun and I was getting that feeling I get, when things are not feeling right.

Guy #4 came over and was actually a really nice guy. He owned a large landscaping company and was very good looking. We talked and laughed, and we were having a great time when the bell rang. I was sad to see him move on, but that is how the game is played.

Guy #5 was very nice also. He was a handsome attorney with a sparkling smile and dazzling personality. I felt amazing chemistry with him, and he looked like he was feeling the same way about me, but then the bell rang again. Guys #6 and #7 were also pretty nice. They were both well-groomed and well versed.

Guy #8 was a nice man, but he looked like he stepped out of the sixties with colorful baggy beach pants and a tie dye shirt with long hair and a leather headband. He fixed motorcycles for a living and surfed as a hobby. Here was a man in my opinion that was not ready to grow up. He had never married; he never had kids and liked to travel to various places to catch some cool waves. With all that, it translated to me as non-committal. I will say there are real winners out there that are real losers, especially when they are in the 45 – 55 age range.

The next four men were wonderful! One was a doctor, one an attorney, another was an engineer and the twelfth one was a general contractor. These four guys were all good looking and were able to hold light, easy conversation. I was attracted to them, and I got the feeling they were attracted to me. I felt pretty lucky.

The last guy, #13 seemed a little drunk and smelled of alcohol. "Wow", he staggered over to my table, and I could not understand a word he said. I had wondered if he had been disappointed after each woman he sat with and decided to have a drink after each ring of the bell. I guess no one had ever explained to him that "you only get one chance to make a first good impression". I just wanted this last session to end because this last guy was just wasting my time. This had become the longest six minutes of my life.

Finally, the bell rang, and I couldn't wait to give my card in. I had chosen eight men and I just felt they had chosen me also. I was so excited to hear from them and to have eight eligible men call me was like winning a dating jackpot. The best thing about speed dating was that I had already seen what they look like so there was no fear of a fake picture or the Loch Ness monster showing up in the place of a falsified profile. I left the restaurant with great joy and hope in the anticipation that I would receive eight calls and dates over the next few days.

The next day I received a call from the man hosting the event with the results of my compatible mates. He told me only one guy chose me out of the thirteen men that met with me. I was completely shocked! I told him he must be mistaken. I had a great rapport with at least eight of them and only one guy chose me. He also told me that more than half the men chose none of the women, so I was lucky to get one. I was bewildered! Even the loser men did not want to go out with me. He gave me the one contact he had for me. It was Michael, the landscaping guy. So now I had to wait for this one man to call me and hope he didn't choose someone else just as well. About an hour after I got the call regarding my contacts or lack of them, my one and only guy called me. We talked on the phone for a while and just like at the speed dating event we had some nice chemistry between us. He asked me out for Tuesday evening, and I was excited because he was a nice guy that looked good, and he chose to go out with me after spending a few minutes with me, so I felt ahead of the game for the first time.

Tuesday night came and I made sure to look my best. I was not going to take any chances with my one and only contact. Michael was thirty minutes late, but he looked great! He was a very good looking man. We talked for a while and then we went out for dinner. Afterwards we went back to my apartment and wound up kissing. He was a very good kisser, but as we kissed it started to become too fast and too much and I had to put the brakes on. I mentioned to him that this was our first date and I wanted to keep it slow.

He asked me, "What's the big deal?"

I told him again, "Not on the first date." He then told me he had to leave because he had to be up early in the morning for work. I wasn't sure if I would ever hear from him again, especially with my track record.

The next day he actually called me and asked me out for Tuesday night again. He wanted to go watch the tennis matches with me which sounded really cool. It was Saturday and I asked him, "What about tonight?" He told me that it would not be good because he was working the entire day in the hot sun, and he would be exhausted. I told him I understood and looked forward once again for Tuesday. On Tuesday he came over to get me and we grabbed a quick bite before we went over to watch the tennis match. We had a nice time and afterwards went back to my apartment.

We started kissing again and once again he wanted more. I stopped him again and asked him what the rush was? He told me he really like me and was very attractive to me and was looking for a physical relationship as well as a romantic one. I told him I was looking for the same thing but not this quickly. He once again said he had to leave because he had to get up early again tomorrow. This pattern persisted for the next few weeks.

A date each Tuesday followed by him trying to get a home run with me, and me trying to slow him down and then Michael suddenly telling me he has to go because he has to get up very early the next day. He reminded me of a small child who when he doesn't get his way, runs away pouting. I had red flags coming up everywhere. It looked like the U.N.

The next time he called and asked me out for Tuesday again, I tried to change the pattern. I asked him if I could make dinner at his place, and he told me his place was a mess and he preferred not. He insisted we just go to dinner to a restaurant as planned. I really felt something was off.

I needed to stop this version of "Groundhog Day". I then insisted that we can go out to dinner, but I would pick him up at his place and then we could drive to a nearby restaurant. He said, "No" and when I asked him where he lived, he also refused to tell me. After that, he told me he was really exhausted and preferred to go out another night. I hung up feeling like a complete fool. This guy was either married or had something big to hide. It appeared to me that he was not looking for a serious relationship but was looking to cheat. I was getting that terrible feeling I get when something does not feel right.

Fifty-nine dollars wasted on this speed dating game. I wondered how many women he contacted the night we met. I appeared to be his Tuesday night. I was guessing all the others got a different day of the week to call their own. It reminded me of the underwear I once owned that had seven days of the week on them. One pair for each day. I was now reduced to comparing myself to underwear. I had never heard from Michael again which was fine with me, but now it was back to the drawing board or should I say the Internet.

Chapter 7 - A Lock & Key Party

I did not want to go back on the internet. I felt I was getting nowhere with that except being in a constant state of obsession. Every time I passed by my computer, I could almost swear I heard it calling out to me.

On top of obsessing over finding the right person, it seemed like I was wasting money. It cost me fifty-nine dollars for the speed dating event and the dating sites cost countless amounts of money also. I didn't know what to do or where to sign up next and I was getting very frustrated without any prospective dates coming up.

I walked back and forth in front from my computer and finally gave into temptation. I was just getting ready to sign back up on Date That Mate again when I decided to check my email first. I noticed an invitation was sent to me for an event called a "lock and key party". This event was being sponsored by the same company that sponsored the speed dating event. It was only thirty-five dollars for this event, and it would take place at a lounge style restaurant on Atlantic Avenue in Delray Beach. It was to take place the upcoming Friday night at 7:30 pm. There were going to be seventy-five men and seventy-five women. "Wow! That is a lot of men in one room in my age group," I thought. I decided to sign up and set my obsessive sights on Friday night. I bought a beautiful outfit, had my hair done and looked great.

I drove to Delray Beach all by myself. I did not have many single friends. Actually, I didn't have any. I was the lonesome dove that was always on my own, looking for love in all the wrong places. All the women I knew were either married or in serious relationships.

I found a parking spot, walked into the lounge, and took a deep breath. There was a reception desk set up for this event when I entered. A woman checked my name off a list and handed me a very big lock on a chain to wear around my neck all night. It was a real Medco silver lock, like one you would you buy in a hardware store. I felt like a cow that was being branded to enter the fields to find a bull to mate with.

I put the cowbell or lock around my neck and entered a very large room that had a very long bar that seemed to wrap around the room. The lock was heavy and hung down right on my breasts. This lock was so big, awkward, and heavy lying against my chest, I figured I would either have a heart attack or become flat chested by the end of the night.

As I entered the room, I saw wall to wall women and men. All the women were wearing the locks and all the men had the keys around their necks. I stood and watched for a few minutes at how this event worked. I observed all the men jumping around from woman to woman seeing if their keys opened any of the locks. There must have been about 150 people in this room, if not more.

This lounge was totally packed, and it appeared people were still coming in. All of a sudden, out of nowhere, a man jumped in front of me and started to put his key in my lock. It didn't fit and he just walked away without saying a word. These men were on a quest, on a hunt and couldn't be stopped.

When they made a fit, which was not too often, they would either get a drink with that woman or if they were not pleased, they would trade their key in for another one. Nothing like putting these women "out to pasture" if they didn't meet your ridiculous standards. Who comes up with these events? *And who am I to talk, since I am the first one to sign up for all of them, I* thought to myself.

Some of the men were really cute and some of the women were absolutely gorgeous with big fake breasts and the big shiny lock that was hanging up high on them like a ledge on a hill. I just wanted to meet a nice man who wanted a sweet down to earth gal. What were my chances of finding that here?

I started to move around the room and as I did, the men just kept coming up saying, "May I"? And the next thing I knew their key was trying to force its way into my lock but with not much luck.

After about an hour or so and over fifty men or so trying their best to unlock me, I decided this was more like trying to get a round peg to try to fit into a square hole. This was not working for me, and I was not having any fun.

The men did not even want to talk. They just wanted to conquer. Finally, about two hours into this cuckoo's nest attraction, a man came over to me, smiled and asked if he could try my lock. I smiled back and said, "Sure". Well, guess what? The key fit! He gave me a great big hug and we started talking. He seemed nice. His name was Art, and he was not bad looking. He told me he was divorced with two grown children, and he had his own contracting business that he had run most of his life, and he just recently sold it and retired.

We talked for almost an hour, and he then asked me if I was hungry and if I wanted to join him for a meal at this little Italian restaurant across the street. I agreed and we walked over there together. It felt great getting out of that meat market event.

As we walked across the street, I didn't feel any great chemistry, but kept telling myself to stop being such a critic. It's not like the men were lining up at the door for me! I needed to try and give him a chance.

We entered this really nice restaurant, and he immediately ordered a scotch on the rocks. I ordered water. I needed to keep my wits about me. We each ordered an entree and the food looked and smelled amazing. The conversation between us was smooth and ongoing. He then ordered another scotch on the rocks. By the time we were halfway through dinner, he was on his fifth scotch on the rocks. This definitely had red flags all over it.

He started getting a bit loopy and when the server came over to clear the plates off the table, he ordered a sixth drink. When he turned around to talk to the server, he fell out of his chair. I was beyond embarrassed and completely mortified. The restaurant staff helped get him off the floor. He was not hurt, but extremely drunk. I just wanted to run out, but how could I leave someone who was not capable to put one foot in front of the other or put two solid words together out of his mouth.

I think the restaurant wanted him to leave because they slapped the check in front of him without asking us if we wanted any coffee or dessert, and trust me, he really needed the coffee. He managed somehow to pull some money out of his wallet, and I prayed it was enough to cover the bill. When he tried to get up, he staggered all over the place and wobbled with me out the door. When we were out of the restaurant, he grabbed my arm and leaned on me with all his weight.

What a night this was! First, I'm a cow in the field with a lock around my neck and now I'm a crutch to lean on. I had been reduced to the lowest form a woman can be in the dating world. As he staggered, attached to me, he was mumbling something I couldn't understand. He looked like he was trying to get back to the lounge where the event was. I hope he was not looking to get another drink. I think he was trying to find his friend that he came to this event with. I was horrified walking back into this lounge with this lush.

When we were inside the lounge, I helped him to sit down on one of the couches and then I left. I ran all the way to the parking lot and got safely into my car. I felt complexly lost and defeated. *"What was wrong with me,"* I thought. Another $35.00 down the tubes. Were there any nice men left here on earth? If this kept up, I would have to and find another planet to live on.

As I drove home, the tears ran down my face. It was back to the drawing board of the internet. I was back to square one.

Chapter 8 - An Old Fashion Mixer

When I got home, I turned on my computer, but just couldn't bear to sign back up on Date that Mate and spend another $35.00 to go back into the jungle of internet dating hell. I checked my regular email account and saw through one of these dating sites, they were having what you would call a dance or a mixer the following Friday night at a place called Club Boca. It was only $15.00 to get in and it felt like a better and more traditional way to meet a man. I was looking forward to this dance and couldn't wait for next Friday night to come. Another week was passing without any dates or bites. I had become so fixated on having a date and finding the one, that when I had nothing planned with anyone, I felt very depressed and extremely hopeless.

Finally, Friday night was here. I asked my neighbor Katherine if she would come with me. She was the only one I knew that would go with me to this type of event. She was also looking to meet a nice man and had not had much luck either. We drove to Club Boca, parked, and when we got to the front entrance, the line was wrapped around the block. We stood on line scouting out the men, as well as what other women there looked like. Some of the men here were extremely good looking and distinguished.

It took about 15 minutes or so to get in. The cover charge wound up being $18.00 and a ticket for one free drink. We walked inside and it was extremely crowded. It was a very large club with many corridors leading to a few different rooms. I walked around and found many eyes were sizing me up. I felt like a monkey that was put into a cage with many apes. As I walked around, many of the men looked familiar to me. Then it dawned on me that many of the guys here were also on the Date That Mate site. I was surrounded by the very addiction I was trying to escape from. I had actually been corresponding with some of the men here through email, phone, and had even had some coffee dates with a few that didn't go so well. I felt reduced to a cliché of a desperate, lonely woman trying to find love after 40. I actually felt ashamed. Every time I came close to one of my past internet encounters, I ducked and carefully snuck into one of the other rooms so I would not be noticed.

I entered into the main room where the DJ was blasting some really great dance music. Katherine was already on the dance floor with a man she just met. She had no trouble with confidence the way I did. I found myself a quiet corner in the back and basically crawled into it watching all the couples dancing. There were tears rolling out of the corners of my eyes. I was so unhappy and wanted to go home. I just wish that I could be in a steady, stable relationship and not in this circus of misfit men that have commitment and chauvinistic issues.

I was about to let Katherine know, I was going to leave when an older and distinguished looking man came over to me and asked me to dance. I said, "Yes" before I knew it, he whirled me onto the dance floor. The DJ was playing a song from the 50's and this gentleman knew how to work it. He spun me around, lifted me and took full control over me on the floor.

I was having a blast and all eyes were on us as we tore up the floor. It was incredible and I was having a blast. The DJ spent the last hour playing 60's, disco and all the party type dance songs. This guy knew it all and I was proud to be his partner. We danced for more than an hour with him leading me with every song that came our way. Afterwards, he led me off of the dance floor with elegance and grace and we found a quiet place near the bar where we sat and talked.

His name was Nathan. He asked me to call him Nate. As we tried to get to know each other the club kept filling up with more and more people and it was becoming harder to hear each other, so Nate asked me if I wanted to go to get something to eat with him at Denny's. I grabbed Katherine and the guy she had been hanging with all night and we drove to Denny's.

Playing it safe as I always do, I drove in my car with Katherine and the two guys who did not know each other drove in Nate's car and we met at the restaurant. Nate waited for me and held the door, and he helped me into the booth we were sitting in. Nate was so attentive to me. I was not used to this kind of attention. He was good looking and quite the gentleman.

After the meal he walked me to his car and asked me if he could kiss me goodbye. I said, "Yes" and he did. It was great and I felt special. He told me he wanted to take me out on a real date and took my phone number. He gently helped me into my car, closed my door for me and we said our goodbyes. I drove off with Katherine feeling ecstatic. I finally met a nice man who truly liked me for me just the way I was.

By the time I reached home, it was very late. My phone rang and it was Nate. He said he just wanted to make sure I got home okay. I thanked him for his concern, and we once more said our goodbyes. *Wow I really met a nice man,* was all I could think as I hung up the phone. This felt so amazing. I met someone who really had true concern for me. Who said chivalry was dead? Oops, I did!

I drifted off to sleep that night feeling relief, contentment and the feeling that I won the lottery. Nate called the next day to ask me out for Sunday night. I accepted, but when I got off the phone, I started to wonder why he asked me out for Sunday and not Saturday. My mind then started its roller coaster of turns where it started thinking about things like; maybe he's married or maybe he is involved in something illegal. I had become so used to these men lying and playing games that when something good came my way, I couldn't trust it. So, while my mind was running away from me with all these terrible thoughts, I shook myself, ran after it and tried to rationalize that I just met him yesterday and maybe he had already made plans for today or did not want to appear desperate. I tried to tell myself to feel happy and look forward to tomorrow.

On Sunday, he picked me up and we drove to a beautiful restaurant. He was easy to be with and a gentleman. He told me he was divorced and had two children and two grandchildren. After dinner we walked around and talked for hours. I was having a great time. We talked about everything. He told me he was new to Florida and that he owned a house on Long Island and also just recently bought a fix-it-up condo on the beach in South Florida. He told me he comes down every other week to work on restoring the condo. His goal is to be able to be in Florida during the winters and go back to Long Island in the summer. He also told me he was looking for that special person to share his life with.

He was a retired electrician with a great pension. I told him everything about me and all that I was looking for. Before we knew it, it was 2:00 in the morning and time for us to leave. He drove me home and he walked me upstairs. He kissed me and told me he would call me tomorrow. I was so excited! I really liked him. Maybe he would be the one! He certainly met all my expectations and my standards on my checklist. I actually felt happy as I went to sleep feeling hopeful, something I have not felt in a very long time.

I had not heard from Nate in a few days. I started to worry like I usually do when something does not feel right. Finally, by Wednesday, Nate called. He told me he was so busy renovating his apartment that he got completely sidetracked and forgot what time and day it was. He apologized to me and asked me out for Friday night.

When Friday came, I was so excited to see him. He took me out to dinner to a beautiful restaurant on the beach and then he took me back to his condo to show me everything he is building and working on. Being with Nate was so exhilarating because he was the first man to actually show me where he lives. This proved to me that I was not just a date, but someone who was important to him.

When I entered his apartment, he wasn't kidding about all the work he was doing. This place was a complete construction zone. It was all laid out in front of me that he was not lying to me that he kept forgetting to call me because he was busy working on the condo. Fixing up houses and apartments had become his new hobby since he retired. He showed me everything he was doing to it, and it was going to be beautiful when he was done. He drove me home and I had another wonderful night with him. He once again walked me to my apartment, kissed me goodnight and told me he would call me over the next few days.

This pattern continued over the course of about two months. He would take me out to dinner once a week, followed by a period of several days that he claimed he went back to Long Island. Not that anything on the surface appeared wrong, but it was just the fact that for a man who claimed he was looking for a partner; this relationship was in reality going nowhere. We were just standing still. When I tried to talk to him about it, he didn't seem to get it, or he didn't want to get it, so I decided for the time being not to rock the boat with him

A few weeks later, when we were out to dinner, he invited me to spend the night in his new condo. He told me renovations are much further along, about 65% complete. I had felt this change in our date night had now taken a step in a different direction and that was good.

He obviously cared about me, so I was probably worrying about nothing these past few weeks.

I picked up some clothes at my apartment and then we drove together to his place. He made me feel very comfortable and his apartment was coming along beautifully. He treated me with great respect, and we just spent the night cuddling and talking. I woke up nestled gently in his arms. I had overthought this relationship and let my imagination run away from me. Nate just needed time to get his condo together and wrap up some loose ends back in New York, so he would have the proper time and attention to give to me. I felt excited and wonderful because things were finally happening between us, and I was looking forward to spending this day with him.

The next morning, Nate was hungry and seemed in a hurry to get breakfast, so I quickly showered, got dressed and soon we were off to start our day by having breakfast together on the beach. He took me to this adorable little breakfast place right on the water. The server came over and we ordered our meal from this great menu that had unique items on it. It was a beautiful breakfast.

We were talking and having the best time when out of nowhere he said, "We need to have a serious talk". I thought he was going to share with me how much I mean to him or how he feels about me. I was not prepared for what came next! Instead of showering me with sweet words, he came right out and told me that he was not in the market at this time for a serious relationship. He let me know that he never again wanted to live with someone and answer to someone.

He also told me, "I want to do anything I want to, such as make a mess, fart in bed all night and come and go as I please."

Confused, I asked him why he led me on these past weeks. He said he wanted to see if he could make it work, but after last night, he realized he wasn't comfortable having someone share his home with him and having to hold back from farting all night long. I couldn't help but think how ridiculous that was. He also added "I can be a gentleman, but I do not want to be one all the time. I really enjoyed acting like a pig and I am good at it."

I was in a complete state of shock. This one took the whole bakery. He was breaking up with me because he wants to fart all night long and he felt he could not do that ever in front of me. Maybe he needs to see a doctor if he does nothing but farts non-stop through the night. Maybe we could be involved during the day since the night poses gas issues for him. This excuse to break up was a first for me.

He also continued to let me know he has been involved with another woman in New York. He was seeing her when he was at his other home in Long Island. I had asked him if he was dating both of us at the same time. He said, "Yes." I asked him if he was capable of farting in front of her or was it just me. He didn't answer me and took me straight home.

We drove in utter silence. I did everything in my power not to cry. I was holding my tears back so hard that I thought I would explode. He dropped me off in front of my building and for the first time he did not help me out of the car or walk me into the building. He could barely wait for me to get out of the car as he pressed his foot hard on the accelerator and took off like a thief.

I ran up to the safety of my apartment and the floodgates let loose. I cried and cried all night until there were no tears left. What was wrong with me? Or better yet, where did these men come from? Did they come from another planet? Did they come out from under a rock? I felt humiliated, defeated, and ashamed. What would I do now?

Chapter 9 - Ronald

I was mortified by my relationship with Nate and how he ended it. After that unexpected disaster, I was hesitant about going back on the internet dating sites. The sites made me anxious and obsessive every time I joined up. I had become an internet dating junkie and I had to try to break the habit before it broke me.

I went to work on Monday with a heavy heart and a lack of self-esteem. I felt so defeated. I was working for a trucking company at the time and when I turned on my computer on that morning, there were quite a few instant messages from a few of our sales agents. We had about forty sales agents working for us, and they would always instant message me when they needed something or sometimes just to say hello.

I was constantly in communication with this one man named Ronald. He was always very nice to me and extremely helpful. His brother was one of our independent agents and Ronald worked for him. We were constantly going back and forth on the computer with each other.

Finally, one day we had decided to send pictures of ourselves through our email addresses. He thought I was adorable in my picture. When I received his picture, I was not very impressed. He lived in Minnesota and had such a great accent; I was expecting a different look. Ronald looked about 5'10", about 160 lbs. and he was bald with a mustache. He also looked about fifteen to twenty years older than I.

I hated being so picky and I did not like when men did that to me, besides it was slim pickings in my neck of the woods, so I decided to give Ronald a chance. It was either Ronald or back to that jungle of hell, called internet dating. We started talking on the phone every night for weeks and then he invited me to come up to spend Thanksgiving with him and his family in Minnesota. I decided to go since I had no one else to visit on this holiday.

When I got to the airport there was a ticket waiting for me. The airplane ride was great, but I was a little nervous about my trip there. I was going to a state I had never been to so I could meet a man I never met before and his family. All I had to go on was a picture he sent to me which didn't give me a lot of assurance. I had to stop thinking about the way he looked. Maybe he would be the one man that looked better in person then his picture. I kept hoping, but at the same time, I kept trying to talk myself into thinking looks don't count.

The plane landed and when I got out, I was looking for someone that fit his description. I looked around and there he was, holding a single red rose. Instead of focusing on the thoughtful gift of a rose, I was focused on how he looked. He looked worse than his picture. They always do! I tried to stay positive, but my word, he was wearing a fringed cowboy shirt, boots from the seventies, a cowboy hat and he had a little itty-bitty mustache. He looked like a not so good-looking cowboy stuck in a time warp.

I looked around thinking there might be a rodeo somewhere in the airport. It was quite awful, and we would be stuck at the hip for the next four days. He gave me a hug hello and handed me the rose. I thanked him and we walked through the airport to get to his car. I was hoping he had a car parked outside and not a horse. We walked to his car and there it was, almost as if I had pulled it from the side of my brain I did not want to acknowledge, a very old, Oldsmobile. He was driving a car from the eighties. I was preferring a horse at this moment. This car was almost the same age as my son, maybe older. I was hoping it had a heater because I just traveled to Minnesota from Florida, and I was freezing.

When we left the airport, we drove to his parent's house. His family greeted me in a very warm and loving manner. The food was set up on a buffet and everyone was doing their own thing and taking their plates into different rooms to eat.

I was quickly able to tell that Ronald did not have a great rapport with his family. He was there with them, but not really interacting with anyone. It was kind of weird.

We did not stay that long. After we ate, we said our goodbyes and hopped into his very old, Oldsmobile and headed to a motel he'd booked not far from where he lived. It was a four hour drive to his neck of the woods. When he finally pulled into the motel parking lot, I was in shock. It was not like I was expecting a five star hotel, but I was hoping for at least one star. This place looked like the Bates Motel from the movie psycho. The room was beyond small and there was barely a blanket heavy enough to heat up my Florida blood. The bathroom sink was all rusty and the shower was an *enter at your own risk* type situation. I wanted to cry. How was I going to make it through 3 nights here?

I asked if I could stay with him at his place. I told him I did not mind sleeping on the couch. He said he lived in a very tiny trailer in the woods, and it was not big enough for a couch and he felt I would be more comfortable at the motel. I jokingly asked him if he had running water. He did not find me amusing.

Soon Ronald left and told me he would pick me up for breakfast in the morning. I looked at my watch praying for the morning and wondering how to make Sunday come quicker. Not only was I bad at internet dating, but I was also a bad judge of character. It's not that Ronald was a bad guy or anything like that, but he was different then I thought, and I could tell in just these few short hours that we were not a good fit. I put a chair in front of the door, slept in my clothes and hoped I would make it through the first night.

Ronald and I spend the next few days going out to eat and just driving and seeing the sights. He was an excellent kisser and a pure gentleman, but I believed he was extremely poor. He would not even show me where he lived and would not talk about his past, or anything! If that wasn't a red flag, what is?

I was counting down the days to go home since my room at the Bates Motel was probably one of my worse motel or hotel experiences of my life. On Saturday, Day 2, we spend the day with Ronald's brother and his family. They had a beautiful house and I finally got to use a bathroom that was modernized and up to my expectations as what a bathroom should be. We had gone out that night to a wonderful dinner in a beautiful restaurant. Thank goodness his brother offered to pay for dinner or there would have been a chance we would be washing dishes all night, which actually sounded better than going back to my motel.

After dinner, Ronald made the decision to start the four hour trek close to the airport since I had a very early flight the next morning. It seemed like it was important to him to make sure I made my early flight because what would he do with me if I had to stay one more day. He probably had no more money for the motel, and he was set against me seeing his place.

The four hour drive seemed like two days. I just wanted to get to the next hotel near the airport for I'd hardly slept these few days and just wanted to get home. This long weekend did not meet any of my expectations which, if the truth be told, were not that high. Ronald pulled into the airport and instead of pulling into a hotel or motel; he pulled into a parking spot. I asked him if he was going to drop me off at a hotel and he told me, you are not going to stay in a hotel, because I thought we can stay in my car all night until you are ready to check in for your flight. Really! It is midnight and my flight is not until 7:00am. Ronald told me he had no more money for motels and there was nothing wrong with sleeping in a car. He does it all the time. I just looked at him, thinking, *there is probably no trailer in the woods either.*

This was so bad! I wanted to scream… I wanted to run… but where to?

This weekend just kept getting better and better! It was like The Sorcerer's Apprentice. It just kept coming, multiplying and I had no control over any of it. Ronald told me to put the seat back and get some rest. I had no pillow, no blanket and when he shut the car off, you could smell the old, pungent smell of his very old, Oldsmobile. I used my jacket as a pillow. I was miserable and under very limited conditions here. This had to be one of the most uncomfortable nights of my life.

I kept hoping we wouldn't get towed in the middle of the night for illegal parking. It was very cold outside, and the car was freezing without the heater on. I must have dozed on and off over the course of the next few hours, each time waking up and feeling like I was hit by a bus. When I saw the crack of dawn, I woke Ronald and said, I need to go and check in for my flight now.

"Thank goodness," I thought. I had never in my whole life been this excited to sit in the airport and wait for my plane. Ronald pulled up to the front and helped me out of the car. I only had my carry on suitcase and my pocketbook. I wonder if it looked obvious to him that I could not wait to get out of here. I wondered how he could not see that sleeping in a freezing car was not fun. I hugged him goodbye, thanked him for everything and ran like the wind into the airport building. I checked in, eventually got on my plane and as usual felt sorry for myself and cried most of the way home.

Chapter 10 - Gary

After I returned home from Minnesota, I was a little depressed and felt completely hopeless. Would I ever find a good man to have a relationship with? Was I asking for the impossible? Was it me? These were the questions that continually ran through my head each day. Where would I look for love now?

I walked past my computer, looked at it, and said, "What the heck!" I opened my internet site and clicked on Date that Mate once again to sign up. I was like an addict, but I paid my fee and reactivated my account, updated my profile and added some new pictures. I told myself this time would be different. After I updated and freshen up everything on my site, I got ready for bed. Maybe when I woke up tomorrow, the man of my dreams would have sent me a message.

When Monday rolled around it was time to go back to work. Of course, the first thing I did was check my emails. I had ten new emails. I went through each one, read each profile and as always, they all seemed like losers or players. As I was getting ready to log off, another email popped up. It was from a gorgeous looking man named Gary. He was an account executive working at a big company and loved to do everything I enjoyed doing. He wrote me a beautiful email, telling me all about himself and what he was looking for. I wrote him back and unfortunately, I would have to wait until I got home that night to check my mail to see if he responded.

It was a long day for me. My obsession and I just couldn't wait to go home to check my mail. Finally, the day ended, and I drove home impatiently hoping Gary had written back. When I got home, my obsession had taken over me completely. With my pocketbook still in hand and my jacket still on, I ran to my computer to log on. It felt like it was taking forever for my computer to turn on and gear up. I finally put in my password and there was no email yet from him. I was so disappointed! I had spent my entire day waiting for this email and just like that, nothing! He was so good looking. What if he found someone better looking than me in this course of the day and was already gone? I couldn't take this pressure and thought process that had taken over my total being. I was so obsessed with this whole dating thing that I actually spend my entire night checking my emails literally every 5 minutes until I went to sleep.

I woke up feeling disappointed and defeated. Of course, I checked my emails before I left for work and there it was. The response I have been impatiently waiting for from him for the past 24 hours. I opened it up and he wanted to talk with me. He included his phone number in the email and told me to call him that night. I happily left for work and felt I was finally in the driver's seat because he would be waiting for me to call him. How unexpected! It was another long drawn out day, but 5:00 came and my obsession and I drove home in hope of having a great conversation with Gary. I did not run to check my emails when I got home, but instead was becoming obsessed with what time to call him, so I did not seem desperate and crazed, which of course I was.

I thought 9:00 would be a great time to call him. It would also make him wonder if I was going to call and it would show him, I have other things to do. How I made it three hours without pulling out my hair or jumping off a bridge was miraculous. 9:00 came and I dialed his number, and to my dismay I got his voicemail. Extremely disappointed I still left a very bubbly message with my number telling him he could reach me up to 11:00. I hung up and of course obsessed over the fact that maybe I waited too long to call and maybe he found someone else. Gary never called that night, and I went to sleep once again disappointed and defeated.

I woke up the next morning and when I checked my phone and my emails, there was nothing from him. I once again got ready for work. It would be another long day waiting for my phone to ring. All day I sat and just stared at my phone. As my obsession and I drove home, it was a long and depressing ride feeling sorry for myself. When I got inside my apartment, I rushed to open my emails to see if he emailed me, but once again nothing.

I threw myself on the bed and cried. I must have fallen asleep and two hours later I was awakened by my phone ringing. It was Gary. I was ecstatic! We talked for a while and he sounded great! He told me all about himself and he actually sounded normal. We agreed to meet at a bar Friday night. I couldn't wait.

I had foolishly convinced myself that this man would be the one. Friday night came and I made sure to look perfect. I walked into the bar and there he was. Finally! I found someone, who lived up to their photo. He was tall, handsome and was dressed amazing and in very good taste. I was so excited to meet him.

Our eyes met each other's glance, and we said our hello's. He seemed very taken with me and it felt amazing for a change. He gave me a big hug and we talked for over three hours sharing some appetizers. I could have spoken with him for days. I was hooked!

When it was time to part, he told me he would call me to set up our next date. My old feelings of disappointment for the night was that he didn't make a solid plan for next time and I would have to wait once more for him to call. I was so bad at being patient and waiting for the phone to ring, but not wanting to sound needy I told him that would be fine. He walked me to my car, gave me a soft, gentle kiss and told me he would call me over the next few days. I drove home happy, content and finally feeling a sense of internet dating achievement.

Of course, the next day was Saturday and I as usual was pacing the floor all day waiting for the phone to ring, hoping that I would get to see him , but he never called. It was as usual a bad weekend of excessive over thinking of what did I do to make him not want to spend time with me especially on a Saturday night, which is always recognized as date night.

By the time Monday rolled around, I figured it was over, but right before I was ready to go on the site to fish out another man, I saw there was an email from him. It said, "It was great meeting you the other night. I will call you one night this week to schedule a date with you." I felt very relieved and tried to figure out why I keep letting my imagination run away with me.

Finally, by Thursday night he called and asked me out for Friday. We went to a beautiful French restaurant near the beach and had a lovely dinner filled with great food, amazing conversation and just a perfect time. He was so easy to be with. After dinner we took a long walk along the shore and watched the sun set. It was beautiful and everything I dreamed of when I saw myself finding the one.

He kissed me and gave me a hug and then once again walked me to my car and told me he would be calling me next week to schedule another date. This pattern continued just like this over the course of the next three weeks. He also always had me meet him somewhere and it is always just on a Friday night with a perfect date followed by days of non-communication. Now why was this not feeling right to me? Maybe this was a new way to date, because it seemed like almost everyone, I would go out with would follow a strange pattern of behavior of some kind similar to this. It was also a little strange to me that such a good-looking man like Gary wanted nothing more from me than a kiss. It was very interesting!

A few days later just like clockwork he asked me to meet him at a fancy restaurant in Boca Raton. I was a desperate woman trying to make something work, so I went to meet him, and I was on a mission to try to see if I could finesse some information out of him and hopefully find out a little bit more about what skeletons he had hiding in his closet.

We once again had a lovely dinner filled with great food and conversation, but when I tried asking him certain questions, I noticed that he was really good at tiptoeing around them. He had mentioned that he lived two blocks from this restaurant so I bravely asked him if I could have a tour of this beautiful apartment that he was always telling me about. Surprisingly, he actually agreed, and we drove in his brand new beautiful car, which I had never been in until today, to his ultra-magnificent apartment located in a penthouse style on the beach.

His apartment was on the 12th floor and WOW was it spectacular! It had marble floors, a view of the ocean from all the large, magnificent windows and an unbelievable gourmet kitchen. I would have no problem living here. Everything was perfect and he was neat as a pin. *This was my type of guy!* I thought as I looked around, examining the apartment.

Once Gary gave me the grand tour, he excused himself to go to the bathroom leaving me alone in the very large living room. I nosily looked around a bit just to see if there was something about him I needed to know for my own protection. (Yes, that is me justifying my snooping actions.) I did not find anything that would point me to the fact that he was married, unless he had two different residences and maybe his wife did not know about this one. "Well, you never know what people are up to," I thought.

As I snooped a bit more, listening with one ear for Gary's return from the other room, I stumbled across a black date book on his very organized desk. I generally do not make a habit of looking into people's private documents, but I was being pulled to this book like a bee is to honey.

This beautiful black book looked very expensive and elegant. Gary seemed to be able to afford the best and even a date book was top of the line. I opened the book carefully while still listening to him coming. When it was still quiet, I turned to the pages in the calendar for this week. Monday it said, dinner with Eva, Tuesday it said, dinner with Susan, Wednesday it said, dinner with Kathy, Thursday read night to relax and review specs for job. And there it was for Friday, dinner with Sharon. Saturday read, dinner and overnight at Jeannette's place.

I quickly went back and forth eyeballing through the past and future weeks. My heart raced quickly like I was being chased by a thief. I couldn't slow it down. This book read like a schedule of a pimp. No wonder I never got more than a slight peck on the cheek or lips and was only able to see him on Fridays. He was so busy getting homeruns all week by the time he got to Friday, he ran out of game.

I was beyond upset! I was trying to keep the tears from coming. I was starting to go into fright or flight mode and all I wanted to do was run and I did! I quickly without thinking dropped his book, grabbed my bag, and ran to the elevator and out the front doors of the lobby. I felt like I couldn't breathe. Thank goodness he only lived two blocks from the restaurant where my car was parked.

Tears started streaming down my face. *Was this for real? Was I just set up on a game show for laughs?* What makes these men think they are entitled to treat women any way they feel fit for them? He was courting a harem of women like he was a sheik. I was beyond discouraged and completely downhearted. Gary had thrown the wool over my eyes and he blinded me. This proved even more to me that I would never find anyone and all I was looking for was true love and normalcy. Does that even exist anymore?

This revelation was such a letdown that took me for a loop. I really had to break my addiction to internet dating and completely stay away from it. It was dangerous. It seemed to harbor men from a different world or planet. These internet sites gave false hope to people. It was a case of looking for love in all the wrong places. I had to avoid all of the wolves in sheep's clothing. I went to bed crying and thinking of where I can turn to find a nice, honest man. My brain was shocked out and overwhelmed and at some point, it shut down and I fell fast asleep.

Chapter 11 - Back to Ronald

After Gary, I was extremely depressed and beaten down. Gary never even tried to contact me or see if I was okay. I guess I was nothing more than collateral damage for him and he was probably used to women finding out and leaving. *No skin off his back*, I figured.

Since my trip to Minnesota, Ronald was emailing me here and there. I guess he sincerely liked me. Well, at least someone did! He was a very nice man and a gentleman. It really was not his fault he was poor and not clever when it came to knowing how to court a woman properly.

Eventually, I started emailing him back and we talked a little on the phone. I wanted to learn more about him, and I started thinking that if Ronald was here on my turf the relationship might be different. This was desperation in its finest moment, but I was willing to try anything. So, Ronald and I spent the next few weeks emailing at home and messaging each other at work. We also started talking on the phone once or twice a week with each other.

We made plans for him to come down to Florida and spend a few days with each other. The good thing about him was I already met him and his family, so I felt safe. I just had to make something work. I hated living on my own, I did not like being single and I was really lonely. I was coming up dry on the internet and frankly it was zapping away my energy and my outlook on life and love. I felt like I was becoming hopeless and helpless. I needed to meet someone the natural way. I just felt like the internet is a falsified means to getting a date and hoping there would be some chemistry; instead of the old fashion way, which was you see someone, and they see you and your eyes meet and there it is: instant chemistry! The way nature and God our Creator intended it to be.

Electronic outlets to find a date just maybe are not real dates. I also felt that the internet had become a playroom for many men and women who were not looking for commitment but were looking to play and just have a good time. You had to be very cautious of who was on the other side of your computer. It was a buyer beware scenario and I was tired of paying for something that had no guarantee of anything, no return and which even posed a danger to my life. I was burnt out and unhappy, so I was settled on making it work with Ronald no matter what it took. At least I knew what I was getting up front.

I picked Ronald up at the airport and we drove in my new car back to my apartment. When we entered the apartment, he looked around and asked, "Are you rich?"

I was a little shocked. I was living in a very old complex and my condo needed so much work, but for me it was affordable. It is amazing how people's perceptions can be so different. I settled him in and gave him everything he would need to be comfortable, including cooking him a gourmet dinner. He enjoyed the meal with me, and we had wonderful conversation that was smooth and free flowing. Afterwards we watched some television together and went to sleep. It felt wonderful to be able to do all these normal, practical, everyday things with someone and I felt happy and content for a change. I closed my eyes and fell soundly to sleep.

Sometime during the night, I was suddenly awoken by what appeared to be the sound of a freight train passing through my bedroom. It turned out to be Ronald snoring. *Good grief!* Did he always snore like this? I tried to shake the bed a bit to see if it would jostle him a little so he would turn over, but he did not budge. I did not want to wake him, so I grabbed my pillow and retreated to my couch in the other room. The next morning, I woke up first and snuck back in my bed. When Ronald woke up, I never mentioned the snoring to him.

We got dressed and ate breakfast and headed out so I could show Ronald some of the sights of South Florida. He had never been here, so it was exciting to show him some of my favorite places and hot spots, including our beautiful beaches. We had a really great afternoon, and it was so nice having someone to experience it with. When evening came, I suggested dinner and a movie and he said, "I will pay for dinner if you pay for the movie." I agreed and we chose a wonderful pizzeria. He had expressed to me that times had been tough, and this was all he could afford. I told him, I love pizza and can eat it every day.

We had a really nice evening together and when we got home, I made him coffee and I had a cup of tea. Ronald was a huge coffee drinker, so I made sure to have a lot of it on hand. We talked for a couple of hours and then went to sleep. Once again during the night, I got awaken again by that freight train that passed through the room once more. I grabbed my pillow and once again retreated quietly to the couch. I had made the decision to talk to him about this the next morning.

I woke up first as always and snuck back into bed. When he awakened, he gave me a big hug and told me how easy it is to be with me. Of course, it was easy to be with me. I was doing all the compromising behind his back. At breakfast I brought up the snoring. He told me that if he is on his back, he snores so next time I should just nudge him and tell him to rollover and the snoring will stop. So that night, right on time the freight train rolled on in, I gently nudged him, but there was no response. I tried it again, but nothing. I realized I could not budge him no matter how hard I tried. This man was a sleeping stone. I grabbed my pillow and camped out once more on my couch.

The next morning, I once more snuck quietly back into bed, and he was still snoring. It looked like the freight train never left my station last night. His snoring was so severe that it sounded like a wounded warthog was in bed with me. I laid there thinking about how to present this current snoring issue without hurting his feelings or sending him packing home.

It was still so early, so I rolled over to see if I could fall asleep with the snoring when I felt something bite my behind. I rolled over and there it was every partner's nightmare. A top set of teeth just sitting there staring at me on my sheets while I, in sudden horror, stared back at them. He never told me he wore dentures, and if he did, shouldn't they be soaking in a jar in the bathroom? I didn't know what to do. Should I wake him up and tell him? Were they his? Was it possible these teeth came in riding on that freight train just passing through and decided to take up residence in my bed? I was beyond horrified.

I left the smiling teeth that attacked my behind where they were. I was not going to touch them or pick them up. I scurried out of my bedroom to find something else to do but think about the naked teeth that were lying helpless on my bed. When Ronald awoke, he had the teeth in his mouth and did not mention anything to me about it. I decided not to bring this up and we went on with our day.

The next two days had the same plot. We enjoyed the time during the day but each night he snored, and I retreated to the couch. At least for the next two nights Mr. Jaws did not show up again. *Thank goodness!* When it was time to say goodbye and bring Ronald back to the airport, he proposed a plan to me. He suggested he would try to get a transfer to the corporate center where I work and then we could live together, build a life and eventually get married. *Wow!* He really cared for me. Someone wanted to marry me. Things were not perfect, but it was a chance for me to get married again and never to be alone anymore.

I had trouble with the snoring, but most men snored. I could turn my second bedroom into a second master bedroom and not have to sleep on the couch or deal with the snoring. It could work! And as far as him losing his teeth, it was not his fault he wore dentures. In the moment, I found ways to justify anything and everything that got in my way of making this relationship work.

When he got back to Minnesota, he worked on getting transferred to the Florida office. When it got approved, he packed up his very old Oldsmobile and drove to Florida to spend the rest of his life with me. He got to my house on a Saturday and spent a few hours unloading his car. I made him dinner and we watched a movie together. Once again when he fell asleep, the freight train showed up for a visit. I still wasn't able to nudge him to get him to roll over. I took my pillow and once again spent a night on the couch.

I was not able to set up my second bedroom as another master because my son was away at school, and I would have to see where he would be eventually living when he graduated before I could do anything, so it was back to the couch. I told him again about the snoring and eventually he figured out I was spending every night on the couch, but he never offered to give me the bed, not even once. I justified my new sleeping arrangement by telling myself, it was this or spending the rest of my life by myself.

My obsession had taken on a life of its own. A week later, Ronald started his new job at my company. We decided to take separate cars each day especially since his position was sales related and he would have to sometimes stay later than I.

The next few weeks started to take on its pattern and Ronald had become very content with it and his life with me. As for myself, I was starting to become bored and a little down. I would wake up each morning exhausted from sleeping on the couch and I so missed my bed.

I worked all day and of course Ronald never wanted to eat lunch with me at work because he does not eat lunch. Every night I would be the one cooking dinner and he told me that he could not pitch in for groceries because he did not have the money yet, so it was all on me. Ronald was working on a 100% commission basis, and it could take a few months until he made some solid deals and start generating steady commission. If I wanted to go out and eat or see a movie or anything, the whole financial burden was on me. I did not feel at this point I was getting anything out of this relationship, but a lack of sleep. Every time I walked my dog Ronald watched me from the window and freaked out if I even said hello to a male neighbor in my building. I guess you really do not know someone until you live with them.

When my birthday came, Ronald gave me a beautiful blue sapphire pendent. It was quite stunning! I had asked him how he could afford this, and he told me he bought it for me before he moved down here. I thanked him and tried it on. It really was pretty, and it felt so nice getting a piece of jewelry from someone who really cares about you. I had not experienced that in a while.

A week later, Ronald got served with papers at work in front of everyone. His wages once he started making some,; was going to be garnished for money he owed, to who, I had no idea. Ronald refused to talk to me about what this was from, and it seemed very serious. I tried nagging him about it to find out something, but he held tight to whatever secrets he was clinging to.

A week later when other claims were coming his way, I told him he must disclose what is going on. He told me that some woman from years ago is claiming he fathered four of her children and he owes her money for them that he never paid. He said it was a lie and she was just trying to extort him.

Now why did this story not sound right to me? If it happened years ago, why is this popping up now and DNA testing can prove it right or wrong so why is he not getting this done. Does he think I am such an ignorant person that I would believe such a story or is he the ignorant one who thinks this story holds truth that I should also see? Ronald had more skeletons in his closet than a haunted house. This story felt so wrong and when I tried to ask more questions, he got very upset and a little irate with me. This was another red flag that he was in serious trouble. I decided to back off and wait till he was in a better mood to discuss it.

The next day we went to work, and he was expecting his first check. Between some sales that had to be put on hold until next month and the garnishment the government was taking out, Ronald hardly got anything worth going to the bank to cash. He started making a very big scene with management in front of everyone. I was so embarrassed I wanted to crawl into a hole. He was screaming and threatening everyone. He was actually getting a little postal and I was scared to go home and be with him alone. I had never seen this side of him.

He was fired immediately and then became more out of hand that two security guards with guns came and escorted him out saying if he comes back, he will be arrested. It was 1:00 in the afternoon when he was walked to his car while he was screaming and cursing under his breath. I did not want to leave. I needed him to go home and cool off completely before I was alone with him. It was the longest Friday afternoon of my life wondering what he was doing and where he was. I tried calling his cell phone all day long and it just went to voicemail which made me even more anxious.

By 5:00 pm I was completely frantic, and I drove home like a maniac praying not to get a ticket. When I finally reached my parking lot, I noticed his car was not there. I was petrified to enter my apartment thinking he could have destroyed everything in his anger or sold all my belongings for money. My mind was running so quickly I couldn't keep up with it.

I entered the apartment with much trepidation and felt an eerie feeling in my gut. Everything seemed intact, but something still felt wrong. I looked around and I noticed there was no sign of Ronald ever living here. Everything he owned or came with was gone, including all his clothes, his hygiene products and his coffeemaker. I checked all my jewelry and things I owned that had value and everything was there, but the beautiful blue pendant he gave me. He took that, I guess claiming it was his. I was so surprised and humiliated that he would just leave without even writing me a note thanking me and saying goodbye.

That night I had a friend change the locks on the door for me. I never tried calling him again and he never contacted me or sent me even a letter explaining things. *What a winner!*

It was a blessing in disguise, but another broken, hurtful relationship made up of me giving and giving and Ronald just taking. I was once again alone and completely broken and shattered. My one true joy that night was being able to get my bed back. The nocturnal tuba symphony had packed up and left on the freight train, no longer to return. This was a blessing, but as I thought about my days ahead, "What would I do now to find a relationship?"

Chapter 12 - MelodyofLove.com

The days had gone by, and I was feeling again so lonely and defeated. The thought of going back on Date That Mate sickened me and actually scared me. While watching television all week, I kept seeing ads for a new dating site called MelodyofLove.com which advertised it as being different than all others. It also cost a lot more than the others. It claims to use a method that matches you on many levels of compatibilities for both men and women to get a solid match. I was drawn to this site like children are drawn to candy. I just had to keep trying. I had to find someone. So I sat down at my computer and my obsession and I joined up on this new site.

I paid the fee, uploaded my picture and profile and then did what I do worst. I waited! I had to wait for a match to be sent to me. This site matches people for you so there was no scrolling through to see who I liked or wanted to contact. The site had to find the perfect match of two people before it would send a notification to both of you. I had no choice on this new site, but to wait. I went to sleep and hoped when I woke up in the morning that there would be some matches for me.

The next morning upon waking my obsession and I ran to the computer filled with hope that here would be a few matches. When I turned on the computer and checked my emails there was only one match. It started with some questions I had to answer that were sent by the guy who I was matched with. I answered all the questions carefully and sent them. Then I had to send him questions and wait for him to return them to me. This pattern of questions and answers without any contact of any kind went on back and forth for days. It was driving me crazy. You could not even see each other's pictures or profile until the question segment was completed, with answers matching appropriate data. If the answers match appropriately, you both moved to the next level, and if not, it was a bust and the match disappeared.

After what seemed like a whole week of questions, I was able to move to the next level where we got to view each other's picture. I finally viewed his picture. He was very good looking. The type of guy I am looking for. I had to click that I was still interested so that I could go to the next level to make contact. So, he would view me and if he was interested and clicked that he was, we would be allowed to make a first contact. I was starting to get excited.

I kept waiting, but nothing and then a few days later I received a notification that my match was no longer interested. What a letdown after all that work. This went on for weeks with a match here and a match there with the same pattern and then a notification that they were not interested. I even got a notification that one of my matches was no longer a member. I can see why! Either my questionnaire profile was not exciting to anyone, or my matches were not good fits.

I couldn't imagine what was going on behind the scenes on this site. I had a great picture up, but not sure too many men saw it because I never got that far with most. This pattern of men leaving the site or just disappearing went on till I was close to the end of the month and the end of my monthly membership cycle. I paid $50.00 for this site and would have liked to have at least a date and one cup of coffee out of it.

I was only getting one to two matches a week that went nowhere except for one man that I had finally got to the end of the questions round with. We finally got to see each other's pictures and while his picture was not the greatest, I was determined to get one date from this site, just to see if this site really even exists beyond the questions and a picture. Finally, we both wanted to move to the next level and the system allowed us to correspond.

His name was Marty and he seemed nice enough. We were able to finally exchange phone numbers and we talked one night, and the conversation seemed nice and free-flowing. Marty asked me out for my first MelodyofLove date. We chose one of my favorite Asian Bistro restaurants. When I got there, he was already there waiting for me. He was nice looking and very tall. We said our hellos and waited to be seated.

Once we were seated, we talked about the menu. I ordered my favorite chicken dish, and he ordered a salmon. We both ordered separate appetizers and when I reached over to try one of his, he snapped at me like a snapping turtle and said, "These are mine. Yours are over there." *Gee, I guess we have our first red flag. He does not want to share, and he almost took my head off for it.*

The conversation between us was not all that great in person as I had hoped from our phone conversation. I was looking for some sort of way to make the hard hit from his snippy remark not sting so much.

Our entrees arrived and his dish looked amazing. This time I asked him if I could taste a piece of it. And there came red flag #2. He exclaimed, "I do not and will not share my meal with anyone. You have your own meal so please stop asking for mine and try to enjoy what you chose." I cannot even explain how a statement like that zaps away your appetite.

More than halfway through my intolerable meal, I reached over to his side where the server put the bowl of lemons that I would need for my iced tea. Marty put his hand in front of the lemon to block me and once again, exclaimed, "Please ask for things out of your reach instead of rudely coming close to my plate while I am eating."

I just looked at him with crossed eyes, there was flag #3 and trust me there was no charm. This date was more like a game show where every time you get a wrong answer the buzzer goes off. This date was going badly, and I was stuck in it. This man was not for me or probably not for anyone who was looking for a human being. Not only was Marty rude, but I could only imagine what he would be like after being in a relationship with him and he's comfortable with me.

Usually, people are at their best on the first date so for Marty he had nowhere to go but down. He seemed like a guy with anger management issues, but heck I was not going to be the one to let him know that. I just couldn't wait for this date to be over. We finally got the check, and he walked me to my car. He told me he would call me, and he hurriedly walked away. I drove home disheartened feeling as usual like there were absolutely no decent men left in the world.

When I got home, I felt a little relieved that this horrible date was over, but as always, my obsession and I turned on the computer to see if I had any other prospects. There had been one other guy emailing me since we saw each other's pictures. I wasn't crazy about the way he looked in his picture, but decided some people are not very photogenic. I emailed him and asked if we could talk over the phone, closed down my computer, and went into bed for the night. My mind wandered on all the events of that night, and I kept thinking that eventually, statistically speaking, I would have to hit the jackpot sometime. That is usually how the odds work. As I lay down to sleep, I prayed there would be a response to my email and this guy would be the one.

When I awoke in the morning the first thing I did, of course was to feed my obsession by checking to see if I had a response. I had one and his name was Ted and while his email or picture did not quite move me, I just felt I had to find a way to make something with him work. My monthly subscription was just about up, and I was wasting a lot of money on these sites without getting any return on my dollar.

Ted wanted to talk with me to and sent his phone number. When I called him later in the day, we talked for a while on the phone. He told me he was 54 years old, but he looked in his picture like he was in his 60's. He asked me when I wanted to go out to meet with him and I actually told him in a few days. I was shocked to hear myself say that. I think I was trying to control my obsession by not being too desperate. I chose Friday, which was two days later, and I felt proud of myself that I was playing it cool.

I also had to admit that I was not all that excited about meeting him. I wasn't crazy about his voice. It was very raspy and kind of hoarse. It was not a sexy voice, but I was doing my best to not be so picky and judgmental.

I picked my favorite Asian Bistro again. I loved that restaurant and since my last dinner date did not go well, I decided to try it with someone else and see if I can have a memorable experience there.

Ted asked me to meet him at the bar. I was hoping we would also have dinner. I cannot go to this restaurant and not eat. I love it too much! I got there before Ted and just in case, put my name down on the list for a table and then took a seat at the bar facing the entrance of the restaurant so I can see ahead of time any single men walking in. It's not that I wanted to be ready to run, but I wanted to prepare myself for the worst.

A man came in and he was walking toward me, and I was hoping it was him because he was gorgeous with a light up the whole room smile, but it wasn't. Another guy came walking in and I prayed it was not him because he was sloppy with bad posture and poor hygiene. I kept saying," Please don't let it be him," to myself. And he magically passed me by as well.

I watched as another man started walking towards me. He seemed worse than the last. This man was coming right to me, and I wanted to make like a ghost and disappear. This man did not look like the picture. He looked about twenty years older than his picture and was wearing very old man styled clothing. This was definitely not my cup of tea or coffee for that matter. He came right up to me. If there was a lake in my view, I would have jumped in it. *Why do these men lie? Somebody please tell me why?* I was not lying about my picture. I actually look better than my picture, so they are getting the better end of the deal. I was stuck now for the entire evening at my favorite restaurant with a man who resembled my great grandfather.

Ted came up to me with his raspy voice and said, "Hi, are you Sharon?" I wanted to say *no*, but for some reason I told the truth. He immediately asked the bartender for a drink. When he got it, he guzzled it down and asked for another. He asked me if I put my name down on the list for a table. I showed him the pager and just at that moment, it started to beep. *Thank goodness.*

He grabbed his drink; hopefully his last and we followed the hostess to be seated. He began asking me questions about myself and I answered the best I could. I just could not stop focusing on how old he looked. I was almost embarrassed to be seen with him because next to him, I looked like I could be a gold-digger.

We ordered spring rolls for the appetizer, and he ordered a third drink. He was either nervous due to the fact that he lied about his age, or he was an alcoholic. Our appetizers came and we started eating.

Halfway through our deteriorating conversation, he had a very tiny piece of carrot stuck to his chin from the spring roll. It was driving me crazy. It just sat there on his chin staring at me. Our entrees came and the carrot was still sitting there like someone glued it to his face.

When he received his fifth drink, I had asked him if he always drinks this much? I thought he would chop my head off for asking that question. He replied, "What are you, my mother?"

I felt horrified! I couldn't wait for dinner to be over. Who were these men that you cannot even ask them a single question without them chewing off your face? I tried to quietly eat my dinner without saying much, but all I could do is just focus on that carrot attached to his chin. If only he would pick up his napkin like most people do and wipe his mouth, maybe the carrot would come off and disappear. I tried to eat but was losing my appetite as the carrot just hung there helplessly. I had gotten an urgent need to take my finger and just flick it off, but I felt that might cause a hostile reaction in this strange old man.

We were finally finished with our dinner, and I was upset that I wasted my whole delicious meal focusing on the carrot and wondering if he was so numb from all the alcohol that he did not feel the carrot pinned to his chin. Finally, when he was all finished eating, he wiped his face with his napkin and the annoying carrot was gone. He paid the bill, and we got up and walked out.

He asked where I was parked and walked me to my car. This gentlemanly gesture got him absolutely no points. I was surprised he could even walk straight after all his drinks. I was dreading telling him I didn't feel a connection and it would be best if we didn't see each other again. I was concerned he might react and become irate, especially after paying for my dinner, but to my surprise he told me to drive home safely, and he was not interested in seeing me again. He told me I was not what he was expecting or wanted in a partner. I was actually rejected by a reject!

I got in my car and drove away. Another dud date! What a waste of my time. I felt sad and disappointed as always and my sense of self-confidence was literally in the toilet. I just couldn't understand how I just kept meeting these awful men. I was continually beating myself up and was lost at this moment. When I got home, I decided to get off of the MelodyofLove site. It did not give me enough options and I had no control over the contacting or timeframe involved with it. I got ready for bed and decided tomorrow my obsession and I would search for a much better dating site where I would be in the driver's seat.

Chapter 13 - Single Mingle

I had been getting a lot of notifications from other dating sites to join. They would send me men's profiles to try to lure me onto their dating sites. Some of the profiles and pictures they were sending me from Single Mingle looked great. The men were extremely good looking with outstanding profiles. If this was just a marketing scheme to pull me in, well it was working.

I checked out the site and it seemed legit, so I joined and sent twenty or so messages to some nice looking men. It felt good to be able to contact anyone I wanted instead of having the system control me and the preferences it thought was best for me. Obviously, that did not work, so here I was back on a regular dating site to see who I could find, meet and fall in love with.

It was great to be able to find so many nice men that I had not as of yet seen on other dating sites. Within minutes of me sending the messages, I had already gotten a few responses. One man in particular caught my eye. His name was Jeff, and he was very handsome. He was a Computer Analyst and had never been married. We started emailing back and forth and after a week or so he asked for my phone number and called me. He sounded great over the phone, and we agreed to meet for dinner on Friday night.

When Friday night finally came, I was very excited. Maybe this would finally be the right one. He had a beautiful voice over the phone and told me he looked just like his photo. I couldn't wait to meet him. We made plans to meet at an Italian restaurant, my choice of course. I arrived first and anxiously waited for him to walk in. Finally, with my heart beating fast, a guy who looked just like his photo entered through the door. It was refreshing to see he told the truth about his picture.

He walked over to me and gave me a big hug. We were seated at once and started talking about everything. We had so much to say, and the conversation was so free flowing, it was wonderful and very comfortable. The chemistry between us was over the top and I was having the best time. I had not had a dinner date like this in years. After dinner we took a long walk and just talked. There just seemed to be a non-stop stream of conversation that we wanted to talk about. It started getting late and he walked me to my car. I did not want this night to end. He gave me a small kiss on my cheek, and we made plans to go out the next night. *Wow, no having to wait for the phone to ring tomorrow*, I thought to myself. I think I finally found a certified boyfriend. I felt so elated.

Saturday night came and we met another restaurant with once again non-stop free flowing conversation. Afterwards we went bowling and it was a blast. Jeff was just the type of man I was looking for: good looking, funny, smart and a complete gentleman in every way. He once again walked me back to my car and gave me a small kiss on my cheek and made plans for the next day, which was Sunday. *Wow, three dates in a row and all on the weekend.* I was in dating heaven.

I was wondering why he had not tried to kiss me, but decided he was a true gentleman and wanted to get to know me first. The next morning, we went out for breakfast. I had not been on a breakfast date with a man in a long time. It felt amazing! We sat forever talking, laughing, making future plans. This was exactly the relationship I was thirsting for, and it had arrived. By the afternoon, I asked him if he wanted to come to my apartment and watch a movie with me. He was hesitant, but then agreed to come.

When we arrived at my apartment, I put a man's type of movie on for him, made some popcorn and lemonade and we cuddled together on my couch watching the movie. After the movie, I asked him if he would like me to cook him a nice dinner. He said, "He wasn't sure." I thought that was a strange comment and asked him if everything was, okay?

I started getting that weird feeling in the pit of my stomach but tried to talk myself out of it. Jeff was putting his shoes on, and he said he needed to leave. I tried desperately to find out what happened. We were just watching a movie so I couldn't have said or done anything to upset him in that small window of time. Why is it that I finally after all this time find a great guy and already on day 3 there is an issue! I begged him to just sit down and talk to me and finally Jeff agreed to that, so we sat, and he talked as I listened impatiently.

He told me that he liked me very much, but things were moving way too fast for him. He said he really was not looking for a relationship. I told him I was confused because his profile said otherwise. He said he knows and apologized for his false profile. He said that every time he dates, and he starts to get close to someone he runs scared. I asked him, "Why?" He seems to have some trouble laying all his cards out on the table, but with my deep questioning and persistence the truth, or was it finally came out.

He explained that he had contracted a non-curable illness that was not life threatening but made it hard to be in a relationship. He told me that sometimes he gets outbreaks, and he was not comfortable being with anyone at that time or having any kind of physical relationship. I tried to find out what his illness was but did not get very far. He told me it was very nice knowing me and walked out my door. He left me in a stupor. I was seriously in a state of shock. This is probably why this adorable man was available and never had been married.

I wanted to cry. I wanted to run and never stop. It was always something and I was so tired and exhausted from all the "somethings" and being in the center of this internet dating jungle of hell. Tears started rolling down my cheeks. He had not tried to kiss me in 3 days and did not really want to come up to my apartment or pick me up on any of these three dates, but as always, my red flags were hidden by my obsessive desire to find the one. I never heard from Jeff again, but days later I saw his same profile was still on the site and wondered if he made up that story just to get out of this newborn relationship with me. Who was he for real? This all was so troubling and hard to swallow.

I was so disenchanted with this dating game that I truly wanted to just quit, but I was so obsessed with finding the one that would change my life and make it better that I couldn't stop. I had become a real internet dating addict. With a heavy heart, I went back on the site and did what I do best; look for someone else to hurt me. There had been so many other men contacting me that I had a large pick of the litter at this time. I started answering some of them wondering what kind of dodo birds I will meet next. Somewhere, somehow there had to be a nice, decent, normal man that was waiting to meet a nice woman like me. I would just have to persevere and plow through until I found one.

I had received two messages from a man named Ned. He looked handsome, athletic and normal, even though I was not sure what that meant anymore. We continued to write back and forth to each other. He was an architect for a firm in West Palm Beach. Finally, he asked me to meet him for a cup of coffee. I was actually relieved to meet him at a coffee house instead of a restaurant for dinner for if the date was not going well, it was easier to leave and not feel guilty that someone you didn't like was paying for your meal. I did not even get a chance to talk with him on the phone. We just emailed each other and planned our coffee date for Thursday night at 7:00 pm.

Thursday night came and with much hesitation I walked into the coffee house. Ned was already there. He looked better than his picture and came right up to me to give me a hug. We got our coffee, sat down in some comfortable chairs we found and talked for two hours. We were quite pleasant and had a nice time. We made plans to go out to dinner the following night, but this time I was trying not to get too anxious about anything and just see where this led to.

The next day I got ready for my date. Ned seemed nice, but they always did until they didn't. I was becoming a critic, but how could I not. My track record was running faster than me. Even so, I tried to look nice and stay somewhat hopeful. We met at a Cuban restaurant and had a wonderful meal. Afterwards we went for a walk, and he kissed me in the moonlight. It was nice and I felt a little chemistry with him. We then went and got some ice-cream and sat outside the ice-cream store chatting away for two hours. I liked Ned and it appears he likes me as well. Trying to keep my eyes open, I do not see any red flags so far. We had made plans to meet tomorrow night to go to the movies. So far, the start of this relationship was on track! I was happy and peaceful for the time being.

When Saturday night came, I had Ned come this time and pick me up. He was exactly on time, and he looked great! I even liked the preppy way he was dressed. We drove in his brand new Infinity to the theater. We got popcorn, soda and had a great time. I felt comfortable with Ned but was trying to hold back my excitement and any expectations of what tomorrow might bring in order to shield my heart and emotions. Ned seemed like a true gentleman so after the movie I invited him up to my apartment for coffee and dessert.

I sat on the couch while Ned sat on my loveseat eating our dessert and drinking the coffee, I put down on my coffee table. As Ned was sitting across from me on my loveseat, every time he reached for his cup of coffee a pink box peeked its head out of the front pocket of his pants. The box seemed to be a pretty good size. It was the size of a large box of over the counter cold medication. What really caught my eye was the pretty unusual pinkish color of the box. I couldn't quite make out what it was, but was trying to look hard, especially every time he reached to grab his coffee from the coffee table. I decided to push back both our coffee cups slightly so he would have to reach a little more so that I could see the first few words and try to figure out what it was. I saw the word Ultra Sen-. *What was this?* I wondered. I needed to see more.

    I moved the coasters with our coffee cups further away from him. He looked at me strangely and I mentioned that I was concerned the cups might fall. He then strained a little further to get them and the box was a moment away from falling out of his pocket. He quickly adjusted his pocket and got that box adjusted back in there. I saw Ultra-Sensitive Condoms. And it was a new box of 36. I was mortified, confused and a little scared to say the least. I think he knew I saw it but was not sure because nothing between either one of us was mentioned. Why would Ned have a mega box of condoms in his pocket? I gave him no reason to believe I was going to be with him today. I did absolutely nothing to make him run out to the store before our date, stock up for a month, and hide it in his pocket. For crying out loud, we had only kissed maybe twice, and it was outside in the street. It was mighty presumptuous of him to think he was getting some and to buy a mega box did he think he was going to get it all night or was this for another date he was planning on going on after he left my apartment?

I was so bothered by this and also by the fact that instead of maybe keeping one or two in his wallet; hidden, he had the economy box in the pocket of his pants where it was visible. I was beyond turned off at this moment. I just could not keep my eyes from looking at that pink box. You would have thought he would at least buy a brand that comes in a box color that matched his pants. I really wanted him to leave before they fell completely out of his pocket and then we would have to discuss them or probably in his warped mind, use them.

I started to pretend to yawn and told him I was getting tired. He asked me if he could spend the night and I told him not tonight!

What nerve he had!

I walked him and his harem of condoms which was still in his pocket to the door. He went to kiss me, but I turned my head quickly which then landed as a small peck on my cheek. I did not give him the chance to say anything more and I firmly closed the door. Maybe others would say I am reading too much into this, but really; a giant box of condoms hidden in one's pocket on a third date! My gut told me to run and quickly. He in my opinion was displaying audacious behavior that I did not want to be part of. Talk about being so over-confident that he assumed he was getting lucky.

So, here's to another date gone wrong. Would I ever find the one? Did he exist? I felt the rate I was going I would be wearing orthopedic shoes before my true love came and rescued me from all these internet dating disasters I was going through.

Ned did try to call me a few times, but I did not respond, and I blocked him from my profile on the dating site. My instincts told me to stay away from him and I needed to stop listening to them for I was making extremely poor choices on the men I was choosing to go out with. I went to sleep with a heavy heart, but at least this time, I felt relief that I did not get caught up in anyone's evil web.

I woke up the next morning feeling defeated, but my obsession and I went back to the site to see if Romeo could be found. I had noticed a professor who taught at one of the universities here in Florida had messaged me. I read through his profile, and he was an older man who taught literature. It said that he was a Yale graduate and had also written several books in his lifetime. He wanted someone to share his life with and his love for books, operas, ballets, and Broadway shows. *Wow! He sounded like a man; every woman would love to be involved with*, I thought as I looked over his profile.

I wrote back to him and told him how much I enjoyed reading, writing and most cultural events. I couldn't wait to hear back from him. Maybe because he was a much older man, he would be different. At least I hoped he would be different.

I received a response later on that night from the professor. His name was Sam. We wrote to each other over the course of several days. He seemed interesting, intriguing and very bright. I couldn't wait to meet him. After the messaging we escalated it to email, and we emailed each other for more than a week until I asked him if we could meet. He wrote back and told me that he would love to meet, but the timing right know was tough. He had classes going on each day and he lived four hours from me. He also told me he would have to wait for classes to end before he could head down my way. I asked him if in the meantime we could talk on the phone. He told me he did not enjoy a phone relationship. I was a little annoyed by his answer. He was okay with an email relationship, but not a phone one? I found this a little absurd especially for a man of his intellect. I had even offered to meet him halfway so it would only be a two-hour ride for each of us, but once again he said, "Not at this time so let's just keep it to emails for now."

This put a real red flag or two up for me, first being that he appeared to be an uncompromising person and the last thing I needed at this point was a man who lived by "My way or the highway." I was getting bored with the emailing, and I wanted to meet him at least once to see if we should even keep emailing each other. Without meeting him, this could all be a waste of time.

One night I felt restless from this email relationship and decided to Google the university he was teaching at. As I went through each department, I could not find his name anywhere. The next day, I actually called the University and after several transfers to the right office and speaking to many people, they confirmed my worst nightmare that there was no such professor or instructor by his name there. Wow! I was scammed!

I emailed Sam pretending that my friend's daughter goes to the university he taught at, and she said she never heard of you, and she was an English major. I asked him if he used a different name for teaching. Well, guess what, Sam never wrote back to me, and I never heard from him again. He also had me blocked on the dating site because I was not able to pull him up. What was the purpose of him just emailing me non-stop for weeks? What joy was he getting out of that? It is so perplexing to me to think someone would go online to one of these sites, devote all this time in creating a perfect profile and picture, and then invest so much time and energy emailing someone you never plan to meet. What kind of mind would devote all he has into something like this?

They need to start calling Internet dating the Twilight Zone dating. Nothing on these sites made any sense or had any type of rhyme or reason. At least this time, I did not go out of my way to meet him, get to know him, like him and then have it end. But I still felt that deplorable and sickening feeling I get when I think this person might be the one and I find out he is not even worthy of walking my dog. So here I am again after a few dates on this site, back to square one with nothing. I thought about putting out a personal note, but then thought about all the weirdo's and fruitcakes that were pouring themselves through those channels and I decided that was probably not a really good idea. I closed down my computer, got ready for bed and cried myself softly to sleep under the covers.

Chapter 14 - Some Really Strange Men

The next morning when I woke up, I cancelled my subscription on Single Mingle and looked at some other dating sites that were out there. I hated the amount of time and effort it took to create logins and a new profile when signing up on new sites. So, in my laziness, desperation and unmotivated mode I made the decision to go back on Date that Mate. I would freshen up my existing profile with new pictures and a new headliner and then my obsession and I would search for the man of our dreams. I paid my money and immediately started pawing through men's profiles like a puppy desperate to find a hidden bone. It was always so amazing how these dating sites made me feel like a kid who just walked into a candy store. Maybe that's why I became so addicted to them. There were so many men of all kinds on these sites, and I dated already so many of them. It was hard to believe up to this point with all this dating and with all these men available that I was not able to get one solid relationship out of it. It was a like tasting a ton of candy and not finding one piece out of all of it that you really like. I had been off of Date That Mate for a while so coming back on it, especially with new pictures and a freshened profile would set me up like a new member. It would also insure me of receiving a lot of hits and messages on the first day or two. I sent a ton of messages and hellos to some men I thought sounded nice and then I shut down my computer and went out for the day.

When I arrived home later in the day, I was anxious as I turned on my computer and waiting for it to boot up. My obsession and I prayed there would be many responses. Finally, when it opened, I had fifteen responses. This was my cue to start weeding through the profiles and respond to those who appeared worthy and discard those who did not.

I had received two responses from some older gent named Bobby. His profile was great, and he claimed to be 62. He looked a little older than that, but I decided to give him the benefit of the doubt. We emailed each other and exchanged phone numbers and he called me a day later. He was quite pleasant on the phone. He was divorced with a married daughter, and he was an art dealer. He told me he traveled the world buying and selling amazing works of art. We made plans to meet Thursday night at a new bar and grill that had just opened.

It was so exhausting getting all dressed up for these dates. I had to make sure my hair and makeup were perfect. It was just so much work and then you had to drive to where you were meeting them hoping they would be a good fit for you. Sometimes they didn't even show up and you were stuck just waiting a while, but then leaving and feeling pathetic because you were stood up. So, when Thursday arrived there, I was getting all dolled up to hope this date would lead to a second one. When I walked into the restaurant I recognized his face, but he definitely looked older than 62. Why do some of them lie and put an old picture up?

Bobby gave me a hug and we were seated and a nice, quiet table in the corner. We had a great meal and he told me all about his art dealings and what he was looking for in a relationship. After our meal we walked around the shopping complex and talked some more. He was pleasant, extremely nice and a complete gentleman so far. I really liked him, but just wished he was a little younger. He was distinguished looking, but really did look like he was in his mid-seventies. I wondered if he really was.

He wound up asking me out for Saturday night and I accepted. I was desperate lonely and longing for some kind of relationship. My pickiness had dropped down by quite a bit. I met him Saturday night at a quaint little Italian restaurant. We had a wonderful meal. Bobby was funny and very charming. Afterwards Bobby and I walked along the grounds of this beautiful complex where the restaurant was located. It was strange, but I was getting the feeling that everywhere we went, people were staring at us. The truth was he truly looked like an old man in very stylish, younger man clothes and I looked about ten years younger than I was so as we walked and held hands, people were probably thinking I was either a gold-digger or his daughter. It was a little uncomfortable.

I unfortunately judge people the same way when I see a miss-match pair like us. I quickly learned that I needed to stop judging people from here on because now I know how it feels when it is done, and I felt terrible about it. Bobby asked me if I would like to come to his house for coffee or tea. I told him that would be great, and I followed him in my car.

He lived in a charming, gated community. Very upscaled! It was an adorable three bedroom type cottage decorated elegantly in good taste with expensive artwork everywhere. He had an unbelievable collection of paintings everywhere. I felt like I was walking through a museum.

He made us some tea served in beautiful floral teacups. It was so dainty! We sat in a room he called his parlor on these luscious silk couches and talked and drank the delicious tea. Bobby asked me if he could kiss me which I thought was so proper and noble, but when he did, I did not feel any chemistry. It annoyed me that when I did find a nice man, there was no spark. And you have to have a spark!

We talked some more and then he kissed me again and all of a sudden, he turned around to me and in a horrible baby voice he murmured, "Please massage my back."

I was a little thrown back by the out of the blue change. Was he just fooling around with me or was this a side I had not yet seen. I totally ignored his plea for a massage and once again he said in baby talk, "Please massage my back."

I quickly jumped up from the couch and told Bobby I had to go. He said "okay" and walked me out to my car. He gave me a small kiss goodbye and I jumped into my car and drove home. He even called me later to make sure I got home okay. He was a great guy, but what was the baby talk about?

I decided to give him another chance and go out with him again. When our next date rolled around, we went to dinner and a movie. Everything was fine until we went back to his place again. We were once again having a nice cup of tea and we started to kiss a bit when all of a sudden, once again in that horrible baby voice he murmured, "Please massage my back." I couldn't believe what I was hearing. "Massage me, pretty please," he followed up.

It wasn't cute for an older man especially one who sells art to act like a five-year-old. I thought of asking him why he was talking like that, but I was so beyond uncomfortable that I just couldn't even talk. Then he said, "Pretty please with whip cream on top."

UGH! What a turn off this was. The last thing I was looking for was an over aged man to breastfeed and diaper. Once again, I told him I had to leave. I told him I was exhausted. And then in that horrific baby voice, Bobby said, "Please don't leave me alone. Let's do a sleepover here."

A sleepover, I thought. *Where? In his crib?*

That voice was creeping right into my bloodstream and if I did not get out of here, it would boil. I went into full flight or fight mode and told him I had to go and without barely saying goodbye, I ran out of there like the flight of the bumblebee. I got in my car and drove off like a bolt of lightning. I was completely done with baby talk man and from this point on; I did not take his calls or answer his emails and blocked him from my profile. Another one bit the dust.

I went back on the internet that night and contacted about twenty men. I figured I would just throw everything up against the wall and see what sticks. I just couldn't understand how these men seem so perfect when you first meet them and then they turn into complete train wrecks overnight. An hour or two later, I received back about ten messages from different guys I contacted. I wrote back and asked them all if they wanted to meet. I figured I would just do some serious mass dating and see if my odds of finding someone decent would come my way.

The next day this man Robert said he would meet with me, and we met at The Coffee House. When he saw me, he seemed a little disappointed. I couldn't imagine why! I looked really nice and was dressed well. He told me right off the bat that he really did not want any coffee which made me uncomfortable to get one. We then walked outside and found a bench to sit down on. This meet up was already not going well. He probably saw me and decided I was not worth spending a cup of coffee on.

I asked him while we were just sitting if everything was okay. He responded to me by saying, "Actually I am very disappointed in the type of body you have. I was hoping for a different body type."

I looked at him in a state of shock and said, "Are you kidding with me? What is wrong with my body?"

He quickly responded, "I am a man who needs extremely large breasts. The bigger the better."

I felt beyond sick to my stomach. Here is a guy who really has many issues on so many levels. I asked him what in my picture suggested I was a porn star. He said, "I was just hoping because the rest of you looked pretty good."

Without any hesitation, I got up from the bench, didn't say anything further and walked quickly away from big boob man. Yikes! Another loser in life. They were just coming out from under the rocks. What a waste of my time!

I had another date a few days later with a man named Jesse. He was very tall, good looking and appeared very nice. We met for ice cream. We sat down with our ice cream to talk, and I asked him what he did for a living because his profile was very vague. He told me he was a professional gambler. I asked him what did that mean exactly. Did he work at a casino? He told me he gambles when he needs money and when he wins big, he enjoys life until he needs money again.

I looked at him like he had three eyeballs coming out of his head. I asked him if he was for real or just teasing me. He said he has been doing this his entire life. I had visions of me introducing him to my friends and family and when they ask what he does for a living, I then answer, "He is a professional gambler." That would go over big! Well, I never went out again with gambler man. I was blocking so many men from looking at my profile; I figured I would run out of people to meet.

A few days later, I met online a licensed nutritionist. I was excited about meeting him because I was really into health, exercise, proper nutrition and holistic medicine. I had been looking forward to this date because I loved talking about nutrition and figured I could learn so much from this guy, but when we met things appeared a little differently than when his profile said. He had a very shallow knowledge of nutrition, let alone knowing anything about holistic medicine. He kept asking me questions about health and wellness and it turned out I knew more than him which led me to believe he was not who he said he was. He was just another man who lied and couldn't be trusted, so I went home and blocked nutrition man from being able to contact me. This was exhausting me. These men were just falling out of trees.

 A few days later I met Robotic man. His name was Marvin, and he felt the need in the first five minutes of meeting him to tell me about the robot he had living in his pants. Some people have a robotic arm, well Marvin had a robotic member down under and it was more information than I needed to know before we even ordered our coffee. And what really touched my nerves was the fact that his robot in his pants was all he wanted to talk about. This man came with baggage and the bag was stationed right down in his pants. Too close for comfort! There was no room in our relationship for a third wheel or robot as he called it, so Robot man was over before it even started.

 A few days later I met Dan, the one hand man as I called him. We met for coffee and every other minute he needed to adjust and re-adjust whatever he had in his draws. This little adjustment routine went on for the whole time we were having coffee. I understand that maybe he had ill-fitting underwear or maybe a bad rash going on but did anyone ever explain to Dan that he only has one chance to make a first good impression. I can't even explain to anyone what it is like to be with a man that is constantly adjusting and touching himself especially when you don't even know him. It was the worst coffee date. He kept adjusting it and I could do nothing, but to focus on his hand being in the wrong place all night, at the wrong time. I couldn't wait to end my date with Dan. That was one of my strangest dates and probably because he did not seem to have a problem with what he was doing or touching. Another profile I had to block. It just kept coming.

A few days later I met George. He was so gorgeous in his pictures, but when I met him, he was another one who looked like he was twenty-five years older than his photos. And to top that off when we met for a date, he actually told me he was expecting me to look younger.

I looked at him with crossed eyes, "How much younger?"

He told me he loved very young girls. He would date as young as eighteen. UGH! What a pervert he was in my eyes.

I asked him, "Why did you meet me then?"

He saw my picture and profile, so he knew I was not eighteen. He said he was just hoping I would be younger. Here was another man not looking for a relationship!

I actually asked him how old he was, to which he replied, "I am seventy-eight and proud of it!" George then told me that I was much too old for him so there was no purpose in having this date. He let me know that he was sorry for wasting my time and he left me sitting at a table like a fool. If my self-esteem wasn't down enough, it was now buried in a hole. I told this wannabe, lying old pervert man good luck with your life even though there was not much left of it and went home to cry.

A few days later, a man named Ed found me on the site and contacted me. Ed claimed to be a lawyer, and I say claimed because I trusted no one anymore. He told me he had a very successful law practice and with not much else to lose, I agreed to go out with him. He wanted to go to a movie on the first date which I found odd, but figured if I didn't like him, it would be the perfect date. We met in the parking lot, and he was driving a very expensive car. He was dressed very preppy, but very expensive looking.

He mentioned while we were walking into the theater that he usually dates women who dress a little classier than I was dressed. And there it came, my first bright, red flag. I asked him, "What is wrong with my clothing?"

He had told me, "Nothing, I just like women on my arm to look like a trophy." I told him I was no one's trophy and would have thrown up if there was a nearby garbage can. And that was my second red flag. We walked into the theater and since he did not ask me if I wanted anything, I told him I would like popcorn and a drink. He actually told me, "I do not buy popcorn for anyone on the first date."

Well now we had the third red flag, and this was no charm. I told him out of spite "Well, I do not like to wear very expensive clothes on the first date."

He looked at me like I was out of my mind. I stopped and bought my own popcorn and drink, and wouldn't you know it, he ate more of my popcorn than I during the movie. That was now my fourth red flag. Anymore and we could have a whole assembly. I wanted to slap his hand every time he put it in my bucket, but violence was not part of who I was even though I did think about doing it. When the movie was over, he walked me to my car and said, "Get home safely." I never heard from Cheap Ed the lawyer again which suited me fine.

As usual my obsession and I were not satisfied, I was determined to find that perfect relationship I dreamed of and would never stop trying until I did. I was so wiped out from all this dating and the men were getting stranger and more bizarre by the days. I was trying everything I had to find a nice, decent man. Was it possible, there weren't any left? I was giving it everything I had but coming up empty day by day. I went to sleep that night feeling defeated, burned out without any hope left. I decided I would look for other dating options tomorrow.

Chapter 15 - Marc

When I woke up the next morning, I felt so empty, so lonely. I searched the internet for other options or ways of meeting men. I noticed an email from a man named Marc from Date that Mate. I looked at his profile and it was a really good one, even though they always look great until they are not. Something pushed me to respond to Marc. He was a pediatrician with his own established practice in Boynton Beach. He played soccer on the side and was very much into health and good nutrition. On paper he was everything I was looking for. He included his phone number on the email and with much hesitation I called him. He had a beautiful speaking voice and we hit it off on the phone.

We each talked about our internet dating stories and it was refreshing to hear that it was not just me, but he was running into same strange women and situations of his own. We made plans to go to an arts and crafts festival that was happening in Miami on Sunday. I was excited, but I decided to Google him and make sure he truly was who he said he was and so far, so good. He was a successful doctor and I actually felt excited about meeting him.

Sunday came and he knocked on my door holding a beautiful bouquet of flowers. This was the first time in all these dates that someone actually gave me flowers. I was smitten with the flowers he gave me and the romantic gesture. He helped me into his SUV, and we drove to Miami. We talked about his practice and all the children he sees each day.

It was a beautiful November day. It was sunny, and the air was crisp and dry. When we got to the festival, we walked around looking at all the beautiful artwork and amazing crafts. It was a perfect day, and I had a great feeling about Marc. We walked hand in hand, and it felt great!

He was very good looking and distinguished. He complimented me and the date was wonderful. About two hours into our walk around the festival, he asked me if I was ready for lunch. I replied, "Absolutely!"

We found a beautiful little outdoor café and we were seated quickly. I ordered a simple, but beautiful salad with chicken and so did he. We had a very pleasant lunch and then the server handed him the bill. He started to fret a bit and called the server over. He started to speak to the server in a very loud voice that was a moment away from yelling. He actually said to the server, "How can you charge this kind of money for two salads, are you crazy man?"

The server tried to calm him down by explaining the type of restaurant this was and the location of it, but Marc was freaking out and did not want to listen to anything the server had to say. This was making me so uncomfortable; I was almost ready to throw the money on the table. This was my red flag to get up and run as fast as I could, but I had the devil on one shoulder, saying, "He's a rich successful doctor so make this work." And I had an angel on my other shoulder, saying, "Leave, run, and go! He needs anger management classes and you witnessing this on your first date."

I did not know what to do and we were in Miami, so I was kind of stuck with him for the day. I had no other way to get home. He eventually paid the bill, and we got up and walked around the rest of the festival. A few hours later we drove back home. He never mentioned the lunch incident, so I decided to give him the benefit of the doubt. I was a desperate woman, so I just felt the need to make this work.

When he dropped me off, he walked me to my door and kissed me goodnight! Wow, He could kiss. He asked me out for the next day, and I said yes.

When the next day came, he picked me up and we drove to see a movie. When we walked into the theater, he did not ask me if I wanted popcorn or a drink, but maybe he thought I did not eat junk since I ordered a salad the other day. We had a great time and once again he asked me out for Friday.

Marc gave me instructions to come to his house. I drove there after work and was actually excited to see where he lived. Marc was divorced with one small son who was eight years old. I pulled up to his house and it looked very nice from the outside. It was a very large two story townhouse. He gave me the grand tour. He was very neat and orderly.

I went into the kitchen to see what he was cooking for dinner and was not too impressed. He had picked up a supermarket rotisserie chicken and made a salad which did not contain much. I was getting the feeling if I continued to date this guy that I would probably lose a lot of weight or at least never gain weight.

I sat down with him to eat and did my best to try to look like I was enjoying the yucky, greasy chicken and the green salad that had barely any color since it didn't contain anything with color because it had nothing in it but some cucumbers and a few pieces of tomato.

I did my best to push these negative thoughts aside and tried to focus on the fact that I was dating a good looking doctor and nothing else mattered. After dinner we sat on his couch and watched some TV. We kissed a little bit, and he was a gentleman in every way. I felt some great chemistry with him, and it was nice. It started getting late and I was feeling tired. Marc asked me to stay over so he wouldn't have to worry about me driving home by myself so late at night. I thought about it and told him, "I would." He gave me a brand new toothbrush and an oversized tee shirt to wear. He put me in the guest room right next to him, but during the night I woke up to an orchestra of horrific snoring. I would have never thought that a slim, healthy, in shape doctor would have a snoring issue that severe.

My room was so close to his that there was no way not to hear it and the bugles and trumpets were playing almost the entire night. Wow, I just could not sleep and was exhausted. I did not feel comfortable in this relationship at this point to turn on the TV or go into his room and wake him, so I grabbed my pillow and quietly snuck downstairs to the couch which was away from all the snoring. There was an Afghan lying over the back of the couch which I took and used as a blanket. I covered myself, and softly fell sound asleep.

At some point, I got startled and was abruptly awoken. When I came out of my comatose state of sleep, I realized I was being carried back up the stairs to my room by Marc. At first, I thought it was a romantic gesture, but then in a stern voice, he said, "If you are going to spend the night here, you need to sleep in bed and not on my couch."

I told him about the snoring, but he just said, "Most people snore, but if you give it a chance you will get used to it because most people snore." I had never heard that logic before, but I tried quickly to fall asleep before he did, but with no luck and sure enough before I could nod out, there came the symphony orchestra once more screeching through the upstairs of this house. I must have spent the whole night looking at the ceiling.

I tried the next morning to not mention anything to him. Maybe he was right, I would get used to the snoring if I gave it a chance. I was beyond exhausted and could not wait to get home so that I can take a nap, a quiet nap. We made some eggs together and then he told me he had his son's soccer game today so he would see me later that night. He walked me to my car and kissed me goodbye. Driving home my mind pondered over many things. I was finally in a relationship and relationships are not perfect, but I found a rich, professional, good looking man and I should be happy about it, but yet something was off. Maybe I had been so unhappy for a long time that I just did not know how to be truly happy. I was going to have to reverse all my judgmental thoughts and paranoia attitudes in order to start to feel happy without having extreme expectations of men and what I feel they need to bring to the relationship. I found myself a diamond in the rough and while some of the things he does are ruff, he was still a good guy and the best I have been able to find. I would do all I can this time to make this relationship work because relationships take a lot of work, and I was up for the challenge.

Saturday night came and we went out for pizza. It was a little strange that so far, he had not taken me to a really nice restaurant. It was always up to this point a quick type of bite or a store bought rotisserie chicken. I did not understand why, but I did not want to ruin anything by prying or asking him why.

After the pizza we went back to his house and watched TV as usual. He insisted that I sleep over again which I dreaded, but I told him I would. He asked me if I would like to sleep in his bed tonight, but I told him I was not ready and would like my own space at this time. Actually, I could not imagine how loud the snoring would be in the same room when it was horrific in the room next door.

We got ready for bed, and he cuddled with me in my bed, tucked me in which was so sweet and then he left. Then in about ten minutes, there came the sound of the symphony orchestra which felt louder today than it was last week. I did not see myself ever getting used to this. It got under my skin, and I was not even in his room yet.

As quietly as I could, I snuck downstairs, pillow and all to the couch where I immediately fell asleep. Once again, I was awoken to Marc carrying me up the steps and putting me back in my bed. Once again Marc gave me a lecture about sleeping on the couch. He told me that the only way this relationship was going to work is if we learned to deal with and tolerate each other's habits and quirks. I could not understand what the big deal of me happily sleeping on the couch was.

Five minutes later, I once again was left to struggle in silence from the loud, horrible noises coming out of his body. He expects us to compromise, but I was the only one giving something up here, sleep!

You would think someone in the medical field would understand the importance of being able to get a good night's sleep, but I guess he missed that lecture when he was in medical school because he had absolutely no concern for my well-being when it came to getting a good night's sleep. The morning finally came after what felt like a month looking up at the ceiling all night. I got out of bed feeling groggy and very unhappy. Marc went off once again to watch his son play soccer and I drove home, eagerly awaiting a very long nap.

The following Saturday was my company's holiday party and for once I had a date for this type of event. Marc came and picked me up for this event. He looked so dreamy and handsome. He was wearing a beautiful Armani suit. I was wearing a new, black, sexy dress. We both looked beautiful together and complimented each other. The party was held in a beautiful hotel in Ft. Lauderdale.

When we arrived, everyone was staring at us, and it was probably because Marc looked so gorgeous. I introduced Marc to everyone I worked with, and they all thought he was very nice and extremely charming. We had a great time at this company event. The food was amazing, and Marc really knew how to dance so it was a great night. This was probably the best date or night, Marc and I had together. Afterwards we drove home to my place and Marc walked me up to my apartment. He came in and he kissed me. He asked me if he could spend the night. I really wanted to say no, but how would that look being in a relationship and telling your boyfriend he could not sleep over because he snores, so I thought about it and said, "Sure."

I also thought that it was my apartment and if I wanted to go onto the couch how could he tell me what to do on my own turf. We got into bed and as usual before I could even fluff my pillow, Marc was out cold snoring away. I tried to ignore the snores and deal with it, but my brain could not, and I was beyond frustrated. I grabbed my pillow and an extra blanket and went out to my living room couch and fell fast asleep, something I needed very badly. When I had awakened the sun was peering into the living room through the sliders. I noticed that Marc did not wake up during the night and carry me back to the bedroom. I thought that finally he was accepting it. I went into the bedroom to give him a big hug and noticed to my surprise he was not in the bedroom and all his clothes, keys, etc. we're not there. I also noticed that my front door was left unlocked. How humiliating this was. Is it possible that he left just to get us coffee or something?

I called him on his phone, and he answered. I asked him where he was, and he politely told me this relationship is not going to work. He told me that he woke up in the middle of the night and once again he found me on the couch after he repeatedly warned me about doing that. I once again tried to explain that the snoring was not allowing me to sleep, and I was exhausted. I asked him if he had any idea how bad his snoring was. He told me I was exaggerating and that I had no idea how to compromise in a relationship. I once again tried to explain how bad the snoring was and how it was affecting me, but he just was not listening to anything I said. He was listening to himself more than me. Marc told me it was time to move on because I was not someone, he could consider a life partner. I agreed and we hung up.

I had been on this road once too many times. Nothing was going to change, and he was the type of man that only saw things one way, his way. The angel on my shoulder was correct. I should have run on day one when we went to the festival, and he had a meltdown for no reason. My obsession with finding the right person was in more control of my situation then I was. I was not that broken up over this as I thought I would be and actually the thought of getting some good quality sleep was more exciting for me at this time.

When I went into work on Monday, on my desk was a Bible. I looked around to see who and why someone would leave this on my desk. There was a new older guy that just started sitting on my row. I asked him, "If he left this on my desk?"

And he said, "Yes."

I asked, "Why would you leave this on my desk?"

His name was Peter and he told me "That I always seem so sad and distracted and he felt if I got to know Jesus, my whole life would change." He asked me to do him a favor and just read it. God can change anything.

I told Peter, It was not necessary, and tried to give him the Bible back, but he was making a fuss about it, so I took it and said thank you. I went back to my desk and looked at the Bible quickly. I thought Peter was crazy thinking this book could change my life. I put the book in my drawer and started my day.

Chapter 16 - New Jersey Jim

I went onto Date that Mate to cancel my subscription, but as usual my obsession was getting the best of me. Before I clicked cancel, I had an epiphany and decided to just look at some other men that live in other states. I have always been told that the men in Florida had the reputation for being players and just more difficult which I firsthand have been witnessing. I put a few feelers out in New Jersey just to see if destiny was awaiting me.

I had lived in New Jersey at one point in time and always felt comfortable there. I sent out about twenty or so emails to different guys that looked pretty decent and had strong profiles. One in particular caught my attention. He was adorable with a very muscular built. I loved men with muscles, and I loved the fact that they worked out which gave me something in common with them right off the bat. I went to the gym every day and was hoping to find that someone to go with. His name was Jim, and he ran a commercialized cleaning service. He was divorced with 2 children and appeared to be decent and normal, not that I knew what decent and normal meant anymore.

I sent Jim a message telling him about myself and that I was interested in him. We progressed to emails and spent over a week emailing each other back and forth trying to learn who we each were. We then exchanged our phone numbers, and he called me first.

On the first call we wound up staying on the phone over three hours. We had so much to talk about and we had great phone chemistry. Jim did ask me why I was looking to meet someone in New Jersey when I live in Florida. I shared some of my dating horrors with Jim and also explained that I used to live in New Jersey and would have no problem ever moving back there. He told me he really did not want a long distant relationship, but after all the great phone conversations we were having, he would give it a whirl and see where it would lead him.

I really wanted to meet Jim, but he told me that we would have to wait a few weeks until Jim's workload held up a bit and he could take a few days to come down to Florida. In the meantime, we talked every single night on the phone for an hour or so. We just had so much to say to each other and the chemistry between us was enormous, enough to make me stop my subscription on Date that Mate.

On Valentine's Day, a big package was delivered to my apartment. I opened it to find a package filled with all kinds of things and a card from Jim that read, *"If I can't be with you tonight, my gift can."* It was one of the most romantic things I ever received. The box was filled with, a pair of cute earrings, a Macy's gift card, tons of chocolate on a stick from a fancy chocolate company and many other things. I felt so happy and blessed to have found Jim. He brought Valentine's Day into my house. It was romantic, thoughtful and for someone who never met me he knew everything I liked. I hugged the package as though I was hugging Jim. I couldn't wait to meet him.

Finally, March came, and it was Jim's slow season at work, so he booked his trip to Florida. I was beyond excited. After all these months, I would get to meet the man I have been so taken with over the phone. I started counting down the days until he arrived, but as it got closer, I started to become more realistic, and my antennas went up. My mind started going like a locomotive, and I started thinking about things like: What if Jim was lying to me about things like I experienced with other men. And what if he did not look like his picture or was missing all his teeth? Maybe he really did not have a job and was unemployed and recently let out of prison. Oh my, what was I thinking letting a perfect stranger from another state come to visit me and let alone stay at my place for a few days. What would happen if I didn't like him after one day and I had to be here with him for four?

I know I was sounding like a crazy woman, and I had to stop over-thinking. I committed to this visit from Jim, and we did have a fantastic, close phone relationship so I just needed to be hopeful and have faith he was who he said he was or appeared to be. I had not lied about who I was, so it was possible either did he.

Saturday came and when I checked his flight it was on time. I drove to the airport to get him and made it just in time to his plane landing. I was so nervous. I waited at the entrance and prayed so hard he would be the man I was expecting. According to the picture, he was handsome, muscular with a beautiful smile. I just hoped I would not be disappointed.

As the people started coming off the plane and headed down the ramp towards where I was standing, my heart started beating a mile a minute. All of a sudden, I saw him, and he did look like his picture. It was a bingo win for me! "Thank goodness!" I thought, watching him get close and closer.

He came up to me, took me his arms and just kept hugging me. We walked to my car hand in hand, and we were both happy and content. It was a beautiful day and Jim asked if we could take a drive to the beach. I thought that was a great idea, so we went there, parked and walked for a few hours enjoying the beautiful horizon and talking like we always do for hours. He kissed me as the sun was setting and it felt amazing. Jim so far was everything I was looking for.

After the beach we drove home to my apartment where I got Jim settled and then we headed out to a romantic dinner where we sat outside, enjoyed some delicious wine, great food and just talked for what seemed like hours. Jim and I had a wonderful time, and it only took for me looking in another state to find this. When we got home, I made up the bed in my guest room for Jim, but we wound up cuddling first in my room and then falling asleep in each other's arms. When I woke up the next morning, the sun was coming up and I noticed there had been no snoring issue during the night. Hallelujah! I was able to sleep with him peacefully and harmoniously.

We spent the rest of the day together and next three days doing everything I enjoyed from going to the gym together, sightseeing, movies, going out to eat and a lot of kissing and hugging. I was having the time of my life and his visit was coming to a roaring end. I didn't want him to go and now understood why people do not like to do the long distance thing. We both felt the heartache as I drove him back to the airport. We promised to continue to talk on the phone every night and he wanted me to visit him next month in New Jersey. As his plane took off, I cried, but felt happy that everything worked out wonderfully between us and that Jim might actually be my happy ending.

We continued our calls every night like clockwork, and he booked my flight for my upcoming trip to New Jersey. I spent the next few weeks counting the days down until it was time to see him again.

When the day came to leave for New Jersey I was beyond excited. My flight got into Newark Airport on time and when I got off the plane there was Jim waiting at the entrance for me with a beautiful boutique of flowers. I ran into his arms, and we hugged and kissed. We drove to his home where he had a lovely dinner waiting for me. It was so surreal! Over the course of this weekend, I met most of his family, his friends, his children and many people he worked with.

Jim was so excited to introduce everyone to me and it felt so wonderful to feel so special and wanted. I was so happy to be with him and be in this wonderful relationship with him. I made the right choice to look out of Florida to find the one. It was a perfect weekend, and it was one more time we had to part from each other. Jim drove me to the airport where we could not stop hugging each other. We said our goodbyes and soon after I was up in the air. While I was at Jim's apartment, I made the decision to leave some personal items in the cabinet in his bathroom and I tucked away a pair of my sneakers in his closet so I would not have to keep bringing the same things back and forth every time I visited him.

I felt sad when I returned home, but we spent the next two weeks on the phone every night. It felt wonderful to have a steady boyfriend even if we were a long distance away. I felt relieved to be out of a relationship with the internet dating sites that I had before Jim had become my whole world. Maybe eventually Jim would ask me to move to New Jersey to live with him. I was completely ecstatic about that possibility but would wait patiently for him to ask.

Another two weeks had passed, and it was time once again for me to take a flight to visit Jim in New Jersey. I had a 3:00 flight and was so excited. I left work early and headed to the airport where my flight was delayed by an hour. Jim and I had plans to go straight from the airport to dinner, so I immediately called him to alert him to the flight delay. He said, "Okay." And then he just hung up. Maybe it was just my imagination, but he seemed a little upset about it. I didn't let it bother me, but just as 3:30 was approaching, they once again announced a second delay on the flight. So instead of my flight taking off at 3:00, it would be taking off at 5:00, hopefully. I had to call him again and this time it was not my imagination, for he sounded downright pissed off. He kind of snapped at me like a snapping turtle and this in no way was my fault. Well maybe he was having a bad day. We all do, I told myself. I had a bad habit of giving all my boyfriends the benefit of the doubt when truth be told; I shouldn't since no one has the right to bite one's head off especially when things, situations and circumstances were out of my control. I just needed to believe that Jim was having a bad day or maybe he missed me so much it was hard to wait so long for my plane to get in. I decided to go with that thought process and enjoy my happiness while awaiting my great weekend with Jim.

    Finally, they started to let us board, but it took forever for the plane to get everyone on and depart. By the time we were airborne it was 5:45 with an estimated arrival time of 8:07. My plane was going to land three hours behind schedule. I finally landed and felt starved and tired. I had not eaten anything since 1:00 pm that afternoon. All I could think about was being in Jim's arms and dining at the wonderful restaurant he was taking me to. As I got off the plane, I kept walking until I saw Jim. He gave me a quick kiss and hug and seemed very annoyed which was making me uncomfortable.

    We got into his truck, and he started driving. I asked if we were going out to the restaurant, he told me about. He snapped at me, "No, I ate already. I couldn't wait all day for your plane to land." I told him I was really hungry, and I hadn't eaten. He erupted at me and barked, "Can you just eat something at my house?" I told him I was looking forward to a nice dinner and he just yelled at me, "You are kidding, right, it is 8:40pm and I'm tired."

    While I just got my first red flag unless you count the earlier phone call with him where he was very snippy when I told him, I would be delayed. This would put me at two red flags and counting.

As we were driving, and conversation was limited he asked me if I would eat something from Panera Bread. I said, "Sure."

We walked into Panera Bread, and they looked as though they were getting ready to close and they were no longer serving. I was absolutely starving at this point. Jim started to have another meltdown. I was a little shocked at his juvenile behavior. Not only had my rose colored glasses come off, but they had fallen to the ground and broke. All I wanted to do at this point was get back on the plane and go home.

We proceeded to get back into his truck as he continued to yell at everything around him. Jim pulled into a diner and as we sat down, he told me to hurry up and order something quickly. *How uncomfortable did this feel?*

I ordered a plain turkey sandwich and he had just a cup of coffee. We did not talk much, and I tried to eat as quickly as I can. After I was done, he paid, and we hopped back in his truck. On the way back to his place, he started to talk normally and seemed his old self again. I guess he came out of his postal episode saga. He told me he was a little irritated. "Is that what he calls it?" I thought to myself. Jim told me he had been up since 4:00 am working on a job and was really tired. I told him, "No worries." When we got back to his house we just settled in for the night, talking, cuddling and then went to sleep. I decided to shrug off all his temper tantrum behavior and fell asleep nestled neatly in his arms.

The next day when we woke up everything appeared to be back to normal. We went out to dinner with his family and friends, took long walks through the gorgeous parks where he lived and hung out at the coffee shops nearby talking and just enjoying life. It turned out to be a wonderful weekend and when he drove me back to the airport Monday morning to go home, I felt a little conflicted. Was Friday night just a meltdown based on a bad day that he did not mean to take out directly on me or was that really scary, angry person who Jim really was? I thought about it the whole way home but made the decision not to just throw away the relationship, but to see who the real Jim was. I also had my niece's wedding coming up in three weeks and did not want to attend by myself. I would kill two birds with one stone by having a date for the wedding and seeing how Jim's personality would be during a family wedding and then make a decision.

For the next three weeks leading up to the wedding, Jim and I spoke on the phone every day and everything between us appeared to be going well. When it was time to fly up for my niece's wedding, I drove with my two sons to the airport for they were invited as well. Jim picked us all up when we landed and even took my children and I out to dinner. He was very nice to my sons and they both seemed to like Jim. They slept over Jim's apartment with me and slept on the floor with Jim's two sons and they all had a blast. All four teenagers were very well behaved and respectful even to each other.

The next day was the wedding and Jim's kids were not invited so they went home to their mom. Jim and I and my sons all drove to the wedding together. It was in a beautiful hotel where I wound up booking for the night a room for my sons and a room next door for Jim and me. When we checked into the hotel and got up to our room, all Jim wanted to do was take a nap. I wanted to walk along the grounds and look at all the amenities this gorgeous hotel had to offer. Jim insisted that I lay down with him and take a nap, but I was not tired, even though he could care less about my needs it seemed.

He laid down and told me I better not leave the room. He was acting like my father, and since I really did not want to get into a fight and ruin my time at this wedding, I pretended to be sleeping until he fell fast asleep. I then got up, snuck out of the room and went swimming in the beautiful indoor swimming pool I spotted on the way in. I swam for an hour and then quietly sneaked back into the room where Jim was still sleeping. I hopped into the shower and then started to get dressed for the wedding which was starting in an hour. I woke him up to get dressed and he was very grumpy.

He got dressed while all the while complaining, then we picked up the boys at their room and we all walked downstairs to the chapel. All my relatives were at this wedding, but Jim was not all that friendly to them. He did not want to dance or walk around or do anything but sit at the table like a grumpy old man. At 9:00 which was only two hours into this wedding night, Jim asked if we could go upstairs and go to sleep. I told Jim this was my niece's wedding and I have not seen my family in a long time and would like to stay and enjoy myself. Jim insisted that I go upstairs with him and told me that my place is with him and if I did not go upstairs with him, he would pack his things, go home and leave me here.

I was shocked that he would talk to me like that and threaten to abandon me here at this wedding all because I was not tired and did not want to go to sleep. I was so embarrassed by his behavior, but because I did not want any scenes or for my family to see how pathetic my life had become, I made the decision to go upstairs with him. My sister was pissed with me that I would leave so early in the middle of the wedding and my sons just watched me walk out against my own will and leave the wedding before they even cut the cake. We went upstairs and Jim went right to bed leaving me sitting on a chair dressed up in the dark without him saying two words to me. I went into the bathroom, changed my clothes and cried for over an hour. When I was exhausted from crying, I crawled into bed and fell asleep.

The next morning was the after wedding brunch for all wedding guests. We went downstairs and it was one of the most beautiful brunches I had ever seen. I was excited to eat, and I was also hungry since we left early last night, and I did not get to finish everything on my plate. All my cousins and my sister were already sitting at a table. I walked over and sat down with them and as usual, Jim looked annoyed. He told me to get over to the table he was at and told me I should be sitting with him, so I got up and sat with him. My children were at another table sitting with all their cousins.

As always, I was the one that had to back down and compromise everything getting absolutely nothing in return. I was the one who paid for the two hotel rooms, the wedding gift for all of us and the plane fare. Shouldn't I be able to enjoy myself at my niece's wedding without feeling guilty or fear that Jim will react in an ill-mannered way and leave me there by myself? We sat alone at a table in the corner, and I was not enjoying the food or beautiful atmosphere. Jim had a cup of black coffee and a bagel and was asking to leave after 10 minutes. I reminded Jim that we had a plan to drive my sons two hours from here to their grandmother's house for the rest of the weekend. He had a full blown out hissy fit and told me he decided he was not driving anywhere but back home.

    I was devastated and once again stuck with a difficult situation that I would have to resolve on my own without any help. This man was definitely not a team player and not my match. I was played a fool once more in my life. There were so many red flags popping up that I felt I was in a red graveyard headed for hell. I had to call my sons grandparents and get them to drive two hours each way in their 70's in order to get my sons to their house. My in-laws are salt of the earth people, so they agreed to come get them with a smile. Thank goodness! Jim would not even let me wait until my boys got picked up and he yelled at me to grab my suitcases so that he could get out of here. Being that Jim had two children of his own, I was hoping he would be more empathetic when I begged him to let me just wait till their grandparents arrived, but he said if I did not leave now, he would leave without me. The scene Jim was creating became so out of hand that I kissed my sons goodbye and told them to hang with their cousins and my sister until their grandparents came and also to text me when they got there.

    We left the beautiful hotel which saddened me because I was looking forward to this wedding all year and now it was over, and I felt like I did not get a chance to enjoy any part of it or spend time with my family. Jim was in a very bad mood the whole way back to his place. Jim seemed to be someone who could only have a decent relationship on the phone. The presence of a human being seemed to always blow his gasket and he became like a racecar that was overheating.

When we got back to his house, he informed me that he was going to spend the afternoon at his pool club with his sons. I told him that I really did not want to spend the entire day in the hot sun, and he leisurely answered, "Then stay home."

"Gee!" I had no choice but to go. We wound up spending all day there. Jim brought for himself everything he needed such as, magazines, books, and a lounge chair for himself and totally ignored all my needs. He was actually downright mean to me in a quiet way. He did not bring any snacks or drinks for me and when I was thirsty or hungry, I had to go to the snack bar by myself and fend for myself. It was a very bad, lonely day and the rest of the weekend was no better.

When Monday morning rolled around it was a relief to my system. I could finally get out of this chamber of torture. On the way out of his place, Jim handed me a large bag of the things I had left at his place over time. He told me, "This is a male household and feminine paraphilia is not welcome to live here so please take your things home with you when you leave." I had no rebuttal to what he just said, and not only was it a male household, but it was also a crazy one I couldn't wait to get out of. I feel I was finally getting off of the set of "One Flew over the Cuckoo's Nest."

I grabbed the package of my stuff and put them in my suitcase with all my other stuff. I had the boys wedding clothes suitcase also that I promised I would take home for them. When we arrived at the airport, there was an additional charge for the extra bag I had. Jim took out a $20.00 bill quicker than I ever saw him take out money. It felt like he could not wait to get me out of his hair and out of his state quick enough. I let him pay and hugged him goodbye. I knew at that moment I would never see him again and it hurt because I did absolutely everything in my power to make this relationship work. I sacrificed my family time at the wedding and did anything he wanted to do and still the relationship did not persevere or work. I boarded the plane by myself going back to my lonely life of nothingness and knew in my heart it would be back to the grind or should I say back on the internet.

As the plane took off, the tears I was holding back came pouring down. There was a young woman seated next to me who was dressed very differently than I was. She appeared to be religious and was quietly reading her Bible. She turned and asked me if I would like her to pray for me. I politely said, "No, thank you."

I was ashamed of what I was feeling and was completely humiliated. I tried so hard to stop my tears, but the more I tried to hold them back, the harder they fell. I looked at the young woman and through my tears, I asked her to pray for me. The young woman never told me her name, but for the entire flight she prayed and read through parts of the Bible with me.

Those were the safest 2 ½ hours I ever experienced on a plane flight. I felt a comfort and peace that I could not explain at that time, for without the wisdom and knowledge of who God really was, it was hard to understand. Little did I know at that time, the truth would come to me later on, when once again, God would show up in my life.

Chapter 17 - Match and Catch

When I got home from New Jersey I received a call from Jim. He told me that his weekend created too much reality for him, and he could not handle a relationship moving this quickly, so we needed to slow it down. This man definitely had commitment issues because we lived 1200 miles apart. If we slowed it down anymore the relationship would not even exist. Jim also has anger issues, and I definitely didn't want to be the bull's-eye of that anymore.

I told Jim we could just talk on the phone once a week and he seemed very content with that. In the meantime, I was still on the prowl to find the relationship of my dreams. I decided to try a site that everyone seems to rave about, so I joined Match and Catch. I carefully created a whole new profile, put up some new recent pictures, then my obsession and I once again had to patiently wait to see who would contact us. I went out for the day to take my mind off of this new site and sure enough, hours later when I returned, I had about 20 notifications from different men waiting for me. When you first come onto a new site as a newbie, you are immediately attacked by so many men who see you as fresh blood coming aboard for them to conquest. I sat down and started going through all these new profiles and I responded to a few of them.

There was one in particular that caught my attention. His name was Jason, and he owned his own air conditioning business. He had three children and appeared from his profile to be very levelheaded, which I know from past experience means absolutely nothing at this point in the game. Jason and I started emailing each other and after a few days, we decided to meet in person.

    We met at a nice restaurant in Boca Raton. Jason was very tall and good looking. *Thank goodness he looked like his picture*, I thought as he walked up. He gave me a hug hello and then we got seated. We were having a nice dinner with decent conversation, but throughout our dinner, his children kept calling him and he kept answering and talking to them. They were 16, 14 and 12 and lived with their mom and this rude behavior that Jason had no control over went on throughout the whole meal. I was not sure what the issues were, but as usual there were already issues. All in all, it was a nice evening. When dinner was over, Jason walked me to my car and asked me out for Saturday night. Of course, I accepted and was tempted to ask him to leave his phone home but thought that might be a deal breaker for him, so I kept my thoughts to myself.

    On Saturday night he picked me up at my place and helped me get into his car like a true gentleman. We went to dinner again and sure enough his phone kept ringing and it was his children again calling him all during dinner; he spent most of dinner apologizing to me. Afterwards we went back to his house. He wanted to show me his lovely house he owned and fixed up. His house really was beautiful, but his phone was ringing all night from his three children alternating the calls throughout the evening. We were trying to talk in the living room and the calls just kept coming.

He spoke with his children more than me throughout the evening And I was starting to get extremely agitated. I asked him if his kids do this to him every day. And he did tell me unfortunately, yes. I was having trouble holding back my tongue and asked him why he just doesn't take away their phones. Jason expressed to me that he felt doing that was cruel and thoughtless. I felt he was acting like a jerk to allow this kind of behavior every day. When he took me home, I knew this would be the last time I would see him. If my batting average was this high when I played baseball, I would be a professional ball player, but unfortunately, I had become a professional dater who could really pick losers. I went home that night and moved onto the next poor soul.

I responded to a man, Jeff, who had been emailing me. He was extremely good looking and dreamy, well his picture and profile were, but most of the time in person, they looked nothing like their picture which to me was so bizarre. He was a sales executive who was divorced with one young daughter. We emailed each other back and forth for almost two weeks. I had asked him numerous times if we could meet in person, but he never responded to that particular question. *Now what was up with that?* In the meantime, I was emailing a few others just in case Jeff was a figment of my imagination.

After another week of emailing Jeff, I asked him if we could talk on the phone, and he actually sent me his phone number. I waited for the right time to call because I hated getting these men's voicemails so I always tried to find the best time so they would be home. If I got a voicemail, I never knew if they received it or what and I could not call again because it would make me look desperate. I had one chance to hit my mark and if I miss, I was out of luck.

I decided to call Jeff at 9:00 pm. Luckily, he answered, and we really hit it off over the phone. We talked for two hours about everything. Jeff and I had amazing phone chemistry. I was very attracted to his voice. I asked him once again if we could meet in person and this time his answer was, "Sure, but let me get back to you with the details." I agreed and we continued to talk some more. After another hour on the phone, we hung up for the night.

After I got off the phone, ending a wonderful conversation, I still felt like I had gotten nowhere with Jeff because we still did not have a date to meet, and he now was holding all the cards. This pattern of talking on the phone and me asking him when we could meet continued for the next two weeks. I felt like I was never going to meet him and all this time on the phone I was investing was nothing more than a waste of time. I started wondering if he was married or involved with someone and just enjoyed playing on the dating sites for kicks. I decided on our next phone conversation if he did not make a date with me than he would become history.

He called me the next night and as always, we had this great aura over the phone. I was so taken with Jeff over the phone that my obsession was having its own obsessions with him. My obsession and I were so out of control that we could not see the forest from the trees. I just had to meet him but was so fearful of rocking the boat with him and causing him to disappear before I ever met him in person. I was also so frustrated with myself for allowing someone I had never met control me like this.

I asked him again about meeting him and told him that we have such amazing chemistry on the phone that we need to meet to see if it is real in person. He apologized for his lapse in getting back to me with the details of our first meet and explained that he has been so busy with work, it has been hard making plans. I told him, "I understood and asked if we could meet Friday night?" He actually agreed and asked me if I would like to meet at the Melting Pot restaurant at 7:00pm. I was so ecstatic! I told him that I love that restaurant and couldn't wait to meet him.

Friday night could not come soon enough. I bought a new outfit and made sure to look perfect. I got to the restaurant at 6:55pm. I asked if someone by the name of Jeff made reservations, but the hostess replied, "There was no reservation under the name of Jeff." I waited patiently. Maybe Jeff put the reservation under his last name which at this point, was not told to me. I checked my watch every few minutes and when 7:15 came around, I started to get very concerned. At 7:30, I started getting that really weird feeling I get when something doesn't seem right. At 7:45 I started calling Jeff, but it went straight to voicemail. I did not know what to do and felt like a complete fool who was still waiting by the door of that restaurant all dressed up and looking like an extremely, desperate and vulnerable woman stuck in quicksand. I tried his phone again and this time like a pathetic idiot I left a voicemail telling him I was worried something might have happened to him, since he did not seem like the type of man that would stand up someone especially after hours of great conversation on the phone.

I left the restaurant finally and cried all the way home and of course rushed onto my computer to see if Jeff had emailed me anything, but there was nothing from him. I cried myself to sleep feeling betrayed and completely played for a fool.

The next day he called. I was somewhat shocked to hear from him. He apologized and explained that he had to take his mom to the hospital for something and he got stuck there pretty late and had no signal on his phone. I didn't know what to make of his excuse, but I was obsessed with this guy and dying to meet him. I even asked him why he did not try to call me when he got out of the hospital, but he claimed it was much too late. He asked me to please give him another chance and meet him again next Friday night at the Melting Pot at 7:00 pm. I tried very hard to rationalize this. I told myself if he was just trying to stand me up then he wouldn't have called me immediately the next day and try to make things right. I told myself if his mom was truly having an emergency, then he would be freaking out and he would be putting all his efforts on helping her. I told myself everything my obsession wanted to hear and while I rationalized both sides of the coin, I ignored all the red flags or any little voices in my head or gut telling me something is really off. Jeff and I talked on the phone the rest of the week and on Thursday confirmed our meet for Friday.

When Friday came, I felt secure that he would be there this time and once again, put on my new outfit that he never saw and made sure once again that I looked fabulous. I drove to the Melting Pot, and it felt like Déjà vu. When I walked into the restaurant it was exactly 7:00 on the dot. I didn't see Jeff and asked if there was a reservation under his name. She told me no and the waiting once again began. At 7:15 I started to get that awful feeling and at 7:30, I tried his phone, but it went straight to voicemail. By 7:45, I knew he was once again standing me up. An old expression played in my head, "Fool me once, shame on you; fool me twice, shame on me."

    I felt like a complete idiot. There I was at the same restaurant, in the same outfit, standing near the same hostess, who probably thought how pathetic someone could be to wait for a man again. How could I not listen to my gut? I tried his phone one more time, but once again it went straight to voicemail. I did not leave a message. I drove home crying once again. I was once again betrayed and played for a complete fool for the second time by the same man who I had never met. I had reduced myself to someone who was willing to allow anyone to hurt or abuse them just to meet a need that so wanted to be filled. I felt so angry and hurt and not really from Jeff, but more so at myself. I got home, got undressed, and hopped into bed wanting to never wake up. I cried myself to sleep for a long time. I never checked my emails or messages because I did not want to know what happened or ever speak to him again. I was embarrassed and ashamed to let someone do that to me twice and had to just move on.

    The next morning when I awoke, Jeff called me on my phone. I forced myself with everything I had not to answer. Curiosity was killing me, but I had to move beyond this and besides curiosity would only kill the cat and what good was that to me. He kept calling and even left a message, but I had to fight my obsession and win. Three times was not going to be a charm in this scenario. I fought with all I had and deleted all messages without listening to him give me another excuse, then I took it a step further and blocked him from my profile, my email address and my phone number. I felt proud of myself for finding the strength not even to find out who went to the hospital this time. I was moving on for he was another man that was not going to be the one.

Later in the day, I went back to the Match and Catch site and responded to someone else who had contacted me. I felt like I was destined to be on these dating sites forever. I started corresponding with one man who had an adorable picture on his profile page. His name was Wayne, and he was a court judge. I was impressed that someone of his background and looks would want to contact me. I cut right to the chase this time when we spoke and said, "Let's meet!" I didn't want to waste days and weeks talking on the phone. I wanted to meet as soon as possible and see if there was anything there between us instead of dragging it out. He emailed me and asked me to meet him at this beautiful restaurant in Coral Springs. He said he would be waiting at the bar for me at 6:30pm. I felt confident this time that this guy would show up. He was a judge, so hopefully he had more morals and higher standards than all the others I have been dating.

As I was driving to meet Wayne, I kept thinking what it would be like to tell people I was dating a judge. *That would be very impressive!* I parked my car and walked into the restaurant. According to his profile he was 52 years old, his height was 5'9" and he was very distinguished with salt and pepper hair. I looked around and no one filled that bill. I just stood there, and this little man came up to me. He told me that he was Wayne and I almost fell out of my heels. This guy looked around 70 years old, and he barely had any hair, and he was barely 5 feet tall. We sat down in the bar area, and I bluntly told him he looks nothing like his profile picture. He told me that everyone changes and magnifies looks and information on their profile. It's part of the game. I told him this was no game to me. I told Wayne I want to meet the man; I will spend the rest of my life with. Wayne expressed to me, "If this is true then physical features should not matter." I told him, they don't, but the lying about it is very bothersome to me. He actually told me to get over it and then we ordered our drinks.

    I really did not like this man, or his mannerisms, and I was not attracted to anything about him. We talked awhile and when I brought up his judge-hood, he told me that he was no longer a judge and his license had been suspended years ago for reasons he didn't want to talk about. And there it was another dud date on every level designed with red flags and signs that read, "*RUN!*" I finished my glass of wine and was definitely in flight/fight mode. When he went to pay for the drinks, he realized he left his wallet home. *How convenient this was for him*, I thought to myself.

    I wound up paying for the drinks and I just wanted to hit him over the head with my wallet. *What a weasel he was!* He tried to walk me out of the restaurant, but I told him I wasn't interested and that he lied about everything on his profile which I took as a betrayal. He just kept going on about how it is no big deal and I just kept walking to my car. *Some judge!* The only thing about him that had judge in it was my poor judgment of his profile. I really needed to learn how to dissect these profiles and find holes in what they were saying so I wouldn't have to keep wasting my time with such horrible men.

    I got home and went back on the internet and started looking very closely at their profile. I tried analyzing and looking for any clues that pointed to the fact that maybe they were not telling the truth. It was difficult figuring out if their pictures were false or from many years ago when they were younger. I found one man who seemed nice and sincere, well I hoped he was. I shot a message to him and to a few others, just to be safe. Basically, I was throwing everything at this point up against the wall to see what would stick. This internet dating had become so exhausting that I was drained from it. When did dating become so hard? But I had to persevere if I was ever going to find Mr. Right.

    I got a response from one of the men I was interested in. His name was Max, and he was an engineer for a firm in West Palm Beach. We emailed a few times and then he asked me out for dinner for Friday night. I prayed that Max would be at least who he said he was. We met at a Japanese restaurant, and I got there first. I hoped he would show up. What a terrible feeling to be stood up and I did not want to go through that again. A good-looking man walked in and thank goodness it was Max. He looked just like his picture. He was about 6'2", he had blue eyes, and was slim with a great smile. We said our hellos and got seated. We ordered drinks and appetizers and enjoyed smooth, free flowing conversation until he suddenly excused himself and said, "I'll be back in a minute."

I didn't think anything about it until he excused himself after each course we had. Maybe his stomach was bothering him. I didn't want to embarrass him, so I did not bring it up. After dinner he walked me to my car and gave me a big hug. I thought I smelled cigarettes, but when I asked him if he smoked, he said, "No." I decided it was probably coming from somewhere in the parking lot and when he asked me out to a movie the next night, I graciously accepted.

When Saturday night came, we met at the movies. He cordially bought me popcorn and a drink, and we sat down. I was excited that he was not cheap and so far, our dates were going very well. During the movie he started excusing himself and getting up about every 20 minutes or so. This was starting to make me very uncomfortable. After the movie I asked him what was going on, but he said, "Nothing." I asked him where he was going when he got up and that he missed most of the movie. He told me he was just going to the men's room, but when we left the theater and he hugged me again, I once again smelled cigarette smoke. I detested the smell of cigarettes.

I asked him again if he went out to smoke all night and finally, he admitted he was in fact an avid smoker. I asked him why he did not state this on his profile. He told me that he likes to date non-smokers because while he is a smoker, he is constantly trying to quit without any luck. He also admitted he smokes two full packs a day which did not surprise me since he could barely sit through dinner or a movie more than 20 minutes. I told him that I appreciated him coming clean and telling me the truth, but I could not date a smoker. I also was sure to tell him if by chance he does quit for good, he could call me and we could pick up where we left off, hopefully not leaving me alone in a movie theater most of the night. He agreed and told me I would be hearing from him soon. I drove home and felt proud of myself that with all my desperation and obsessions, I let him go and did not settle for someone who smokes. Of course, it was easy to let someone go when you could come home to a complete candy store of men waiting on the internet for you to just click your mouse and wait for a response. And of course, that was the first place I went to when I got home from my date with the smoker.

    I barely took my shoes off before my obsession was nudging me to respond to someone who had been sending me messages. He was very good looking in his picture and had a decent profile. I responded back to him and within minutes I received a response. His name was Thomas, and he was an attorney. I was excited to meet him. According to his profile, he was tall, athletic, good looking and accomplished. We were meeting the following night at The Coffee House, and I couldn't wait.

    The next day after work, I came home and got ready for my meet and greet with Thomas. I made sure I looked perfect and then drove to meet him. I felt happy and hopeful. I figured eventually the odds would fall in my favor and I would reel in a good man. I couldn't keep meeting duds and losers the rest of my life. It was impossible to have this many dates and not hit one correctly. The odds were getting ready to work in my favor. I could feel it that night.

I walked into The Coffee House and looked around. I didn't see anyone that resembled Thomas, so I patiently waited. I was just sitting in a chair awhile when a very big man and I mean big was sitting in a chair across from me had yelled out, "Are you Sharon?"

I looked at him and said, "Yes!"

He said, "I am Thomas." I looked at this man and was shocked. He was so big he could barely fit in the chair. And I am talking like 400 pounds big. He was slouched down in the seat with this huge belly hanging on his thighs and his huge chin hanging down on his chest. He had these enormous flabby arms that were hanging over the chair's armrests with nowhere else for them to go. If I didn't know better, I would have assumed he was Jabba the Hutt from Star Wars. I was mortified. I heard of lying, but was this man for real?

I simply told him I was leaving and that his picture and profile was a complete and total lie. Thomas told me he did not lie and was stung yesterday by a bee. I looked at him and said, "Must've been a very big bee." I then walked out, or more like ran out, of The Coffee House and right to my car.

When I got in my car and closed the door, I took a deep breath and the tears started falling down my face. Were these men serious? What were they thinking? I drove home and peeled the covers off my bed and went right to sleep. This internet dating was not working for me. These men were nuts and I was just blown away from this last one. It was so much work planning these dates, getting all dressed up, and then driving to meet them and then they wind up being a circus act instead of a date. This was becoming too much for me to bear. I cried myself to sleep and hoped I would feel better in the morning.

When I woke up the next morning, I did feel better, but my dilemma was, do I stay on the internet continuing to look for someone, or should I look for love in other places? So far, I have been unsuccessful doing both. My obsession was pushing me to go back onto the Match and Catch site, while my heart was saying no more. I had rationalized to myself that I paid for one full month, so why waste the money. These dating sites were like slot machines in a casino; you just could not stop until you win, and you want to win big. I just couldn't stop, and my obsession was winning because here I was pathetic as one could be searching through the profiles still thinking my one true love will magically appear.

I kept getting messages from a man named Peter. He was 6'5", had sandy brown hair and owned an importing and exporting manufacturing company. He sounded great, but of course I had to stop putting too much into their profiles until I met them to see what was true and what was not. I just had to keep trying and being hopeful. I just knew the right man was out there probably searching for me as well.

I responded back to Peter and then he asked to meet at The Coffee House that evening. This was quick! At least I would know the same day if he was a keeper. This was becoming quite a game. How far-fetched would his profile be from who he was? I was starting to make bets with myself over these things; unfortunately, I was losing all the time.

I drove to The Coffee House and when I got inside, there he was, just like his profile. He was so tall and extremely good looking. I felt relieved. We said our hello's, got our coffee and sat down outside chatting away for almost two hours. Peter was everything he claimed to be and more. *Finally*!

It was starting to get late, and Peter asked me if I would have dinner with him on Saturday. I told him I would and drove home excited feeling like maybe he could be the one. He seemed real, sincere and beyond good looking. I felt like I hit the jackpot. It took forever for Saturday night to come, but eventually it was here. We met at a nice restaurant that we both decided on and when I arrived, he was already there. He was my type of man always on time. He kissed me hello and we were then seated. We had a wonderful dinner filled with great conversation. We both enjoyed swimming, writing, reading and long walks. So far Peter was everything I have been looking for. He was old fashion and appeared to be the type of man that takes good care of a woman.

After dinner I followed him back to his house. He lived in a very large house in a beautiful development. It was a four bedroom sprawling ranch. It appeared to be about 3,500 square feet or more. The house was very outdated though and needed a full remodel and of course, a woman's touch. *I could be very happy in this house,* I thought to myself. It also had a very large pool and backyard. My first date with Peter and my obsession was rapidly conjuring up future plans with him. I had to stop doing that, but after all my dating disasters, I felt entitled to dream and make it come true. I felt I earned it.

Peter gave me the main tour and made us coffee and dessert. We talked for an hour or so while we drank our coffee and we both seemed to really like each other. He told me he was looking for a woman who could work hard, save money with him and be a real team player in the relationship. I agreed with Peter and also added that I would like someone to work out with and take nice vacations with. Peter stopped me in my tracks and said that he doesn't believe in vacations. Instead, we need to work and work non-stop because this is the time we have to save for our retirement. He believed that vacations were a waste of money. And there it was my first very large red flag. Amazing, it does not take long when dating to show its true face.

I looked at Peter in complete shock. I really wasn't sure how to answer him. I really was not sure if I should run or give him the benefit of the doubt. Maybe, he was just being careful and testing women to see their reactions to things and to make sure they were not looking for a sugar-daddy. I was also thinking that if this was the only issue with Peter, then I am sure over time, I could coerce him into taking a small vacation once a year. He had everything I wanted in a man. I owed it to myself to at least go out with him a few times and get to know the real Peter. I was almost sure that statement he made wasn't as bad as it sounded. I went home that night and tried not to think about anything other than I was in a relationship with someone who was good looking, successful and very nice.

We had plans the following Friday to meet early in the evening at a pool club where Peter lived. This pool was a training pool and had many lap lanes for swimmers to practice laps in. In the pool we each had our own lane and swam for about 45 minutes. It was a lot of fun doing this. I had never found a man that enjoyed doing laps, so this was special. After we were done, we collected our things and went back to his house to shower to get ready for dinner. He had three big full bathrooms in this house.

After we both showered, I asked him, "Where are we going to dinner tonight?"

He looked at me and responded, "Either we go out to a restaurant tonight or Saturday night. I make a point at only eating out one night a week."

I asked him, "Why?" and he told me he does not like spending money on restaurants, especially when we could eat the same things at home. I told him that I do not like going out every night, but I do enjoy going out once or twice a week and going out for breakfast on Sundays. Peter did not agree with me and felt it was throwing money away. I told him I was really hungry from swimming, to which he responded that he could make me a sandwich. I totally was not in a sandwich mood, but I bit the bullet and ate the tuna fish sandwich he made me.

Afterwards we watched TV. He had very few channels and did not believe in spending money on frivolous things like cable. This frog dressed in a prince's clothing was turning out to be a real cheapskate. Is it possible, he was really poor? I would need to find out as red flags were just popping up out of nowhere. I started asking Peter questions in a round-a-bout way regarding his business to try to see if he was related to Scrooge or if he was sincerely struggling with finances. We talked about his business, and it sounded like he had a profitable business and was doing well. From most of his answers, it sounded like he was just cheap.

He also talked a lot about retirement and kept mentioning that he plans to work as long as he can, maybe all the way into his seventies so he could just sock away money. He said, if I were with him, he would expect me to work till I am that old also so we could have a fruitful retirement. I started thinking to myself, fruitful? By the time we retire, we will be able to pay for a nursing home.

This man was planning my life and my retirement and I had not even spent a night with him yet. It was pretty presumptuous of him. I started to get the feeling that this relationship was not going to go anywhere except to work. Peter did not believe in vacations, restaurants, cable, or even updating his beautiful house. The kitchen and appliances were from thirty years ago and his furniture was well, let's just say my grandmother had nicer furniture when she was alive. I could never live my life like this. I am not a fancy, jappy type of woman, but I like nice things, including going out, shopping and living in a house, even if small that is modern and up to date. This could be the reason Peter was available for dating. According to his profile, looks and occupation, generally men like this are zapped up in a moment and by beautiful women, but I am sure most ladies fled when they saw the life, he profiled out for them to live.

I also felt a little edgy around Peter. He seemed to be a bit of a worrier. He spends too much time thinking about what will happen tomorrow instead of enjoying today. I needed to be with someone who knew how to relax and take life one day at a time. Peter made me too nervous, and I really didn't need that because I knew how to be nervous and anxious on my own. I drove home from his house knowing that he was not the right one for me. It was no big surprise. While he was a very nice man, we are absolutely a bad fit. I was not going to settle for someone just for the reason that he checked a lot of checkpoints on my list. The things that were really Important to me and truly mattered were not present on Peter's list.

When I arrived home and called Peter to let him know I was safe, I told him I did not think this relationship was going to work and thought it would be best not to see each other again. He told me he could tell my heart was not in it and told me to take care of myself. We hung up for the last time. I felt sad and let down, but I did the right thing and Peter did prove to me there are really nice, sweet men out there looking for love and commitment. I felt I was getting closer to finding the one. If only I could find a man like Peter, but without all the quirks and idiosyncrasies. I decided to go back on the dating site and try once again.

Chapter 18 - Men Who Fell Off the Face of the Earth

I had been messaged by a man named David for two weeks before I decided to respond to him, since he showed so much interest in me. He looked nice and had an interesting profile. He claimed to be somewhat of a thrill seeker. He had climbed Mount Everest in his younger days which made me very curious to know if he had all his toes and fingers or did, he leave some on the mountain. He also used to jump out of airplanes and continued to enjoy sports such as Parasailing and boating. This is probably why I never responded to him. If his profile is for real, then we truly had nothing in common. My choice of thrill seeking was a child's small coaster in an amusement park. The only thing I ever jumped out of was my skin which I seem to be doing a lot lately with all this online dating. But time was not standing still for me, and I needed to widen my horizons if I was going to meet someone soon before I was too old to date.

I received David's response and he wanted to meet for dinner. We met at one of my favorite restaurants that had live music and dancing on Friday and Saturday nights. It was a beautiful Saturday night and I figured since he was a thrill seeker, he probably liked dancing since it kept him moving. We met in the lobby, and he was very handsome. He was 5'11" with dark hair and a nice physique. He had made a reservation which also showed me he had some class. I finally, had a date with a man who took the time to do things properly and fashionable. We were seated at a beautiful booth, and each ordered a glass of wine. When we ordered, we both ordered the catch of the day special. So far, we had food in common. While we waited for our salads to come, he asked me onto the dance floor. He was a good dancer, and I was having a great time. So far, this was the perfect date. David was a complete gentleman and fun to be with. He was charming and very attentive to me and my every need.

Our food had arrived, and we sat down to enjoy a stellar meal. We talked about everything for well over two hours. We even ordered coffee and shared the most amazing, huge piece of decadent chocolate cake. It was so delicious! We ate our dessert while still keeping the conversation flowing and alive. We seemed to actually click and have a lot in common. I really was in awe with this guy. We even made plans for the following night. I was ecstatic.

He asked me if I wanted to dance some more before we left, and I did. The music for the night was all the oldies. *What a great night*, I thought to myself as the night continued to get better and better.

After dancing, we then went back to our table and David paid the bill; he then excused himself to go to the men's room. I sat there happy and content daydreaming of what our first kiss would be like. I was sitting for quite a while subdued in a romantic fog when I looked at my watch and realized David had been gone about twenty minutes. I didn't want to bother him in the men's room especially if his stomach was bothering him, but after another fifteen minutes I started to worry. I asked my server since he was a male, if he could please check on him and he did. I finally found a nice guy who seems to like me; I hope he didn't die in the bathroom. That would be tragic!

The server came back and told me there was no one at that time in the bathroom. I asked him if he could get someone to check the women's room for maybe he wandered into the wrong bathroom. The server looked at me like I had three eyeballs in my head. I told the server it was my first date and just in case he was sick, I did not want to wander into the bathroom and embarrass him.

I was starting to get that terrible feeling I get when something feels terribly wrong. This wonderful magical date was turning into black smoke. Where did he go? Before long, I had to give up my table. Thank goodness he paid the bill before he left. I decided to scout the entire restaurant, bar and dance floor to make sure he just didn't wander somewhere. Maybe he bumped into someone he knew, started talking and lost track of the time. It could happen. I even tried his phone, but it went straight to voicemail. I searched everywhere, but there was no sign of him.

I was standing on the edge of the dance floor like a wallflower. I looked and felt pathetic. I got ditched after dinner, but why? I just couldn't figure this one out. It had been a perfect dinner and perfect date. I went outside, but I saw no sign of him. I felt so hurt, so betrayed and so rejected. I could not make heads or tails out of this situation. He ate, danced, and paid the bill. Why disappear when he could have just walked out with me, said goodbye and just never called me again. What is wrong with these men? What tune plays in their head? I drove home with tears rolling down my cheeks.

When I got home, I just let the faucet of my emotions drain. I cried and cried. He just disappeared. I felt like a bride left at the altar. I was confused and lonely and just didn't know what I could do differently. I had to stop obsessing and move on, but it was so hard. I went to sleep and when I woke up the next morning, I was still kind of bummed out that this really nice man who I really liked for no reason whatsoever wined, dined, danced with me and then disappeared into thin air. It is so hard to let this go and hard to wrap my brain around it, but who could.

As always, I went back on the internet to be someone's next victim. I was responding to many men who contacted me over the past few days and weeks. I was completely discouraged but kept plugging or keyboarding along. My obsession was pushing me harder and harder to find someone. It had become at this point more than finding the one. Now I wanted to conquer and to win. After all the bad and ridiculous dates, it had become a conquest to prove there was some sort of normality in the dating world, especially the internet dating world. I was now out to prove to the world that it was possible to find a nice and normal man and I would not stop until I did.

I started corresponding with a man named Victor. He was tall, good looking and worked for a bank as a financial investor. One of his hobbies was cooking. According to his profile he loved to cook and would win a woman's heart with his food. His specialty was Italian food and it sounded yummy. There were so many wonderful attributes in this man's profile; it was kind of exciting reading it. I just hoped he was who he said he was and really did know how to cook. All this dating had turned me into a pessimist and a very judgmental woman.

My life had taken a very strange turn and was being dominated most of the time by doubt. In any case I made plans to meet Victor Friday night at a little Italian restaurant in Boca Raton. When Friday came, I drove to the restaurant waiting in the lobby for him to show up. As soon as he walked in the door, I knew it was him. Victor looked exactly like his picture with a sparkling smile and a bubbly personality to go with it. He was holding a small little gift bag which he handed to me. Inside was a book called, *Under the Tuscan Sun.* Victor told me his hope was to find the woman of his dreams and take her to Tuscany for a two week vacation. Now here is a man who likes to go on vacation! It was a little too soon and a little presumptuous, but what a sweet gesture on a first meet.

We were seated at a lovely table and enjoyed a delicious Italian meal together with great conversation. I prayed all through dinner, he wouldn't get up and go to the men's room. It is amazing how old habits die hard once you have them.

During dinner, Victor was telling me all about the exotic meals he loves to cook. His favorite dish to make was Shrimp Diablo. He told me he could make it better than any restaurant and he had it down pat. I told him I would love to try it. He offered to come over my apartment and cook it for me. So, we made plans for him and I to cook the dish together the next Friday at my house. I would make the appetizer and dessert and he would make the main dish. He told me he would pick up and bring all the ingredients for the dish. I was so excited about cooking with him. I was also ecstatic that we made it through a lovely dinner, and he was still here. Victor walked me to my car and gently kissed me goodnight. I was excited driving home and I had a terrific night.

The following Friday took forever to get here. I decided to work a half day on Friday so I could buy everything I needed for my appetizers and dessert and get the house clean and make myself beautiful. I set a beautiful table with care and love and made an amazing antipasto salad. It looked beautiful like it just got picked up from a restaurant.

I made my semi-healthy dessert that everyone enjoys using a parfait glass, whip cream, yogurt, layers of berries and a chocolate sliver on top. It looked truly scrumptious! I made three of them in case he wanted another and put them in the fridge to set and chill. My table looked perfect with wine glasses, fancy napkins and all.

I was just finishing up my hair and makeup when I looked up at the clock and noticed it was 5:45pm. I told Victor to be here at 6:00pm. He was picking up the groceries we needed and then we were going to cook together in my kitchen. I started getting excited. I was rushing to finish my makeup and felt a little anxious. When I finished, it was already 6:15pm and I looked around my apartment to make sure everything was in place. Everything was perfect from the scents of the candles burning to the lovely tableware I set.

When it was 6:30pm, I started getting antsy. I knew he had a lot of groceries to pick up and it was his first time coming here so he had to find his way. By 7:00pm I started getting slightly concerned. I decided to call him to make he was not lost. The call went straight to voicemail. I left a lovely message and decided he was probably using his phone for directions so that is why he couldn't pick up. At 7:15pm I tried his phone again, but once again it went straight to voicemail. I decided to send a nice text message, just letting him know I was worried about him.

I started pacing around my apartment and that feeling I get when something doesn't feel right was starting to creep in. I looked at the clock and it was now 8:00pm. He was officially two hours late and I was officially disgusted and downhearted. Could this really be happening? Am I getting stood up again for no reason? It can't be! Maybe I fell asleep and I'm dreaming. I just spent all this time cleaning, setting up, and preparing food that cost me money. I even took a half day off from work. Was he kidding? He couldn't have called me earlier and just cancelled like a normal human being.

I plopped down on the floor and just sat like a little child crying. My mascara was running down almost going into my mouth. I must have looked like a mutant from a bad horror movie and to be honest my life felt like a horror flick that was ending badly. My dating life was nothing more than an abomination of a bad nightmare. Would this ever end? Would I ever meet a decent, normal man? Was I asking for unrealistic expectations? I just didn't know what to do or where to look anymore.

As I was sitting there crying and over thinking my situation like I typically do, my phone rang. For a moment I was hopeful, but then I saw it was Jolie from the next building. I told her what had happened with a heavy heart, and she felt so bad for me. She told me to come over and bring the food I made. She and her husband were just getting ready to watch a movie and they would love to have me join them. That was so sweet of her, but what a change of events for the night. A lovely romantic dinner was turned into me being a third wheel in my girlfriend's house with her and her husband.

I decided to try his voicemail one more time before I left. Once again it went to voicemail. I decided to send an email also. I knew it made me look desperate, but I was. I looked at myself in the mirror. I had become a truly desperate and frightened woman. I had allowed men to define who I was and transform me into someone who felt so insecure and invaluable.

I decided in that moment to not allow this man Victor to rule my mind or my heart. I shut off my phone completely, cleaned my runny makeup and took the appetizer and delicious desserts to Jolie's house to watch a movie where I would not have to be alone. Jolie and her husband were in awe over my dessert. It was a good thing I made three of them. I sat and watched the movie with them. We had my antipasto salad and Jolie had pizza delivered so it turned out to be a nice meal. We watched the movie and had popcorn and wine and I did my best to try to forget what Victor did. I felt sad but refused to be broken. I went home after the movie and went straight to bed. I never turned my phone back on that night and never checked my emails.

Chapter 19 - Good Men Gone Bad

The next morning when I awoke, I turned my phone on. There were no missed calls or any emails from Victor. He was another bad guy who became dust in the wind. I went on the internet to see if I had any messages from anyone else interested in me from Match and Catch. I came across one from a man, Greg. If his profile and picture were accurate, which most of the time it was not, then he was drop-dead gorgeous! He was so handsome; I couldn't stop looking at his picture and was wondering why anyone who looked like that would even need to be looking for love. You would think love would just find him.

I decided on a whim to respond to him, figuring I would not be anyone he would be interested in. Against my better judgment as always, I started emailing with Greg. I felt I did not have much to lose and was curious to see if he really was as gorgeous as his picture. We made plans to meet Friday night at a local bar and grill. When Friday came, I made sure to look my ultimate best in case he really was extremely good looking. I drove over to the bar and grill with low expectations so I wouldn't be that disappointed if he was not who he said he was. When I arrived, I did not see anyone who looked like Greg, so I grabbed a table and waited.

About ten minutes later, this gorgeous man walked in. Wow! I hit the jackpot. He was beautiful just like his picture. He hugged me and we ordered drinks and some appetizers. We talked and talked for about two hours. Not only was Greg gorgeous, but he was charming and electrifying. He was everything, so far, that a woman would want in a man. He was a retired detective from Connecticut, so on top of everything he had that mysterious, alluring bad boy aura about him which was a turn on or at least most women think it is. We had such a good time and our personalities seemed to be in sync together.

After we ate, Greg walked me to my car and asked me if I wanted to go to a dinner and a movie tomorrow night. I told him, "Absolutely!" We made our plans for tomorrow, he kissed me goodbye, and I drove home. I drove home like a princess who just left her prince. I was excited and couldn't wait for tomorrow night. Maybe I was finally getting lucky.

Saturday came and I took a long time to get ready for my date with Greg, Mr. Gorgeous. The only negative about dating a very handsome man was you felt you had to look great every time you were with him. I found a really nice man so I wanted to do everything I could to keep him. I put on a new pretty outfit, did my hair and makeup carefully. I was letting him pick me up at my place. I was so nervous and excited I felt like a schoolgirl.

My doorbell rang and I went to answer it. There he was looking magnetizing and pulling me right into his trance. He was wearing nice, fitted jeans, a black V neck sweater and a pair of loafers. I was stoked! We left my house and got into his car. He was driving a beautiful high end Lexus SUV. Everything about him was perfect. We had sushi at a nice Japanese restaurant and then drove over to the movie theater. He wound up holding my hand through the whole movie and I was tickled pink. Afterwards we sat in his car and talked and kissed a little bit. He was quite the gentleman. I really enjoyed his company. We then drove home to my place, he walked me inside, kissed me goodnight, gave me a hug and then asked me if I would like to come over to his place for dinner Friday night. I said, "Absolutely, and I will bring dessert." He then left. What a perfect night!

Friday night couldn't get here any sooner and it was the day before New Year's Eve, so I had my fingers crossed that he would ask me out for that night so I wouldn't have to be alone. The holidays were always hard when you are by yourself with no one to enjoy them with. I drove to his condo which was located on the beach. When I arrived, he had made sure to have a parking space reserved just for me and actually came out to greet me and walk me into his building. He lived up on the 10th floor in a gorgeous apartment building. His apartment overlooked the ocean from almost every window. It was breath-taking.

His place was exquisite and unusually clean. It was so immaculate with no clutter or stuff anywhere that it looked like it was being staged for an ad. It actually felt a little sterile. It was decorated modern and in good taste. The only real peculiar thing was there were no pictures of him or anyone anywhere in the apartment. No knickknacks or paraphernalia anywhere to be found. There was nothing showcasing any events or anything from his life. The other police officers and detectives I dated had all kinds of mementos and souvenirs that highlighted their livelihood and showcased their life being a defender of crime. He had nothing anywhere showing anything. It was weird and eerie. It really felt like this apartment was staged for our date. *I hope not!*

I tried so hard to turn down the voices in my head about things I was finding that felt wrong. I really liked this man and wanted it to work. I had to let my hair down a bit and have a little faith that there really might be some good men around and maybe, just maybe Greg would be one of them. I shrugged these thoughts off and walked over to the beautiful table he set for us. He cooked a beautiful dinner and chose a good wine. Greg made a romantic toast to start off the dinner and then we ate. Everything was so delicious just like him.

We did the dishes together which I found romantic and then Greg told me he had three movies he choice that I might like. Two of them were romantic comedies and the third was an action film. I chose the action film. In my own mind as much as he was trying to please me, I was trying to please him. We snuggled on the couch with popcorn and a blanket and watched the movie. We kissed a little, held each other and really enjoyed the movie.

After the movie, I told him it was getting late, and I had a long drive home. Greg insisted that I stay over so that he did not have to worry about me driving home. I thought that was so sweet but thought it would be better at this point in the relationship to just date for a while without any sleepovers or learning too much about each other too soon. I wanted to take this nice and slow and give it a chance to grow. I told Greg I prefer to go home and in response, he smiled his million dollar smile and walked me to my car. He kissed me goodnight and asked me if I had any plans for New Year's Eve. I told him, "Now I do!"

I got in my car, and he told me he would see me tomorrow. "I will make the plans," He said as he closed the car door. I drove off feeling elated, content and falling for this beautiful man. I also had a date for New Year's Eve. Hooray! I finally made a real connection with someone who made me feel safe and special. I was elated.

The drive home went quickly and just as I was stepping into my apartment, my phone rang. It was Greg and he told me he just wanted to make sure I got home okay. My heart skipped a beat. He told me he would call me tomorrow and let me know what the plans were. We said our goodnights and my head was spinning. I think I finally found a decent man. I went to sleep that night feeling safe and protected in a bubble, finally not having the urge to go back on that internet, for I found Greg.

When I awoke in the morning I got dressed and went on a mission to find the perfect dress. I wanted to look beautiful that night. I must have gone to at least 12 stores before I found a dress that just wasn't a dress but made a statement. I needed it to say beautiful, sensuous and fashionable in a bold way. I found matching shoes and then went home to shower and spend time doing my hair and makeup. Greg was a beautiful man, and it was important that I felt beautiful when I was with him.

Around 2:00pm the phone rang, and it was Greg. My heart always skipped a beat when I saw his name light up on my phone. I answered excitedly, but he sounded a little different. He told me that while I am a very nice woman, he took the morning to think about it and feels that I am not the right girl for him. I took another look at my phone thinking, *Who is this? Could this be a wrong number?*

I asked Greg, "What happened between the time I got home last night and now?"

All he had to say to me was, "I feel like we are not a good fit."

I asked Greg," What about our date tonight?"

He apologized and said, "Tonight is not going to happen for us, but you will find someone who is better suited for you." He then abruptly hung up.

I was left sitting on my bathroom floor with my brush in my hand in a stupor. I felt like my entire world came crashing down. "What just happened?" I was very confused and misguided. Why would he drop this bombshell on me and a few hours before we were so supposed to go out? What kind of a person does this to someone for no good reason? I felt nauseated and completely sick to my stomach. I didn't know what to think or what to do. I felt helpless and hopeless and just broke down like a child crying with everything I had.

I cried for Greg, and I cried for every bad date and person who ever hurt me. The tears came so violently, I couldn't stop. One of my friends, Rachel came over and I just ran into her arms bawling my eyes out until finally there was nothing left. I felt like I could hardly breathe.

She and I tried to rationalize the situation but came up with nothing. I told her about how his apartment was so sterile and staged-liked. Rachel felt that because he was so gorgeous, and had it all, he probably went onto the dating site this morning and found someone else he wanted to spend New Year's Eve with. He sounded to her like a player. It could have been that I did not show any signs of wanting to quickly get physical with him so maybe he found someone else for the evening that would be an easier score for him. Obviously, he had no emotions so it was no skin off his back who he would hurt. She told me to be careful with overly good looking men because they can have anyone, they want, and they usually do.

It was now New Year's Eve and too late in the day to get a date so not only did I get hurt by someone I cared about, but now I would spend that night on my own left with my thoughts and all my sadness. Rachel told me her sons were in for the holidays and they were all going to a club to dance. She asked me to come join them. I didn't want to go anywhere, but stay and drown in my self-pity, but she told me if I did not come on my own, she would drag me out of the house. I got dressed, but my face looked like a punching bag from all the crying. I did my best to cover it up with makeup and hoped I did not start to cry again, especially when I saw couples out on the dance floor. I decided to return the dress and shoes I bought for that night because I wanted no memories of what was to be and then what was.

I spent the night with Rachel and her sons watching them dance and have a great time. I did my best to smile, but my heart was so heavy and not just because I was starting to really like him and trust him but mainly because of the deception, lack of truth and the absence of empathy he showed when he called to end it. It was just an unexpected turn in my road that reinforced my negative beliefs in the dating world, especially online. The end of this terrible day could not end any sooner. The worse came when it was midnight and everyone celebrated, kissed and hugged and I had no one to celebrate with. I gave it all I had to hold back my tears and prayed for Rachel to be ready to go home. Another year gone and I was still on my own with no rainbow in sight.

When I woke up the next morning, I did not feel any better. I decided to take a look at the dating site to see if I had received any new emails. I also felt that meeting someone else, good or bad would take my mind off of Greg. My obsession with finding someone was just pushing me to the limit and in all directions no matter what the cost. At this point in the game, it was not just about meeting the man of my dreams, but about getting into a relationship, any relationship so that I could finally get out of this dating world and off the dating sites. I did not know how much more I could take from this dating sub world which was making me crazy. If I stayed on this path, I would eventually end up in a dating anonymous group or be someone's headliner for a Dating for Dummies Book.

I checked through my emails and came across one from a man named Scott who also was very good looking. I responded back to him. I also started emailing a few other men with good profiles. Scott responded back and told me he was an architect. He said he was newly divorced with no children. We emailed each other for days. He seemed very nice on email, but I did not want to keep emailing without meeting for I found it to be a waste of time. I asked if we could meet and finally, he agreed.

There was a concert in Mizer Park, and we agreed to meet in front of one of the stores there in the parking lot. I thought this would make for a very cool date. When I entered the parking lot and parked, there he was standing up against his car waiting for me. I got out and greeted him. He was very cute just like his photo. He had a sort of preppy, professor type of look to him. He was about 6 feet tall, dressed very nicely with a nice built. We said our hello's as he took my hand, and we walked over to where the concert was playing. We found a seat on a nearby curb, not exactly nirvana, but I guess being our first date he did not want to pay for tickets so that we could have real seats. I didn't overthink it this time. My expectations were pretty low from all the dating blows and bruises I had experienced.

It was a two hour concert and by the end of the second hour, my behind felt like it had saddle sore from riding a horse all day. We got up and walked over to the coffee shop to get something to drink. We each got a latte and sat down in a chair. *Thank goodness!*

We talked for an hour or so. I enjoyed conversing with Scott. He was funny, handsome and very clever. Physical attraction was very important to me, even though I truly tried to not make it the most important thing, but you had to have it or there was no spark. And everyone needs a spark to fall in love. It started getting late and he walked me to my car and kissed me goodnight. It was a nice first kiss and I was a little smitten by him. He took me in his arms and hugged me. It was a great genuine hug that felt so nice. He must have felt the spark also because he just stood there for a while hugging me. He then put me gently in my car and told me he would call me to set up another date. I wish he would have made a plan right there and then because with my obsessive personality, lack of patience, and all my dating experience so far, waiting for the phone to ring was like waiting on death row for me. Slow and timeless! I liked Scott a lot and had a really nice time but did not want to get overly excited about him since my track record with some of these men were not good. I got home and went to sleep. I prayed I would hear from Scott tomorrow so I wouldn't have to pace the floor over the next few days.

Three days had passed, and I had worn out the carpet in my apartment waiting for him to call or email or something. In the meantime, to ease the pain and suffering of waiting I contacted other men on the site. I really wanted Scott to call. I just kept playing the reels in my head over and over trying to understand why these men are so difficult even after a great date. I could find no rhyme or reason to any of this.

My annual companies' cocktail party was coming up in two weeks and I was hoping I would not have to go alone. The weekend had come and gone with no word from Scott. It looked like maybe he had come and gone also. I was making plans to meet another man when after a week had gone by that Scott called. I didn't want to sound desperate or too anxious, so I picked up the phone in a very uncaring, nonchalant matter. Scott wanted to know if I wanted to meet for a drink on Thursday which was the next day. I desperately agreed even though I would have enjoyed dinner, better than just a drink, but my obsession and I agreed to meet and at least find out why it took him so long to call me.

We met at a charming little bar in Boca Raton. We had a drink and shared an appetizer. He never made mention about dinner, so I decided not to bring it up either. We wound up having another great night and he then proceeded again to walk me to my car where we once again kissed and hugged. He once again put me in my car and told me he will call me to set up another date. I decided to get a head of myself and nip this in the bud right now by inviting him to my work's upcoming Cocktail party next week. He took his time answering me. I told him it was next Saturday night, and it was at a beautiful hotel where my company spares no expense and the food and entertainment every year is stellar. He actually told me he would love to go and then he told me he would call to get the details for next week. I was so glad I took the initiative to ask him. I was excited to walk into the party next week with a man as charming and good looking as Scott. I couldn't wait.

The weekend slid by without a call from Scott. I was starting to wonder if there was something he was hiding from me, but I decided to hold off until the party before I flagged him red.

On Tuesday, Scott called and told me he had been so busy with work that he just did not have a moment to call before now. Normally that kind of statement would get my goat, but this time I was on a mission to bring an extremely handsome man to my company party and would not let anything get in the way of that. I asked and confirmed with him about Saturday night. He told me he would be there and even had his suit pressed for it. I asked Scott if he wanted to pick me up, but he told me it would be much easier for him to meet me there because he was working on Saturday and could be running slightly late. This didn't feel so good, but it never does with these men. I wanted him to accompany me that night no matter what the cost and beggars cannot be choosers. I agreed to his needs and asked him to please touch base with me on Saturday before the party just to confirm all was well. He said, "Okay." And then we hung up.

I booked a room at the hotel where the party was being held and received a reduced rate. I just figured since Scott was not driving me home and these parties always went so late that it would be safer for me to drive home in the morning. My thinking was also if it got really late maybe Scott would need a place to sleep. I decided to just in case he stayed to make a reservation in the morning for their spectacular buffet brunch. It would be amazing to see Scott two days in a row and plus it would prove whether he wanted more of a commitment with me. It was a romantic setting, and I was excited about sharing it with him.

On Saturday afternoon, Scott called to confirm our plans for the party. I told him about the room I booked and the breakfast buffet the next day. He said it sounded great and he would pick me up before the party at my room. I was so excited. I went out and bought a beautiful black dress, packed my suitcase and was off for a lovely party with a wonderful man.

I got to the hotel at 3:00pm which was my check in time. I had a gorgeous room with a view of Fort Lauderdale and the hotel's gorgeous pool. Their pool was heated, and I had time to kill so I decided to take a swim before I got ready. I was happy and felt great. I also felt in control because it was my company, my party, my hotel room and all my plans, not his. It felt good for a change to navigate a situation.

After the swim, I went back to my beautiful room and spent a lot of time getting ready for the party. I wanted to look great for Scott, the people I work with and for once, myself. When I was done, I have to say, I looked really nice and felt beautiful! The party started at 7:00pm and it was 6:45. I nervously and impatiently waited for Scott to knock on my door. At 7:10, I started like always to worry. It would be so humiliating if I got stood up and had to go by myself especially after I told everyone I was dating this really good looking man.

A few minutes later, there was a knock on my door. It was Scott. He looked amazing in his beautiful Armani suit with a beautiful sapphire blue shirt. He took one look at me and said, "Wow!" He stepped in my room, took me in his arms and gave me a deep kiss hello. I was transported into a different dimension for that moment. I grabbed my evening purse, and we walked arm in arm to the elevator.

While in the elevator, I did make mention again that I had this room for the night and a reservation for a great brunch tomorrow.

When we got out, we proceeded to walk into the party. Together, we were Mr. and Mrs. Perfect. When I walked in with him, I could feel everyone's eyes sizing us up. For the first time in years, I felt magnificent. Like I was really someone special! The evening was sublime. The food and music were great. Scott was a really good dancer, so I had so much fun with him. We really had a blast together.

After the party, Scott walked me upstairs to my room and came in for a while. He kissed and hugged me as he always did, but I felt like he was holding back something. I asked him bluntly if he wanted to stay with me, but he told me that he did not and was getting tired and needed to go home. I actually begged him just to lie down on one of the beds so he would not have to drive home so late, but he outright said no and wanted to be in his own bed. I told him again about the brunch tomorrow that I had pre-paid for. I asked him if he wanted to come back tomorrow for it. Scott grabbed his jacket, kissed me goodbye and told me as he was walking out the door to enjoy the brunch tomorrow. And then he was gone! He had a good looking woman who was there for him, paying for everything and tomorrow and he just leaves her alone and walks away. Was he for real? I wonder what he would say when he called me in a few days. Once again feeling troubled and defeated, I got undressed and jumped into this beautiful bed in this beautiful room by myself. This was not the scenario I had pictured earlier in my head.

When the morning came, I packed up my stuff and walked downstairs to take a peek at the room the breakfast buffet was in. What a beautiful, elegant room and the food on the buffet were incredible. I wanted so badly to eat there, but I recognized so many couples and families from my workplace and the party last night and I felt too humiliated to go in by myself, sit down and eat alone, especially after everyone saw me with Scott last night. I just couldn't handle sitting there looking pathetic and alone. I was even too disgraced to ask the hostess at the desk for my pre-paid money back, so I walked away from the restaurant, checked out quickly and ran to my car like a bat out of hell before someone spotted me that I know. I didn't want anyone to ask me any questions, especially when I had no answers.

I was glad when I got home and was in my own surroundings. I waited for days for Scott to call me. I thought he would have at least given me a call to thank me for a beautiful night and for inviting me, but he never called. I emailed him saying hi and asking how he was, but he never responded. A few weeks went by and nothing. Dead silence. I always felt something was off with Scott. Maybe he was married or in a relationship with someone else, but you can get a feeling by someone's mannerisms, and the pattern of behavior and timing that keeps repeating itself.

I never heard from him, and he blocked me from being able to see his profile, so it was now once again time to move on once more with no reason behind it. It was getting harder and harder to go out with anyone. I trusted no one and knew it would probably end badly before it rarely started, but if I gave up dating then I would never meet anyone. *If you don't play the lottery, you will never win,* so I kept trucking through the dating site like I was climbing Mount Everest.

I was searching through profiles and emails I had received these past weeks. I was reading one from a man named Jeff. Like all the others he sounded great and looked nice. I guess I would just need to keep tugging along until that special one waiting just for me showed up. I decided to respond back to Jeff and to a few others. Jeff seemed like a fun man. He skied several times each year and enjoyed scuba diving as well. He responded back to me and asked me if I wanted to meet him for dinner that night at his favorite Japanese restaurant. I told him it would be great to meet him and got ready for my date. I got dressed and drove to the restaurant.

When I walked into the restaurant a man was waving at me from one of the booths. I walked over to him and sat down. He looked a little older than his picture and a little heavier. This did not shock me anymore because I had gotten used to false pictures and lies. Jeff was very nice though, with a very happy go lucky type of personality. As we talked, I was able to figure out he seemed to have no cares in the world. Little did Jeff know I cared about everything for the both of us!

We had a wonderful dinner with no expense spared and we talked about everything for the next few hours. Jeff shared stories of his adventures as an avid scuba diver and skier. I had skied years ago and had been really good at it, but scuba diving wasn't my thing, but of course if I found the right man, I could learn to love many things that interested him.

After he paid for our meal, he walked me to my car and kissed me goodnight. I had a great time and he asked me out for following night. I was overjoyed and accepted. It was nice having a date where the guy made actual plans for the next date right then and there. What a revelation! He put me in the car and even told me the name of the restaurant and time where we would meet tomorrow. I felt like I was making dating progress, finally. I drove home and an hour later, Jeff texted me to make sure I got home okay. He also confirmed that he would see me tomorrow.

The next day came, and I tried with all my might to not get too excited about seeing Jeff again that night. I rationalized that if I had low expectations and it didn't work out, then I wouldn't get too upset over it like all the others. He called me during the day and told me since we were meeting at the Italian restaurant near my house, would it be okay if he picked me up and we drove together. I had told him, "Yes." This experience was much better and more traditional than this new type of dating where you just keep meeting somewhere. I got dressed and waited patiently for him to arrive. While I tried not to be excited, old habits with me just seem to die hard. At 7:00pm on the dot, there was a knock on my door. It was Jeff. He kissed me hello and I gave him a tour of my apartment. When it was time to leave, he helped me put on my jacket and we walked downstairs to his car, which he then helped me get in. So far everything with Jeff was going well and he did things a little more old fashion than most of the other men I went out with, which made me believe the results or the outcome of dating him might actually turn out in my favor for once. I drove with him to the restaurant feeling happy and content.

This little Italian restaurant we went to was near where I lived, but I had never been there before. It was romantic and cute. It was a little hole in the wall that was so perfect. We had a delicious dinner with wine, dessert and a man walking around playing the accordion. We sat and talked for over two hours. Afterwards we came back to my apartment. I made coffee and talked again for what seemed like hours. He told me about his big scuba trip coming up in two weeks and he wanted me to join him on it. Jeff was a certified diver and very knowledgeable about this sport. He was going to Key West with some of his buddies and their wives. He told me that when he had long dives, I would be able to hang out with the other women.

They were staying at a beautiful, five star hotel and there would be so much for me to do, including: taking a beginner's diving class, helping him clean all the gear, shopping in beautiful stores there and so much more. He told me he would pay for everything. Jeff was really trying to talk me into going with him and if I wanted this relationship to work, I would have to take an interest in his hobby, so I agreed to go with him as long as he did not force me at any time to dive if I felt uncomfortable. He agreed and gave me a great big hug. The next two weeks were perfect between us. We went out to dinner a few nights a week and saw two movies. I was in a true relationship with a four day vacation coming up with him to the Keys. Life seemed almost perfect.

The day before we were supposed to leave, I started packing. I had bought two new bathing suits for my trip. I wanted to look perfect for him. I felt this trip could really be the icing on our cake or relationship, so I wanted to make sure everything went smoothly. I decided to turn in very early because Jeff was picking me up at 5:00am in the morning. I had just laid down to go to sleep. It must have been about 9:30pm when the phone rang. I saw it was Jeff, so I picked up. He asked me if I had a few minutes to talk and I said, "Sure." He explained how important scuba diving was to him and he really enjoys it the most when he has a strong partner diving with him who can be there to support him in the water. I reminded him that I was going to be taking lessons so I could be that partner in time. He told me he thought that was great, but in the meantime, he met a woman online this week that was also a certified diver like himself and he decided just for this trip he would like to take her instead of me. He felt it would be in his best interest and that should also be important to me.

In that split moment, I do not know what threw me off the edge more. Was it the fact that a few hours before he was supposed to pick me up, he asked another woman to go in my place or was it that all these weeks together he was still online looking at the dating sites trying to meet other women instead of trying to make a relationship work with just me. I started to feel that panic button in me come alive and I started to fight for this relationship by reducing myself to a desperate, pathetic woman who was begging to be taken instead of the new woman he just chose to go.

I went on to tell him that I spent time and money shopping for some things I needed for this trip and even took the time off from work. Jeff apologized but told me this is for the best and that he would take me with him the next time he went. I asked him where this woman who he just met these past few days would be staying on this trip and he told me in his room, where else?

I asked him, how can he be with someone else if he liked me? He just started saying how I was being very selfish, and I was making it all about me. I started to actually beg him, but then caught myself from going about it. My obsession wanted to beg and scream and cry, but, my common sense kicked in, better late than never and reminded me he was just another player looking for a better game to play. He was still on the internet while we were dating and he uninvited me the night before our trip that we planned together and then chose another woman he just met to bring instead of me. He then turned everything around telling me it is my fault that he needed to bring someone else because I did not know how to scuba dive.

He ended the conversation by telling me I am a selfish person. I knew in my unique moment of common sense, this relationship was over, done and probably never really had a chance. It was another bad relationship. It was another train wreck waiting to happen. It was another bad man. I slammed the receiver on him while he was still balling me out and justifying his ways.

I blocked him from my phone, emails and dating site, and cried for which seemed like hours until I finally fell asleep. The last thing I was looking forward to tomorrow for was waking up the next day and having to face once more what happened. I was supposed to be on my way to the Keys for a fantastic trip with Jeff and now, because I was also off from work all day, I had the privilege of thinking about this the entire day. I slept late the next morning and wondered what I would tell everyone next week when I went into work because everyone knew about my upcoming trip and was happy for me, and now they would all have to be told I didn't go because I was dumped the night before. I stayed in the house all day and continued to cry and mope.

Chapter 20 - Run Like the Wind

I was having a really bad day and what was worse is that I had nothing to do for the next three days. I had also requested Monday off. I had three days to keep imagining how much fun it would have been in the Keys with Jeff. I tried really hard not to think about it, but my obsession seemed to have a mind of its own. I kept walking by my computer, but I was trying not to go online and pick out another loser from the pack. I was so obsessed with looking for another man; I couldn't control my thoughts, let alone my hands.

I turned on my computer and started checking emails from all the men contacting me. While I was scrolling, my mind began to wander, and I became reflective of my experience with online dating. *Why do we become so addicted to these sites? Is there something subliminally hidden in these dating sites that pull us in at all times like we were alcoholics or gamblers waiting for the next high or win? I always feel compelled to come back to this dating site which has held for me nothing more than bad dates with negative consequences.* The more I thought about it or tried to talk myself out of it, the more I was drawn to it. I sat down like a junkie and went through tons of messages and profiles. I was trying to dissect these men and figure out who really wanted a relationship. I tried to find some clues or patterns of unusual behavior, but I was not a detective, just a lonely woman looking for love.

I came across one profile I liked. He was a trial lawyer in the Fort Lauderdale area. He lived on the ocean and loved boating and all outside sports. He was very good looking, but in a non-ostentatious way. He had a very serious and sophisticated look in his pictures. His profile stated he wanted someone just like himself, solemn and earnest. I had a feeling about him. I sent him a message and then spent over an hour pacing back and forth hoping he would answer quickly, like he had nothing better to do. I might have been acting like a pathetic, obsessed woman, but at least it got my mind off of Jeff and this long weekend.

An hour later, a reply came from the lawyer. His name was Andy and he sounded wonderful. He wanted to know if I had ever been to this particular mall in Fort Lauderdale that has the most amazing food court. He wanted to meet there tomorrow at noon. I responded back and agreed to meet him there. He told me he would be waiting for me in front of the bakery that was in the center of the food court. I was excited about this and at least it got me out of the house.

The next day came, and I got ready to meet Andy. I decided to wear comfortable shoes instead of heels just in case we hit it off and we spent time walking around the mall. I drove east to where the mall was located. It was a long drive for me, but it was a beautiful day with a great lunch and man awaiting me. I parked right outside Dillard's because a friend of mine told me it was the easiest access to the food court. I walked through Dillard's and sure enough, there was the food court right by the Dillard's entrance to the mall. My friend was correct.

This food court was huge and unique and right in the midst of everything. I couldn't wait to eat. There were beautiful healthy dishes, all kinds of salads and all the fruit and produce looked sparkling fresh. I felt like I died and went to food court heaven. It was spectacular just like Andy said it was. Even the bakery was extraordinary. They had beautiful baked goods displayed in such a way, it looked like all the muffins, croissants and breads were dancing. Everything smelled freshly baked and out of the oven. It was all so mouthwatering.

I hadn't spotted Andy yet, so I just walked around surveying everything. I was checking out the ice cream booth when a man tapped my shoulder and said, "Are you Sharon?"

I said, "Yes."

He said, "Hello, I'm Andy," and he shook my hand. He told me to look around and decide what I want and then we can get acquainted while we eat. I stood looking at him in supreme shock. This was absolutely not the guy from the profile I chose. This man standing here resembled a homeless man on the street. His hair was rattled, matted and his clothes were in bad shape. All his fingernails were dirty and discolored. I felt sick to my stomach. There was no way this man was a lawyer; well, he may be one that was barred. I could barely look at him, let alone have a meal with him.

All of a sudden, my beautiful day and this wonderful food court turned cloudy, and I went into fight or flight mode and wanted to just run and get out of here. I looked around and tried to figure out how to get out of here without any confrontation from Andy. Andy had asked me what I wanted to eat, but I told him I was having trouble deciding. He suggested we split up, get our food and meet back at the register so he could pay for everything. This food court had a central register system like they have in Disney World. I agreed to do that and as soon as he walked away and I saw he was ordering something at one of the counters, I ran and took off through the mall like a bat out of hell. I kept running. I never looked back. I just kept running and running. When I hit the entrance to Dillard's, there was a guard standing there and as I was running, he grabbed my arm and said, "Ma'am is everything okay?"

I said, "It will be if you let go of me." And I kept running straight through the store, never stopping or looking back. I ran to the back door and ran straight to my car. I got into my car so quickly; I almost took my hand of. I drove away just as quickly like my life was depending on it. At this point I was very hungry and beyond disappointed. First, I was so upset that I wouldn't get to experience the magnificent food court I was so looking forward to and second, I was so taken back at the size of the lie Andy created by putting up bogus pictures of himself and probably a false profile. Luckily, he didn't have my number because we never talked on the phone; we just emailed to plan this date. I would have to block him from my email when I got home. I drove all the way into Fort Lauderdale for nothing.

I got home, ate a tuna sandwich, sat down and just cried. I cried for what just happened and I also cried for all the bad people in the world that feel they have to lie and pretend they are someone else; all they do is waste your time and energy, especially in the dating world. I couldn't stop crying. All this day did was add more salt to the wound and it hurt. Not only couldn't I find the love of my life, but these men were so deceitful, I couldn't even find one to be friends with. I spent the rest of the day home crying on and off, watching television and trying to talk my obsession out of convincing me to go back on the internet.

Of course, my obsession won out and I obsessively, without any control, had to check my messages. Mr. Right was somewhere, and I had to find him. I had gotten two messages from a dentist in Lantana, named Don, and a retired accountant named Max. I checked out both their profiles and pictures and against my better judgment, I decided to respond to both of them. I really wanted to tell them to be up front and show your true self, but I figured that would scare them away and have them thinking I was a psycho or something of that nature, so I didn't. I sent emails to both of them, shut down my computer and went to sleep for the night.

The next morning when I woke up there was a message from Don, the dentist. He wanted to meet me at the Wellington mall and take me to a restaurant of my choice. It was a far ride for me, but I loved that mall and it had very nice restaurants. It was a beautiful day, so I decided, "What else do I have to do," and I offered to meet him at 4:00pm. I spent the day getting ready.

Before I left, I checked his picture again. He was very good looking with a great smile, as it should be for a dentist. Maybe Don would be the one! I drove a whole hour to get there. I arrived at

3:30pm and decided to walk around a bit. We were meeting by the entrance where the food court was. Now that brought back a memory of the last food court, I met someone at.

At 3:50pm I passed the food court to see if Don was waiting for me, but the only man standing there doing nothing was a tall, very thin, scrawny man with disheveled clothes and unkempt hair. I still had ten minutes, so I went into another store. When I came out, I went right to the meeting entrance we had agreed upon. It was exactly 4:00pm, but I didn't see Don, just that same scrawny man was still standing there. At 4:10, I started getting that feeling I always get when something feels wrong. Don was still not there, and that same scrawny man was there just waiting and looking as though he was waiting for someone. Either I was being stood up or that scrawny man was my match.

I started to feel the blood rush to my head when all of a sudden, the scrawny man came up to me and said, "Are you Sharon?" I was in shock! Of course, he recognized me. I was every bit of what I disclosed in my picture and profile, but Don, it was as if he stole someone else's profile and picture. Is there such a thing as identity theft dating? If this guy is a dentist, then I am a brain surgeon. His teeth were horrible. They were all crooked and yellow. His clothes were old and tattered. I just stood there in shock looking at him in horror.

With such regret and disappointment, and without even thinking, I blurted out, "You look nothing like your picture, not even close!"

He said, "The picture was a few years old." I told him he was a liar and once again without thinking, I went into fight/flight mode and started running out of the mall to my car. Don started running after me, but I picked up the pace even in my heels and flew into my car. Without looking back, I took off and drove away, leaving him standing in the parking lot staring at me like I was the one with the problem. What were these guys thinking? The tears, as always, started running down my face. It was a lot of work driving here, not to mention all the wear and tear I am putting on my car for nothing. I was horrified! My dating situation was getting worse. I couldn't trust anyone at this point. I got home, barely ate anything and cried myself to sleep. I felt I would never find anyone and would have to do this acrobat of dating for the rest of my life.

I woke up the next morning and had to go to work. I was depressed and exhausted from trying so hard to just meet a normal man but getting nowhere. Dating had become a bad job for me that I was stuck having to continue working at. I got through the whole day without checking any emails. When I got home, I wasn't sure if I should keep trying to meet someone through internet dating, but there was no other way. Everything else I tried did not work for me either. I decided to check my emails. I couldn't resist. I was addicted and a glutton for punishment. I had become so overly obsessed with the dating sites; I seriously needed an intervention program or treatment plan to get off of them.

    I had reduced myself to a dating cliché and wasn't even aware of it. I had been emailing with the retired accountant Max. Again, he had a nice picture and profile, but what did that really mean? I was hesitant to meet him. I actually told him about some of my dates and he asked me to meet him just for a cup of coffee and give him a chance. He told me it was a new picture, and he is who he claims to be. I agreed to meet him the following night for coffee and was prepared this time for the worst. In the interim, others kept messaging me, but I decided before I responded to them, that I would give Max a chance and just focus on him until we met.

    According to Max's profile, he had a lovely three bedroom home in a very up scaled golf development in West Palm Beach. He lost his wife a few years ago and was in great need to find a partner and his next soul mate to live out the rest of his years with. It sounded good to me if only he really meant it. I did a search online of the development and boy was it fancy. You had to have a lot of money to live in there. There were restaurants inside and many amenities. I was actually getting a little excited about meeting him. Maybe, finally he might be the one.

    The next night came, and we met at a popular coffee shop in Boca Raton which was close to the half-way point for us. I drove there, parked and walked into the coffee shop feeling hopeful. When I walked in, he was already there, and he actually looked like his picture. *Hallelujah!* Max appeared to be a man in his early sixties, about 5'11" with salt and pepper hair and a decent average built for his age and height.

We had a great conversation, and the time just flew. He told me about the development he lived in. There were golf courses everywhere, and everyone drove around in golf carts, even to get to the huge clubhouse and all the restaurants that were located on the grounds. He had asked me if I would like to come up on Saturday so he could take me around in his golf cart and show me everything. I agreed to drive all the way there and spend the day with him. He walked me to my car, we hugged goodnight and said we will see each other Saturday.

It was a good first date with a lot of promise and it felt good to not be lied to or deceived. Max really seemed to be everything he said he was, and it felt good for a change. I couldn't wait for Saturday to come. Maybe I finally got it right and I would no longer have to be alone and continue to play this dating game. I went to sleep and slept peacefully for the first time in a while.

The rest of the week went slow. Max and I spoke over the phone once or twice, but I was anxious to see him again and just couldn't wait. I did not go back onto the dating site during this time because I wasn't interested in finding new men. I was hoping Max would be it.

Finally, Saturday arrived. It was a beautiful day. I put on a pair of thin jeans, a pretty, pastel cotton top and playful, but comfortable, strappy sandals. I did my hair and makeup very carefully. I wanted to look perfect, especially since we would be together during sunlight hours. After I was ready, I happily got in my car and drove up to West Palm Beach. Max had emailed me the directions to his home. It took me without traffic a good hour to get there. There was a guard gate, but Max left my name at the gate, so I had no trouble getting in. I drove through the development looking for Max's house. This development was magnificent. Each house was bigger than the next and it was so big inside here, it was like an enormous self-contained city. There were golf courses all around, as well as little shops and restaurants. I could easily learn to love it here.

    I kept driving until I reached his block and came to his house. Max was outside waiting for me. He gave me a big hug when I got out of the car, and we walked hand in hand into his house. His home was beautiful. It was a three bedroom, spacious and charming ranch that was decorated in a soft and cozy manner that could use a woman's touch. The floors were all wood, even in the kitchen which made everything warm. The place was decorated simply, but in good taste, and I was impressed with how nice everything was and how immaculate it was. He made us some delicious iced tea with lemon and we sat and drank it while I admired his kitchen. I pictured myself cooking for him in this oversized kitchen with an enormous island that I always dreamed of having. Max startled me out of my thoughts when he asked me if I would like to take a ride around the grounds. I quickly came out of my dream mode and told him, "Of course."

We got into his golf cart, and he started driving up and down the hills of this majestic neighborhood. We passed other folks who were also on their golf carts. We waved to each person or couple as we passed. Everyone was so friendly. It was like being on the set of a movie. I guess I would be so happy all the time if I lived daily in nirvana. Max took me inside the two big clubhouses on the grounds and introduced me to people he knew. He showed me all the golf courses, the golf house, the restaurants and all the little shops that were there. I was having a blast. I hadn't had a nice day like this in a long time. Everything was just easy breezy.

We stopped off and played a game of shuffleboard with some of Max's friends and had a drink by the tiki bar. Since we were only driving a golf cart, I wondered if the drinking limits applied to them also. By the time we got back to his home, the sun was starting to set, and he asked if he could take me out to dinner. I said, "Absolutely!" I was having a great time and did not want the day to end.

Max took me to a little Italian restaurant outside the development. It was his favorite place. We had an amazing dinner with wine, music and great food. I was overwhelmed by everything. I guess this was what real dating was like. It was hard for me to tell or know for sure since I had no real experience the past few years. All I know was that I was in heaven and did not want to leave. After dinner we went back to his home, and he made a pot of coffee for us, and we talked. He then put a movie on, and I must have fallen asleep because at some point, Max was nudging me to wake up. It was about 11:00pm and I was groggy and tired, probably from being out in the sun and fresh air all day.

Max told me it was time for me to wake up and go home. I was a little taken back or too tired to understand what he just said. I felt wiped out and with an hour drive home and it was all highway, I felt too tired to make the trip. I told Max this and asked if I can stay over in his guest room. I told him that he wouldn't even know I was there. Max told me that he does not do sleepovers and because I have such a long ride home, it would be best to leave immediately.

I looked at him like there were three eyeballs popping out of his head. I said, "Are you serious?"

He said, "Yes, and maybe now is a good time to lay down the ground rules of our relationship."

"*Relationship*," I pondered. This was only our second date. He continued to state his rules and let me say, those red flags that were not present all day, were popping up like toaster strudels in a toaster.

He went on to tell me that there will never be sleepovers and he is not looking for someone to live with, nor will he support anyone ever again like he did with his wife. I asked him, "What about that partner and soul mate you said you were looking for?"

He told me that he was looking for his next soul mate, but this time wanted someone who would live not too far from him so they can be together all the time, but no sleepovers or living together, ever! He also went on to mention that everything he has and owns will be given to his children and grandchildren when he is gone. The woman that he is in a relationship with will be independent and have her own place and her own money.

Well, I guess that disqualifies me as his mate, I thought.

He also went on to say that he does not mind paying for dinner once in a while, but not all the time. After he read me this riot act of his, he hurriedly put me into my car with my purse and jacket and told me to drive carefully. He also let me know that he would call me during the week to plan our next date.

I drove away in a state of shock. *What just happened?* I was also lost in this gigantic neighborhood at night in the dark feeling exhausted and dismayed. He gave me no directions out of here and there were like six guard gate entrances so it was important to find the correct one so I could immediately get onto the highway and not waste time going in the wrong direction. I pulled up to one the gates and asked the guard for the best exit out that was closest to 95 southbound. Trying not to let my tears flow from my eyes, I listened to the guard's directions and held back the tears with all my might until I reached the highway and then the waterfalls opened up like Niagara.

I was devastated with the right to feel this way. What just happened? Did I miss something? I was completely baffled. Who did these men think they were? There was so much entitlement in this world.

As the tears fell, all I could think about was it me or them who had the problem? I just couldn't do this anymore. Does Max truly think that I would go out with him again? He was offering nothing in this relationship, but abuse.

As I continued to drive home, the rain started falling. Between the bad visibility, my tears flowing and my exhaustion, I am surprised I did make it all the way home without calamity. When I finally made it into my apartment, I changed my clothes, took a shower and climbed into bed. That self-complacent, self-absorbed man never even called or texted me to make sure I made it home alright. I guess calling to check on me was a no-no on his list of rules. I cried until there were no tears left and finally drifted off to sleep.

When I awoke the next morning, I felt beat up. I just didn't know what to do anymore. I felt hopeless and helpless, but I knew I had to do something different. The first thing I did was block Max from my phone, dating site, and email. He was a horse of a different color that I was not looking to ride again. I thought about my dating failures all day and surmised that maybe it was a Florida thing. "That was it!" Men in Florida probably have an entitlement issue or maybe they have been overexposed to craziness because of too much time in the hot sun. Just then, I had a bright idea! I would go back on the internet and find matches for myself in other states. I was tired of Florida anyway and needed a change.

Chapter 21 - Looking for Men in Other States

I went back onto Match & Catch and set new perimeters to bring up profiles only in some other states. I felt I had to do something different; try something new. A few hours later I received a message from a man in Chicago. His name was Tom. He was an engineer and born and raised in Chicago. I did ask him up front why he would pursue someone who lived in Florida and his reply was, "I am looking for my soul mate and I have not been able to find her here in my state." I have to say that the word soul mate gets used too often and freely. These men throw it around like footballs. I wonder if they even know the true meaning of that word.

I responded to Tom asking him many questions. I also disclosed to him my reasoning for looking for love in other states. I wanted to be as up front with him as I could so if he wanted to retreat, here was his chance. I told him about the false pictures men here in Florida have put up and all the lies about who they are, what they do and what they want. I told him it felt like a breeding ground for everyone running away from their true self.

Hours later Tom sent to my email five more pictures of himself and his business card stating what he does for a living. I thought that was adorable that he was trying to prove to me he was who he said he was and trying to sooth my distrust about dating. After many emails I was impressed with him. He seemed honest and open about everything. We wound up emailing each other for weeks. He then asked me to Skype with him so we could see each other and see if we want to pursue this any further and I agreed. So, we started to Skype and since we were pleased and comfortable with each other, we met each other every night online learning more and more about each other's lives. This was actually a great way to get to know someone and unless someone else was pretending to be him, which would make no sense, I got to see who he was each night. I was content for now with my new cyber boyfriend and at least for the time being it felt nice to not have to get all dressed up, drive far and meet someone who was not who they were supposed to be.

A few weeks into my cyber relationship, Tom asked me if I would fly to Chicago to meet him. I wasn't too thrilled to fly to Chicago. I was actually enjoying having an online, no frill relationship. In actuality, I was actually scared to meet him. If it did not work out or went badly, I would lose my cyber buddy that I looked forward to meeting online every night. We even had dinner together while we were conversing together on the computer. It was a very sweet, safe romance. I was very content with this new type of relationship but knew sooner or later I would have to meet him, otherwise he might think I'm a cyber-stalker or some kind of a nut job.

We made plans a week later for him to fly down to Florida instead and stay in a hotel in Fort Lauderdale. *Thank goodness he was coming, instead of me going to him.* He arrived on a Friday night very late, so we just talked on the phone, but our plan was to meet for lunch on Saturday at his hotel which had a restaurant inside.

Saturday came and it was time for me to drive to Tom's hotel and meet him in the flesh. We had become great friends via the internet and phone, and I wanted so much to have that connection in person. I made sure to look my best and I drove over to where his hotel was. I was so excited to meet my best friend, but at the same time I was scared. I entered the hotel lobby and there he was. He ran over to me and gave me a big hug and kiss. We walked over to the bar, sat down and got a drink, and chatted for a while. While sitting there, Tom laid his hand on my thigh, but I pushed it away. He then proceeded to put his hand once again on my thigh and once again, I pushed his hand away. It was a little uncomfortable, but I was trying my best not to make a big deal out of it.

He then asked me to have lunch with him in the little café restaurant at the other end of the lobby. It was a beautiful hotel with many amenities. As we got up to go, he grabbed me and once again hugged me and gave me another kiss. At that moment, I felt a hand slip down my back onto my behind. I kind of jumped and broke our embracement. Tom seemed to feel an entitlement to put his hands wherever he wanted or was I being paranoid. I wasn't sure, but just because we are internet buddies doesn't mean he has the right to touch me the first time he meets me. First of all, I had trust issues based on prior dating experiences and second, I was a lady looking for a gentleman and a gentleman does not touch without permission especially in the middle of a hotel lobby in front of everyone there.

We sat down for lunch and instead of Tom sitting across from me, he hopped into the booth almost on top of me. We ordered lunch and it turned out to be a terrible hour that never lived to end. I spent the entire time pushing his hand off of my leg. I was so busy pushing him that I did not have both hands available to pick up my sandwich with. Every time I made an attempt at explaining my discomfort with this, he totally ignored me and kept doing it.

After lunch we made our way back into the lobby. I was so turned off. *What else is new?* All I could think of was this guy was looking for a quick feel and probably a lot more. I just couldn't wrap my head around the fact of him flying all the way here just to pursue me physically when he can just do that in Chicago where he lives with women there. It was a little mind blowing.

I sat down in the lobby, and he asked me to escort him back to his room claiming he had an amazing view I needed to see. I told him I was not comfortable going to his room so early in our relationship and he once again discounted what I said and told me he had a great bottle of wine he picked up for us and we could drink wine, watch a movie together, and cuddle. I didn't think he really wanted to cuddle. I bet getting me sloppy drunk and taking advantage of me was more on his menu.

Once again, I told him no and he grabbed me in the lobby and started to nuzzle my neck. I pushed him away and told him I needed to leave. I started walking to my car and he ran after me, screaming that he came all the way from Chicago and that I owed him. Owed him? What do I owe him? The only thing I owed this guy was a slap on the wrist and a kick where the sun doesn't shine.

I ran quickly into my car, started the engine, and took off quickly. When I looked back in the rear view mirror, he was standing in the parking lot with his arms flaring up in the air still yelling at me. I felt deceived and let down once more from a man from another state who I thought was my friend and respected me. Boy am I the worst judge of character. I just couldn't play this dating game, let alone win at it.

I got home, feeling lucky I got out of there on time and decided to try once more to find a nice man from another state. I did a search for men in Michigan. That seemed like a nice quiet state. I found a few men who sparked my interest. I sent messages to three of the men I found and spent the rest of the day obsessively waiting for one of them to respond. About three hours later, I received a response from a man named Mitch. He was a project manager for a big firm in Michigan and told me his firm had an office in Miami and since he was getting tired of the long cold winters in Michigan, he thought if we wound up together in a relationship, he would be able to transfer down here. This really excited me. I finally found a man who knew what he wanted and would make a commitment to it if things worked out.

Mitch had a great picture and profile, and we had a lot of things in common. He was athletic and worked out every morning, like I did, before he went to work. He was divorcedand never had any children. We emailed each other for a couple of days and then he asked if he could call me. I emailed Mitch my phone number and he told me he would call me late Saturday afternoon. I was so excited; Saturday couldn't get here fast enough.

Finally, when Saturday arrived, I spent a good part of the day pacing and hoping Mitch would really call me. At 4:00pm an unknown number rang on my phone and sure enough it was Mitch. He appeared, so far, to be a man of his word. We talked on the phone for almost two hours. I loved his voice, and he made me laugh. It was a long way from everyone else making me cry. He had a soft, gentle, but funny manner about him. We were able to talk about everything. We had great verbal chemistry, and I was ecstatic.

At 6:00pm we finally hung up. We both had things to do, but after that call he was calling me every day for the next two weeks. At the beginning of the third week since we started talking every day on the phone, Mitch told me they needed someone to execute a new project in the Florida office. He decided to volunteer for it, and it got approved. I was overflowing with joy. He also told me the project could take up to six weeks or more too complete which would give us quality time to get to know each other. I just couldn't wait. Once Mitch had all the details and dates, he emailed everything to me. He would be flying here two weeks later and staying in some executive suite his company owns in Miami. I was beyond excited. I had a really good feeling about all of this and felt my life was about to finally change for the better.

The next two weeks dragged even though we continued to speak on the phone each day. Finally, Sunday came, and Mitch called me after his plane landed. He made plans for that night to meet with me at a little Greek restaurant in Fort Lauderdale which was the half-way point for each of us. We also both loved Greek food. I spend most of the day getting ready and tried to look my best. I only had one chance to make a good, no great, first impression.

We were meeting outside the restaurant at 7:00pm. We confirmed this time at 6:00 that evening and then both left to meet. I got there at 6:50pm and waited out front like we planned. At 7:00pm I still didn't see him but decided to check inside just in case he got there before me, and they seated him at a table. He told me he made a reservation, so I checked with the receptionist, but she told me there was no reservation under his name. I gave her my name just in case he felt compelled to put it under me, but it wasn't under my name either. I went back outside and hoped we were not at two different restaurants. I decided to sit on a bench outside and wait. He also did not live in Florida, so this was all new territory for him. I needed to be patient plus I just spoke with him an hour ago.

It was 7:10pm and I wasn't sure if I should worry or not. I thought of calling him but didn't want to give the impression of being an overly impatient woman who freaks out at the littlest thing, so I waited. By 7:30pm I was pacing outside, and it was time to put my patience mask on because I was starting to freak out.

I called Mitch and his phone said, "The phone number you are trying to reach is no longer in service."

Huh?! I tried again and again and kept getting the same message. I checked my phone and text messages, but nothing from him. I just stood there not knowing what to do. Maybe his phone went out of service because he didn't pay his bill on time. It was now

7:50pm. I was beyond bummed and completely blown away. Who was this guy and why did he stand me up?

I actually waited for him until 9:00pm like a pathetic fool. I then walked to my car and drove home constantly trying his phone, but still getting the same out of service message. The tears of humiliation were rolling down my cheeks. This really hurt! When I got home, I ran upstairs and immediately checked by email to make sure nothing bad happened to him. *Look at me still giving Mitch the benefit of the doubt.* There were no emails from him, so I sent one to him to at least get some closure on this situation. The email I sent came back undeliverable. I went onto his profile on Match and Catch and tried to message him, but he blocked me. *Is he kidding?* Was this just a game he made up to keep me going for weeks and then have me drive to meet him, but he never even came here. Who would waste this kind of time and energy? He spent hours on the phone with me and emailed nonstop. What do I do now? There was nothing left to do. I plopped into my bed with no food, no hope and no respect for myself. I felt defeated, confused and extremely exhausted. I couldn't do this anymore. I went to sleep knowing for sure I would never meet someone.

Chapter 22 - Alex

A few days passed and I was just so discouraged and hopeless. I checked my emails to see which men were contacting me, but actually felt disinclined to respond to anyone since whatever I did differently or changed, I still wound up exactly in the same place. Nowhere. I decided not to date anymore, but my obsession still wanted to, so I gave in and checked my messages on the dating site. There was nothing worth responding to and the next week or two I laid low until something worthwhile came my way.

About two weeks later, I received a great message from a man named Alex. He was a retired chef and baker from New York. He was much older than me, but very good looking and distinguished. I felt very compelled to write back to him; even after all I have been through. I just felt if I don't play the game, I will never win. My common sense told me to let it go, but my obsession was pulling me like taffy on a stick. Well as usual my obsession won, and I responded back to him. He immediately responded back to me and wanted to meet me at a restaurant of my choice near my home. Well, that was a little different, just cutting to the chase, instead of non-stop emails and phone calls which waste time and end up in no man's land. With Alex, I figured I could get right to the meal and if things go south, then it was quick and easy, like ripping off a Band-Aid real fast. We agreed to meet for dinner the next night at 7:00pm at one of my favorite Thai restaurants and I figured at least I would get a nice meal before it ended. Of course, that would only be if he showed up.

The next evening, I drove to the restaurant. I did not get as dressed up as usual because I just did not have the motivation to put so much work into something I was so unsure of. I was becoming burned out by giving these dates 100% and they all ended up being dud dates, so I looked good, but decided to keep it simple.

I got there exactly at 7:00pm sharp. A very tall, distinguished man was waiting in front. I prayed it was him because whoever he was, he looked good. I walked over to the good looking man and asked, "Are You Alex?"

He replied, "I am, and you must be Sharon." Alex looked even better than his picture so that was a good start to the night. He took his hand and gently guided it to the small of my back and led me into the restaurant. We had a glorious meal with wonderful conversation that went on for a few hours. We finally got up to leave when it looked like they were getting ready to close. Outside was an ice cream shop and he suggested we get some so we each chose a cup and with our ice cream, we walked around the entire plaza a couple of times. Alex and I had a great energetic chemistry between us and it was apparent to both of us that there was a spark. As we continued to walk and talk, Alex told me he did not want this night to end. He told me he was going away tomorrow for a three day golf outing in Tampa but would be back over the weekend and he would love to catch a movie with me. I told him, "That sounds like fun." He then walked me to my car, gave me a kiss goodnight and closed my car door. Driving home I tried not to be too in awe of him and this fabulous date and chemistry we have because speaking from experience, who knew if I would ever hear from him again.

A few days later over the weekend, Alex called me, just as he said, and we went to the movies. We had popcorn and soda and had a great time. He held my hand through the movie. It was very romantic. Afterwards he took me back to his twelfth floor ocean view apartment. It was a beautiful place with the ocean shining in from every window. It was also decorated impeccably and immaculately.

We sat outside on his terrace listening to the sounds of the ocean and watched the waves crashing against the shore. He made us coffee and he had a delicious homemade chocolate cake he said he baked for me last night. We sat in awe of the ocean and each other, eating our cake and talking once again for hours. When it started getting late, I helped him clean up and bring everything in. In the kitchen, he gently took me in his arms and kissed me. He then gently took me by my hand, and we walked downstairs to his car. Alex opened the door and put me in. I was mesmerized by the whole evening even though I was really trying not to like him so much which was becoming almost impossible.

We drove home hand in hand in the car and it was just an enchanted evening that I couldn't even make up in a fairytale if I tried. He helped me out of the car and walked me to the door of my apartment where he once again gently kissed me. Alex could certainly kiss, and I could certainly let him non-stop. He told me goodnight and told me he would call me tomorrow to make plans for the upcoming week and then he left. I was in a state of astonishment and complete amazement. I wanted to run. I wanted to jump as high as a kite and I wanted to scream out over every rooftop all my joy and elation, but I was scared to really celebrate or invest too much into this too soon. I needed to calm down, take a breath and try to go slow with him. Time would tell if celebration and rejoicing were in order.

    Alex called the next day like he promised, and we made some cool plans for Saturday. We wound up spending the day riding bikes up and down Fort Lauderdale beach and stopped for lunch at an adorable outside beach café and when we got back to his place later in the day, we swam in his pool located outside his building which overlooked the ocean. We paddled around like two children in the pool chasing each other, splashing each other and just having a wonderful timeless day. I had brought a change of clothes with me because Alex said he had some friends coming over for dinner that night, so I wanted to clean up and look refreshed. Alex wanted his friends to meet me so that meant he really liked me which was so exciting for a change. Upstairs in Alex's apartment, I showered, got dressed, did my hair and make-up while Alex prepared a gourmet dinner for all of us. He had even made his own bread. I was stoked! I helped Alex set the table. We used his elegant China and fancy linens. I felt like I was playing house and it felt good. I guess this is what a real relationship feels like.

When his friends arrived, we started with appetizers and wine. They were wonderful people and the women accepted me very easily like they knew me for years. The meal was delicious and mouthwatering, and the night went by perfectly. Alex and I cleaned up together after everyone left. We chatted and laughed together as we cleaned. It was so much fun being with him that the cleaning did not feel like a chore. It had gotten pretty late so Alex asked me to stay over. I told him I would love to but was a little uncomfortable since it was a very new relationship. He told me not to worry and he made up the bed for me in his guest room. *What a gentleman.* We kissed a little bit, cuddled for a long time and when I started getting drowsy, he tucked me in, kissed me goodnight and closed my door. I woke up in the morning to a beautiful breakfast perfectly laid out on the terrace overlooking the magnificent ocean. It was like being on vacation. We sat on the terrace listening to the waves break and ate and talked and as always had a wonderful time.

After breakfast we took a dip in the ocean, walked along the sand hand in hand and then went out bike riding for the day. We stopped for lunch and looked at some antique shops and just enjoyed each other's company. It was so wonderful spending all this time with Alex and the day ran away from us as the sun started to gently set on the horizon. We went back to his apartment where we showered, got dressed and then set out for another beautiful dinner in a simple, but quaint Italian restaurant.

After dinner we went back to his place where we kissed, cuddled and watched a movie together wrapped up in each other's arms. At 11:00pm, Alex said, "I should get you home. I know you have to work tomorrow." I didn't want this weekend to end. I wanted to stay in his arms forever, but when reality seeps in, then it's time to go home. Alex drove me home, walked me to my door and kissed me goodnight. He told me not to look so sad for we would see each other during the week and spend next weekend together again. He smiled and laughed, his charming laugh, and then left. This time when I entered my apartment, I knew for sure I was in a real relationship. I was happy, content and felt like a child who just wanted to jump up and down in sheer pleasure.

It was a wonderful week for me, and it went by very quickly. Alex called me every night and on Wednesday he came over and took me out for dinner. Saturday came and once again we had a spectacular weekend. I got to meet his children and his grandchildren and everything between us appeared to be moving forward and in the right direction. I was, for the first time in the longest time, happy. This wonderful pattern between us continued like this for the next couple of weeks and then one night we were sitting on the couch after dinner and out of the blue he asked me why my youngest son lives with his dad and not me. I explained that when I moved out of Boca Raton into a different area, my son did not want to change schools or leave his friends so he asked if he could live with his dad and stepmom because they had a house in the area his school was in. I have a sensational relationship with my ex, and I love my children so much that I just want them to be happy, even if it is not to my benefit. I told Alex I saw my son all the time and spoke with him every day. Alex seemed very bothered by this and he explained that his last ex-wife had a drug problem that was never disclosed to him until a year into their marriage and she wound up losing all custody of her sons. He told me that he has a trust issue with this and my son not living with me is putting up a red flag for him. I told him I do not drink, and I do not do drugs and if it made him more comfortable, I would take a drug test for him. He told me not to be so ridiculous and dropped the subject.

After that night, things started to change and get a little weird between us. The phone calls and date nights started to diminish. I questioned him about this, but he told me I was letting my imagination run away from me and that everything was fine.

Over the next week or so, things got even weirder. I was barely seeing him at this point and when I called him, most of the calls went right to voicemail. One day I tried to reach him, but again right to voicemail. I was starting to become worried and at the same time annoyed. I had invested a lot already into this relationship, including my feelings, so I got into my car and drove to his apartment. He let me in but was cold and distant. He told me he needed a little space for the next few weeks because he was busy and had some important projects he was working on. I asked him, if I could spend the night and he responded, "No, not tonight, but I will call you in a week or two and we will make plans then to go out."

I walked out of his apartment and ran to my car crying. I felt devastated. I was falling in love with Alex and my heart was breaking. I got home and went into bed, hardly able to close my eyes. He didn't even call to make sure I got home okay. What was happening and what could I do to fix this before it was too late? I cried myself to sleep.

I woke up the next day feeling depressed and exhausted. Three weeks passed and I still had not heard from Alex. I decided not to call him or chase after him. If he truly cared about me, he would try to contact me or at least see how I am. I felt proud of myself for not making an attempt to call him, even though it was killing me, but I did not let my obsession win this time. I needed Alex to prove to me he missed me and this time I was not going to take less than that.

About five weeks later since our last contact, Alex called me and asked me out to dinner. I cordially accepted and prayed that he was over whatever mid-life crisis he was going through. I made sure I looked perfect so he could see what he had been missing. I did not want to give him any reasons to walk away from me again. We had a nice evening and he explained to me he was busy with things that had come up and he also wanted to try to make another go at this relationship because he really cared about me. Over the next few weeks, we appeared to be back on track with our relationship and dating schedule, but things felt different between us and not like it used to be when we met. He seemed to run hot and cold with me for no apparent reason. Once or twice when I stayed over and woke up in the middle of the night, I noticed Alex was not in bed. I quietly went to see where he was. I sneaked over to where his office was because I saw a soft light on and with the corner of my eye; I saw that he was looking through profiles on Match and Catch. I tiptoed back to bed so he wouldn't catch me spying on him and did my best not to cry and just get through this night.

The next day when I woke, I decided not to mention what I saw last night and did my best all day to please him. We had planned that night to meet my sons for dinner so I did not want anything to ruin it, but he was so distant. He didn't want to kiss or even hold my hand. He just kept saying he was not in the mood right now.

The dinner with my sons went well. Alex was very nice to them, and my boys were very respectful and polite the entire night. On the way back to his place after dinner, Alex was so quiet. I felt like I was walking on eggshells with him. I just didn't know what to do. Alex got undressed, hopped into bed without a word leaving me sitting by myself on the couch. Trying not to cry, I waited until he fell asleep and then I went to sleep and just hoped, sleep would find me.

The next morning when I awoke, Alex was sitting on the terrace with a cup of coffee staring blankly at the ocean. He hadn't cooked any breakfast like he always did for me and barely looked at me when I sat down to join him. I needed to say something, so I asked him if something was wrong. Alex told me that this relationship was not working, and he is not happy with me anymore. He also said it's not me, it's him; I often wondered why people use that line. Of course, it's me. It's about Alex not wanting *me* anymore. I needed to really know the truth. I asked him if it was because of my sons. He told me it was not my sons. They were great! He said he just did not want to be in this relationship anymore.

I had absolutely nothing in me left to fight for him. I was exhausted from trying all these weeks to make this relationship work. I was drained, defeated, unwanted and probably not relationship material. Alex did not want to talk or even be in the same room as me, so I got dressed, packed my things and told him I was leaving. He just stayed on the terrace barely blinking an eye and didn't even say goodbye. As I walked to the door to leave, I passed his office and from the corner of my eye, I saw he had his computer turned on and there was Match and Catch turned on in full view. I guess he was on this morning also. He didn't even feel compelled to turn it off while I was here in case, I saw it. He must have met someone else and needed me to leave so he could take her out.

I walked out the door and he never even got up to help me out or say goodbye. Was I that awful that I was not even worth the word goodbye? I ran to the elevator and could not make it to my car fast enough. I felt the waterfall of tears forming and did not want anyone to see. When I got into my car, the waterworks gave way and exploded. What Alex did to me was just wrong and what's worse is he had not a care in the world that he hurt me. I had finally had a real relationship with someone I was falling for and I still did not get any closure or idea of what happened or what I did to cause this demise between us.

I really loved him. The thought of now having to go back on the dating sites and look for someone new was just too much for me to bear right now. I was a complete wreck and now I had a broken heart to mend. I got home, climbed into my bed and cried the rest of the day and night. My whole world had just fallen apart for no apparent reason, and I was left alone to pick up all the pieces by myself.

Chapter 23 - Steve

Over the course of the next few weeks, many men were contacting me from Match and Catch. I was still feeling the effects and heartache of what Alex did to me, so I ignored most of the men trying to reach me. One guy names Steve was relentless. He was sending me messages non-stop. I responded to him just so he would stop sending them. He was recently divorced from Delaware with three teenage daughters. His wife left him for another man, and he was devastated. He told me he was new to Florida and did not know many people. Steve owned many medical supply centers in various areas and states. He appeared to have a lot of money but presented himself in his profile and emails as a very down to earth man. We exchanged phone numbers and talked on the phone on and off for a period of two weeks.

I was not ready for anymore bad dates or bad relationships, but he kept pursuing me for dinner and finally I agreed to meet him, thinking after one date, he will probably fall off the earth like some of the others. I chose the restaurant and city I wanted since I needed to feel like I was in control for a change. Steve showed up right on time to the minute. He was good looking and charming. The good looking ones were generally charming until they went in for the kill and their true colors appeared. He hugged me hello and sat down and we had a nice dinner with smooth flowing conversation. Steve was very easy to talk with, but I did not want to like him too much because if he disappeared, I would once again be the one with the bruised heart and feelings. All in all, it was a nice dinner and a lovely night. Steve appeared very down to earth like his profile projected and he told me that was a quality he liked about me. Afterwards he walked me to my car, kissed me gently goodnight, and told me he will call me after next week because his sixteen-year-old daughter was coming in to visit and he would be spending all his time with her, but would love to get together with me after she went back home to Delaware.

A few days later out of the blue Steve called just to say hello and to see what I was up to. His daughter was there, but he wanted to just hear my voice. I told him, "Today is my birthday, but I have no plans to do anything." He told me that he would not feel good about himself if he let me sit home on my birthday by myself and asked to have dinner with him at the restaurant of my choice with my sons and his daughter. I agreed and choice a Japanese hibachi steak house. I thought having the chef cook and entertain us would take the pressure off of everyone having to make idol conversation because we would all be busy watching the guy cook, especially since the kids never met each other and it was my favorite food.

I made the reservation and Steve arrived with his daughter exactly at 6:00 pm as planned. His daughter's name was Carly, and she was a very sweet, beautiful young lady who got along wonderfully with my sons. *Thank goodness!* The kids even discussed during dinner seeing a movie after. It was a great dinner with everyone singing happy birthday to me and Steve even had a card with a small picture frame that said, 'Happy Birthday' on it, and he wrapped it beautifully. I felt special, and for the first time in a few weeks I was not thinking about Alex. When my son and Carly announced, they were going to see a movie, we all decided to go to the movie together as a group. It was such fun! He bought each one of us popcorn and drinks and I felt content, instead of how I felt this morning when I awoke and thought my birthday was going to be a total wash out. It was a great night and I really enjoyed being with Steve. He had a very mysterious aura to him which I was attracted to. After the movie, we all walked together to our cars. Steve gave me a big hug, wished me happy birthday again and told me he would call me next week.

The following week we had a beautiful, romantic dinner together and talked about everything. He told me he really enjoyed my company. I was starting too really like Steve and that scared me. After dinner he walked me to my car and kissed me goodnight. He was a good kisser and we really meshed. He told me several times since I met him that I was very different than most of the women he was meeting, but he needed to be honest with me. *And there it was!* In this dating game, there is always something that comes up!

I braced myself because I couldn't even imagine what he was going to tell me. Steve continued to tell me he was just recently divorced and didn't want to dive so quickly into another full blown relationship or marriage, but really enjoyed being with me and he wanted to continue spending time with me. Now what part of my profile did he miss while reading? It had to be the part that said I'm looking to get married, and I do not want to be on the dating fence!

I asked him, "Why did you contact me since we clearly do not want the same things, and you kept pursuing me until I accepted to go out with you."

He gave me a typical answer: he really liked my profile and picture. He then continued by saying, "Let's just continue to go out and see where things lead to." I then agreed to this kind of relationship which down the road, I would find out was my first mistake. He kissed me again and his kiss just made it impossible to walk away from. I had to face it, I was completely lacking willpower and strength. I did find it amazing how such a great and perfect night could turn to not so great in a spilt moment. I got in my car and drove home, but this time I did not cry. Maybe I was not supposed to get married. Maybe God had a different plan for my future. That thought did not help me feel better. It just made me deal with what I could not have or find in my life in a better way.

A few days later, I was driving home from work in one of the worse rainstorms I ever drove in. It took me over two hours to get home, and by the time I made it upstairs to my apartment, I was soaked to the bone. What a miserable Friday night, but at least it was the weekend. I changed my clothes and just plopped down on the couch after a long week of working and a long night of driving. It felt great to just cuddle with my blanket and watch television as the rain plowed down outside.

As I was starting to doze off, my phone rang and woke me. It was Steve. He asked me if I was up for pizza and a movie? I actually told him, "No." I just wanted to do nothing but veg out. I felt wiped out by the bad weather and never ending trip home from work. Steve suggested he could bring the pizza to my place. This man was relentless when he wanted something. I didn't want him to come over because my apartment was a mess and I did not feel like cleaning, so as always, I went against what I wanted and agreed to go to his place.

I put on a nice pair of jeans and grabbed a movie that I wanted to watch. He only lived a few blocks from me, but it was back out into the monsoon I had to go through to get there. He left the garage door open for me so when I arrived, I could just pull in and not have to get wet. He was a gentleman! He ordered a delicious pizza and when it came, we sat on the couch with our pizza and watched the movie I brought over. We spent the next two hours cuddling, making popcorn and watching the movie. It was nice. Steve really was easy to be with and I did enjoy his company.

It was getting late, and he asked me if I wanted to stay over. He offered me his daughter's room to sleep in since she only came every few weeks. I really wanted and needed to go home, plus I needed to keep this relationship on the low down since he was not looking for anything serious. I told him I would be fine going home and gathered my belongings. It was important that I looked like a self-made independent woman because if he wasn't seeking a serious relationship, the last thing he would want is a clingy, dependent woman who needed to be with him all the time. He helped me into my car, kissed me goodbye and I drove home carefully even though the rain had turned into a drizzle. It had been a perfect evening with no conflict, but as I climbed into bed, I wondered what direction this strange relationship would take.

    The next day as I was getting ready to go to the gym, Steve called me asking what my plans were for the day. I just told him I was going to the gym to swim in their indoor pool. He told me, he loves to swim and asked if he could go with me as my guest. I said, "Okay." He picked me up at my place. I had a full change of clothing with me just in case, Steve had any plans for us, afterwards. We both swam laps in the big Olympic pool for an hour or so, changed in the locker room and on the drive home, he asked me if I would be interested in coming over for a barbeque. I agreed and we went together to the supermarket to get the groceries we needed for a nice meal. He barbequed steak and chicken and I made a beautiful salad, corn on the carb, and rice. We sat outside on his patio having great conversation as we ate dinner and shared a bottle of wine. It was a perfect night right after another perfect day. We talked for hours, and it must have been 1:00am when we noticed how late it was. Steve insisted I stay over because he was too tired to drive me home, but as always, he was the perfect gentleman and made up his daughter's bed for me.

    The next day when we woke up, we went out for breakfast and spent the whole day together at the beach. I had all my pool stuff with me from the day before which he washed for me the night before. He really was a gem. On the way to the beach, we stopped off at a store and he bought me suntan lotion, sunglasses, and he also had packed us a cooler with sandwiches, snacks and drinks. We had such a beautiful day together. After the beach, we went back to his place where we got showered and cleaned up and then he took me out for a beautiful dinner. He might have told me he did not want a serious relationship, but Steve was really romancing me to the max and I loved it.

After our dinner, he drove me home, walked me to my door, kissed me passionately and left me staring out into thin air like a deer with headlights in its face. When I entered my apartment, I sat down and just reflected on this unbelievable weekend with him. Steve might have not wanted a real relationship, but maybe he was falling for me and his non-relational plans he had were flying out the window. I decided to just stay cool and calm and let this relationship go where it wanted and not try to over think it or alter the outcome so early on. *Let the chips fall where they may.* I was happy for now and for a change, I wanted to cherish these feelings for as long as I could. Maybe, just maybe, I would find what I was looking for!

This wonderful pattern with Steve continued for the next six weeks. It was like a dream come true. We spent all our weekends together going to movies, great restaurants, the beach, the gym and so much more. Because of what Steve did for a living and the important people he met, he was a sponsor for the big arenas that hold concerts, sports events and more, so we got to go to all kinds of events and attractions as VIP guests and sit up in the penthouse level. I was really enjoying being part of Steve's lifestyle.

One Saturday on the way to the beach, he asked me if it would be okay if we stopped off to meet his realtor at a penthouse condo he was looking to buy. He told me he would love my opinion on it. I was flattered and excited to see this swanky apartment since lifestyles of the rich and famous had never been on my horizon. We met his realtor outside the building and Steve introduced me to her as his girlfriend. I was pleased that he called me his girlfriend, instead of just his friend.

We took the elevator to the penthouse which in this building was the 25th floor. The elevator door opened up right into his apartment. It was very cool. The apartment was huge. One whole side overlooked the intercoastal waters while the other side overlooked the ocean. *Wow!* This penthouse had four large bedrooms, three of which had their own bathrooms and showers. The master was its own city, with a humongous sitting area, a closet that was bigger than my whole apartment with built ins and other bells and whistles, and a tremendous kitchen that invites you to sign up for a live cooking show. When we got to the closet, I noticed that it was huge. You could not stand at the entrance of it and see the back, you had to walk through the closet to see all of it.

Steve took me aside and asked me if this is a place that I could see myself living in one day. I said, "Of course." I felt elated and honored that he was thinking these things. Was Steve planning his future included with me? Could it be? As we finished our tour, my head was spinning with excitement. I was the happiest I had ever been and yes, I was falling in love with this man, and I believe he was falling in love with me. Finally, I found my match!

Our lives just kept folding into each other's week by week. I started staying over his apartment on the weekends. We made dinners together, attended each other's events, and really both enjoyed each other's company. Even though he was renting for now, he had a gorgeous, expensive rental in a beautiful development, so I enjoyed spending time there with him, instead of my place. We were really building our lives together and talking about our futures when, and of course, there is always a when, Steve started all at once to become a little distant and I wasn't sure if it was me being paranoid or on high alert regarding any changes I noticed, but he was acting different. I decided not to ask him, but instead to observe and see where it goes. It could have just been by imagination running away with me.

About three months into the relationship, we spent a Friday night and Saturday together like we always did and had a great time. When I woke up Sunday, I asked Steve If he would like me to make him a beautiful dinner for that night. He looked at me and said, "That would not be a good idea today."

I asked, "Why?" Steve told me, very bluntly, that he was going out on a date that night so he couldn't spend the whole day with me." I was blown away like a hurricane hit me. I just broke down continuously crying and right in front of him. Steve held me tight, but also reminded me of our first few dates where he was very clear about not wanting a full-blown relationship. Through my tears and labored breathing, I did my best to express to him that we were spending all our time together and he was the one constantly calling me and asking me out, asking me to stay over and inviting me to everything he was going to. I told him, I just assumed we were getting more serious and taking it to the next level.

Looking at him with a tear filled face, I bellowed out, "I figured you had changed your mind regarding your relationship status. I just took your lead with this."

Steve told me like he did weeks ago that he liked spending all this time with me, because I was different, very nice and a breath of fresh air, but he wants to date and is in no way in love with me and probably never would be. I was overwhelmed and shocked at that moment by grief and was crying so hard, I was practically gasping for air. Steve didn't know how to stop me from crying so he just kept holding me telling me everything will be alright. I tried to pull myself together as to not portray to Steve I was a raving psycho, but I couldn't stop the tears because my heart ached. I just wanted to go home so I let go of Steve, packed my things and started walking to my car. He told me to try to have a good day and take it easy and he would touch base with me the next day. Why do men think we can take all this heartache they provide for us and just shrug it off like it's no big deal? I didn't want to make things any worse than they already were, so I just waved goodbye and drove home. I spent another day in my life crying all day and walking around like a zombie in a state of shock.

Steve called me the next day and asked me out for dinner. I really wasn't sure how to navigate around this. On one hand, he never promised me a rose garden, but on the other hand, is he to blame for my state of mind after spending all that time with me, discussing our future together and romancing me night and day. Because he spent all his non-working time with me almost every day doesn't that come under the term intent to lead one on? I feel like I was once again played for a fool, but here he is again calling me and wanting to go out with me. I just was not sure what to do, and I was falling for him on top of everything. I felt in my heart of hearts that I just had to find a way to get him to fall for me and make things work. Maybe I could try to be everything these other women were not and show him how foolish he was for not committing just to me. So, in my warped obsessive mind, that became my newly revised plan. I would be perfect for him in every way until he could not live without me.

    Steve's birthday was coming up and I decided to make a very big deal out of it and plan a wonderful night he would never forget. I made reservations at a fancy restaurant, got tickets for a show, I bought him two expensive beautiful shirts from the store he shopped most at, and made an order for all kinds of chocolate to be made in the shape of aspirins, band aids and other medical type supplies that were affiliated with his line of work. I planned an entire night of fun, gifts and other surprises for him. I filled up a large entire shopping bag with a night of pampering and fun for him. There were fancy towels, bubble bath, salts, moisturizers all in chocolate scent, for he loved chocolate. My plan was to create a spa night for him especially since he had a very stressful job and business. It would include a massage, bubble bath, relaxing music that I purchased for him, and even special chocolate teas that I ordered for him just for that night. I had everything planned out and I spent a lot of money on everything but knew none of his other girlfriends would go through this kind of trouble for him. Even my birthday card was spectacular. I wanted

Steve to see how creative, inventive and thoughtful I could be. I was fighting for this relationship, and I needed to win.

The Friday night before his big birthday night, I called him and asked him if he wanted to get pizza. He told me he had a friend taking him out for his birthday.

I asked, "Who?"

He told me, "Just a friend."

I kept trying to prod him to find out if it was a woman or a man. Finally, getting disgusted with my pushing, he told me everything I didn't want to hear. Steve told me it was the lady he has been dating. She was taking him out to a restaurant on the beach for his birthday. The tears started running down by cheeks. Steve must have sensed something in my voice when he told me because; he asked if I was, okay? Not wanting to ruin any plans I had for tomorrow, I decided to lie to him and tell him I was okay. He told me to enjoy my night and he was looking forward to spending his birthday with me tomorrow. We then hung up and of course, I was beyond upset. It was ruining my mood for tomorrow, but I brought it on myself with all my hounding, nosiness and obsessive love for him. This would now be a very bad night for me as I imagined them together walking arm in arm and embraced, as one, under the moonlight on the beach.

At some point that night I must have fallen asleep but was then awakened to the sound of my phone at 2:00am. It was Steve calling me. I picked up the phone and to my dismay he sounded drunk. He told me he was on his way home from the restaurant. He also told me he had an entire bottle of wine together with his lady friend and they danced on the beach in the moonlight. Wow, Steve just kept taking that knife and turning it round and round until I could barely breathe. I asked him If he should be driving?

He told me, "Absolutely no, but my date put me in a cab, and I will have to pick up my car tomorrow." Steve asked me to stay on the phone with him until he reached home. *Sure, she gets all the fun and I have to stay up and babysit him.* I wound up staying on the phone with Steve for close to an hour until he was home and in his house. I listened to his entire drunken mumble jumble as he spilled out all the details of his night. When we finally hung up, I realized, not that this was a surprise to me, but I was nothing more than a desperate, pathetic fool. I cried a little more and fell back to sleep.

The next day was Steve's birthday. I sent him a Happy Birthday email and told him to pick me up at 5:00pm because we had dinner reservations for 5:30pm. He asked me if I could drive to his place at 5:00pm instead. I didn't know why, but not wanting to rock the boat with anything, I agreed to come to him. I spent the good half of my day fussing over myself. I had to look perfect! I had no idea what this other woman looked like, but I had to somehow look better than her. I bought a beautiful new sexy dress with matching high heels and made sure my hair and makeup looked great and professional. I thought I looked really great, but of course my obsessive compulsive soul did not agree and thought I could look even better.

I got into my car with all my presents and surprises and of course, my overnight bag so that I could stay over. When I arrived at his house, he asked me what all this stuff I had was.

I told him, "They are your surprises for later, but I would like to give you your main birthday gift now." Steve seemed very taken back when I handed him the box, like he didn't really want it. He actually asked me if he could open it later, but like a little girl, I said, "No, open it now." He opened the beautiful card and read it with absolutely no reaction and then he opened the box that contained the two very expensive shirts I thought he would love, but all I got was a measly thank you and then he put the box containing his new shirts in the closet. I then handed him the beautiful gift basket I had made up that contained all the chocolate medical supplies attached with a beautiful poem I wrote just for him. If he didn't look thrilled with the shirts, you should have seen his face with the basket of chocolates and the poem. He looked like someone just punched him in the gut and he needed to throw up. He once again put the basket in his closet and never read the poem and then asked me what the other shopping bags were for. I told him they were a surprise for both of us when we got back home later.

We drove to the restaurant and had a very quiet dinner. Steve was not his talkative self that night and when the check came and I took it, insisting to pay, He abruptly said, "No!" And he paid for the meal. We then drove to the Performing Art Center which thank goodness I paid for in advance so he couldn't take that pleasure away from me. I reserved great balcony seats right on the wall and we watched a great show. He seemed a little better after the show and we talked about the show on the way back to his place, which was nice.

When we got inside, I asked him if he was ready for my next surprise. He started opening the different shopping bags and pulling out all the tissue paper and as he looked through everything, once again there was that look of disgust on his face. He asked me if we could save these things to use another night. I was completely devastated! What kind of man would not want to be pampered and fussed over on his birthday by a woman? I had spent so much time, money and planning and all he did was walk over to his laptop and start doing some work on in, avoiding me at all costs.

I asked him if he wanted to watch a movie with me, but he told me that, "Something came up at one of his centers and he needed to respond to it immediately." He added, "It would probably be best for you to go home tonight since I will be working most of the night and wanted no distractions." I felt humiliated and actually embarrassed. Steve did not want me there and was using work on his birthday no less to get rid of me for the night. I had been just about throwing myself at him all night with no reaction on his part. I just stood there, not sure of what to do. I decided to stand strong and not cry this time. I just didn't want him to think I was nothing more than a cry baby. He was totally ignoring me, so I grabbed my purse and jacket leaving everything else behind, in hopes of forcing a call back date and said, "Goodbye." We had not even had the beautiful cake I made up for him. He just waved goodbye, without even walking me to my car like he always did. He did make sure that he screamed out that he would call me tomorrow and then I shut the door and got into my car.

    I waited until I was out of his development before I allowed the waterworks to turn on, sending my mascara sliding down the cheeks of my face like an avalanche. My guts were telling me Steve did not seem too interested in me anymore and that maybe he found someone else to take my place. *What was it about me that men got tired or bored with?* As always, I blamed myself for everything that went wrong with these men. When I got home, it was the first time Steve didn't call to make sure I got home okay. I knew in that moment waiting for my phone to ring that it was over. I felt in my heart of hearts that he found someone else. I was in love with Steve very much, but unrequited love really hurts. How would I heal once again from another broken heart? I cried the entire night, going over all the details and events of the night. I believe Steve was upset about all the gifts I got him because he knew the relationship was ending and didn't feel good about everything, I bought him and all the money I spent. If Steve had a conscience, which I am not sure about, then he would feel guilty about all I was doing to make his night special.

    I awoke in the morning like a zombie after having maybe an hour's worth of sleep. Between all the crying and my mind going through every detail of the relationship from the beginning to now, there had been no room for sleep. I was waiting impatiently the entire day for Steve to call me. It was torturous and hard not being able to call him or send a text or email. When Sunday was over and I was able to go to work on Monday, I felt a slight relief from the waiting and memories of a bad weekend. The week went slow as I constantly was checking my phone and email for a message from Steve, but nothing the entire week. By Saturday, I was a complete mental case desperately just wanting to hear his voice. Listening more to my obsession than wise wisdom and reasoning, I called his phone, but it went straight to voicemail. I did not leave a message. I then spent my entire Saturday writing and re-writing an email to him straight from my heart stating, "If we can't be lovers, can we at least be friends?" It was a well, thought out email filled with friendship, love and gratitude. I never received a response back from Steve. It was totally over, and he did not even want to know me as a friend. I cried the whole weekend once again and then with a wounded and heavy heart, I had no choice once again, but to move on.

Chapter 24 - FBI John

It had been a few weeks since Steve and I broke up and I thought maybe if I started dating again, it might accelerate my healing process, so I did a search on Match & Catch and contacted a few men. One older gent responded to me. He was a professor at a college in Orlando, but also had a residency in Hollywood. His name was Peter. He was a lawyer who taught classes instead of practicing law. He was about ten years older than me, and we spent the next week emailing back and forth to each other and then he asked me to meet him. The following Monday was a holiday and a day off for me, so we decided to meet since we both did not have to work. We made plans to meet at the halfway point which was Vero Beach and where all the great outlets were. Peter and I made plans to meet at 11:00am and start by visiting all the outlet stores and then having a beautiful lunch at a restaurant he chose right on the beach.

When Monday arrived, I had to hurry to get dressed and look my best because it would take me over an hour to get to Vero Beach and I wanted to stop off quickly at The Coffee Hut and grab a latte. I got in my car and quickly drove over there. When I entered the parking lot, I couldn't believe the line; it was completely out the door and beyond. I quickly checked the time and decided I had a little bit of time to wait. Maybe the line would go fast.

While in line and feeling frustrated because of the long wait, I accidently under my breath mumbled, "Doesn't anyone stay home and make their own coffee in their own kitchen anymore?" A very good looking man in front of me heard my snide remark and turned around and looked at me. Boy was he good looking.

He replied to my comment by saying, "I don't see you making your coffee in your kitchen." I was so embarrassed because I did not think anyone heard what I said. I apologized to him for being rude, but he smiled at me with the most charming smile and said, "Trust me, everyone feels the same way. No one wants to stand in line for this long for a cup of Joe." He then put his hand out and said, "I'm John."

I shook his hand and said, "I'm Sharon" We talked a bit while waiting which made the line go so much faster. I told him I was on a dating site and was driving today to Vero Beach to meet this man for the first time over at the outlet center. I also explained to him that the man I was meeting was a college professor from Orlando and we thought Vero Beach would be a good halfway point.

John seemed a little shocked by what I just told him. He told me he was a retired FBI agent, and he felt this type of dating was dangerous. I thanked him for his concern and told him we were meeting at the outlets for shopping and lunch and there would be people around me at all times. John still seemed concerned and did not understand why people had to go through these internet dating sites to meet someone.

John was extremely good looking. He told me he was 58 years old, but looked 50, except for his gray hair. He was divorced with three grown children and like me he was a bodybuilder dressed in a nice pair of shorts, a tank top, and had a firm body and muscles bulging out everywhere. *Ooh la la!* He was like something out of a magazine. You could tell he thought a lot about himself by his body language and his FBI cocky type of mannerism that gave him much confidence like the actors on those police shows.

I was very amused by him and was really enjoying our talk which made this line from hell move faster or at least seem like it did. When we both got our coffee, we walked out of The Coffee Hut together. John was still talking up a storm. He had the gift of gab, but I was enjoying him. He told me to wait a moment because he had something in his car, he wanted to give me, and so I checked my watch and hoped he would hurry. He came back and handed me his business card. He asked for mine. I hesitated to give him my phone number, but when he smiled that dazzling smile and flexed his muscles, my card somehow slipped out of my wallet and into his hand. I told him I really had to go, and he told me to be safe and call him if I ran into had uncertain issues and needed help. *Wow, my very own FBI agent, just in case I need one*, I thought to myself as I walked away from John giggling under my breath.

John really did think he was all that, but truth be told he was very different and unique then the average men you meet on the street. He was much too good looking and cocky for me. I already had my share of conceited and overly good looking men who did nothing more than break my heart. I threw his card away and hoped he wouldn't call me, which he probably would not.

I drove to Vero Beach to meet Peter. I was hoping he would be a nice man for a change and if not, I was excited to visit this outlet center. I had never been there before. I heard this was one of the best outlet centers and had great stores. It was a beautiful day, and I was actually content to just drive there and shop.

When I arrived at the outlook center, Peter was already there and waiting for me where we had made a plan to meet. He, of course, looked better in his picture, than in person. His clothes also looked slightly tattered, and he had so much less hair than his picture showed. I wonder if he lost some on his way here riding in his convertible with the top down. There was no real attraction, but after meeting Mr. Gorgeous FBI Man, it would be hard to top.

Peter hugged me hello and we went store by store looking at everything. It was so much fun, and the outlets just went on and on with so much to see. We tried to hit almost every store, but it was impossible, so we decided to go get lunch and come back after to finish our shopping excursion. We went to a beautiful restaurant on the beach. I followed Peter there to play it safe. I ordered a beautiful seafood salad, and we talked about what we were both looking for. Peter had a different agenda than I did. No surprise to me! He was looking for a younger woman who basically would be at his beck and call. He told me that the woman he chose would quit her job and he would support her as long as she cooked, cleaned and performed whatever tasks he required. He was not looking to marry her, but just have her be in his life. This man in a round-a-bout way was looking for a sex slave or maybe an indentured servant. I also wondered about these men because I believed most of them did not read the women's profiles but were just interested in the picture because there was no compatibility with Peter as with most of the men I met online. I just listened to all Peter's wants and needs as far as a woman was concerned and happily ate my lunch so I could get back to shopping at the outlet centers, hopefully by myself.

    When we were both finally done with lunch, I told Peter I wanted to go back and shop some more. I was hoping he would just say goodbye and go his own way, but to my unfortunateness, he stayed by my side in all the stores like a puppy in heat. I even tried to over shop to wear him out, but nothing worked to get rid of him. After a few more hours of this ball and chain at my side, I told him I was tired, and it was starting to get dark so I should leave. He walked me to my car and out of nowhere grabbed me to kiss me. I strategically found a way to break his grip and slip out of his embrace. I told Peter I am not in a kissing mood and grabbed my keys and quickly entered my car and locked the door. As I drove away, I looked out my rearview mirror to see him standing there alone where I left him with arms flared up in the air at me. Goodbye and good luck, I thought as I drove off. Another dud date I could add to my repertoire of strange men.

    I got onto I-95, which was nearby, but was hoping this late to hit the turnpike, which is where I wanted to be, because it was safer. I was not seeing any signs for the turnpike and had a long ride home.

My phone rang but I did not recognize the number so I hesitated to pick it up, especially in case it was Peter trying to reach me on another line. I didn't pick it up, but then ten minutes later, it started ringing again. I decided to just answer because the ringing was annoying me. I picked it up and after hearing his voice, I realized it was FBI John, who I guess had nothing better to do then call me and find out how my dysfunctional date went. When he asked about Peter, I just changed the subject by telling him I was onI-95 but could not find any signs to merge onto the turnpike. He told me he knew this route like the back of his hand and would have no trouble navigating me there. *Of course, he would.* Sure enough, I had to get off a particular exit to pick up the turnpike there and he did stay true to his word that he knew this route well. I got on the turnpike and felt much safer. John asked if he could stay on the phone with me until I got home. I agreed to this because it made the trip go faster.

For a whole hour we talked about everything including his fascinating career. We actually had a strong magnetic chemistry between us, and I was enjoying my ride home because of it. John led me right into his driveway where he was standing on the phone with me waiting for me to pull in. He only lived about five minutes away, so I did not mind another view of this gorgeous man and his muscles. I got out of the car and stretched my legs. I thanked him for talking to me the entire time I was driving. I told him, "This was better than a cup of coffee." John gave me a big hug and I could just feel his muscles flexing. I was trying not to swoon over this man, but he was making it hard not to and I got the feeling John was the type who always got people to do what he wanted them to do. We talked in the driveway for another hour and then I told him I really had to get home because I had work in the morning. He gently reached toward me and pulled me close to him and gently kissed me. *Wow, I think I saw stars.* So, John was gorgeous, intelligent, had a bad boy, high octane career and boy could he kiss. I was in really big trouble! I could have stayed and kissed him all night, but I left. He told me he would call me the next day and I believed he would.

I went home, took a shower, jumped into bed after a long day and dreamed of John's strong arms. Most of my days go bad, but today turned into a great day and I dashed off to sleep thinking all happy thoughts for a change.

The next day, John called me while I was driving home from work. He asked me if I wanted to come over. I couldn't resist and went straight there. I assumed we would have dinner together, but as always, I assumed wrong. I had asked John if he wanted to go out and get a pizza, but he told me he had eaten already and was not hungry. I, as usual, put my needs on hold and decided not to tell him I was starving after a whole day of working and not having the time to eat much. We hung out in his family room watching television and cuddling. I was so into him, but not once did he ask me, knowing I was coming from work, if I wanted anything. I just hope he was not being cheap. I would have paid for the pizza. I tried to not think about my stomach and focus on this delicious man who actually wanted to hug and kiss me. It was amazing.

John told me all about his pension, all the properties he owned, the collectibles worth money that he owned and his house which was all paid off. He was also receiving social security and was running a small part-time security business. This man had it all except for a meal or snack to offer me. After about two hours, I told him it was getting late, and I needed to get home to get ready for work tomorrow. He walked me to my car, kissed me goodnight and told me he would call me tomorrow. I got home and devoured some chicken and pasta I had left over. I couldn't figure John out yet, but in time I would.

The next day after work, I went home and made myself dinner. About two hours later, John called. He was hanging out at the bar of one of his favorite restaurants and asked me if he could stop by on his way home. I told him he could, and in about five minutes there was a knock on the door. He came in and I gave him a tour of my apartment. He liked it and thank goodness it was clean. We sat down together on the couch and talked. He looked gorgeous. He was wearing tight designer jeans, a V-neck shirt that profiled his muscles and a pair of brown casual loafers. I was blown away from him. I think he should be arrested for looking that good! We wound up kissing and cuddling for a while and then he left. John was a gentleman who up to now had not tried anything other than kissing me. It made me feel secure and safe. I still had no clue where this relationship was going but tried hard not to like him too much and was trying just to go along for the ride.

On Saturdays and Sundays, my days off from work, I would go to the gym each morning, and then with sticking with my own rituals, would grab a latte from The Coffee Hut which was right across the street before I headed home. John hung out there every morning with a group of his buddies who were also retired. After I got my latte and I spotted him, I went over to kiss him hello and join him while I drank my coffee. John pulled away from me casually not allowing me to kiss him. I sat down a little shocked from his reaction to my greeting. He did introduce me to the other men and women sitting there, not as a girlfriend, but just as someone he knew. I watched John engage with everyone at the table. He was the center of attention, and you can see everyone admired him, including himself. After about an hour everyone got up to leave, including John. He said goodbye to me and left me sitting there without an acknowledgement. I was a little bewildered and taken back but did not want to call him and ask. I did not want John to know I was upset and didn't want it to look in any way like I was chasing him.

The next day, which was Sunday, John acted the same way toward me, and I did not hear from him the entire weekend, but when Monday night came, he stopped by, out of the blue, to hang out with me and watch television. We sat on the couch and kissed and cuddled a bit and then he left to go home. I did not know what to make of this strange relationship and did not feel comfortable talking about it with him.

For two weeks this same pattern of behavior was still prevailing. Monday through Friday he would either stop by my house to hang out after he was finished eating or drinking at his favorite bar or if he wasn't going out to the bar, he would ask me to come over so that we could kiss, cuddle and watch television. On Saturdays and

Sundays when I would stop off at The Coffee Hut after the gym to get my latte, he would be talking with all his buddies and would totally ignore me and barely gave me a hello. After all these weeks, I had never had a meal with him or went out anywhere together with him. In front of others, he was so cold, distant and standoffish that it felt like he was embarrassed to be seen or affiliated with me. I knew I had to walk away from this deranged relationship, but I felt stuck in quicksand. I was drawn to him like a moth to a flame.

The following week I found out I needed some surgery on my gums and my dentist was in Boca Raton. He gave me a pill to take before the procedure that would make me relax and sleepy, so I needed someone to drive me there and back. I was scheduled for Friday and took the day off of work. I decided on a whim to ask John to take me and he actually said he would. He was at my door 8:00am sharp as planned and helped me take the pill. I was scared but having John there with me made it easier. When I walked in with John to the dental office, the assistants were all commenting to me. "Where did you get this hunk from?" They knew I wasn't seeing anyone, and they thought he was drop dead gorgeous, which he absolutely was. I wish I could have told them he was mine, but the truth was he was not, and probably would never be. I had no idea what I was to him and might never find out.

After the procedure I was groggy. John helped me into the car, and I must have slept the whole way home. When we got back to my apartment, he took care of me. He gave me an ice pack to put on my mouth. The dentist had given me about ten stitches, so it was a little swollen, sore and still partially numbed from the shots. He put me in bed and covered me then he gave me my pain pill with water and stayed with me for a few hours, just to make sure I was okay and not having any reaction to the pain medication.

    We started watching a movie in my room, but I must have at some point fallen asleep. When I woke up, I felt okay. The pain was bearable and the pill that made me sleepy had worn off, so I was feeling much better. John told me he needed to go, but if I needed anything to just call. I thanked him and he left. I spent the rest of the weekend on my own taking care of myself. I didn't see John at all the whole weekend though he did call once, the next day after the surgery, to see if I was okay. I was too swollen to go to The Coffee Hut for my latte even though I craved one. I was hoping John would ask me if I wanted anything from there, but that never happened. I spent the whole weekend in the house dreaming and pretending John was here with me, taking care of me. It was hard to always be alone especially when you have surgery or you're sick and you have to fend for yourself without any help from anyone. Having John take care of me on Friday was like a dream come true and I yearned for more.

    The following week I was able to go back to work and my mouth was healing nicely. My strange relationship pattern with John started up again with him popping in to watch television with me during the week and ignoring me at the coffee place on the weekends. This was definitely not healthy for me because while John was somewhat in my life, in some form, I was not sure exactly how. It just couldn't be defined. What I was sure of was that I was totally and certifiably falling in love with John and could not tell you why. He never took me out or anywhere for that matter; he never told me how he felt about me and ignored me completely when there were other people around.

I also became very absent minded and clumsy whenever I was with him. I was totally not myself. I would lose all self-assurance, control and intelligence when he was near me. I never had this happen before with anyone and the only way to stop it was to break all ties with him, but how? John was like a big, delicious chocolate chip cookie that you just couldn't stop eating. You had to have more. I wanted him so badly and was not able at this time to completely walk away from him, no matter how bad he treated me. He was like no other man I met. He was gorgeous, had an unbelievable physique, was well educated, and being a former FBI agent just added that self-assured and audacious personality that made him charming and alluring to all he met. John could walk in a room and all at once everyone there was drawn to him like a magnet, especially me.

One Sunday, I was coming out of the gym and rushing to look great and get to The Coffee Hut before John left. I was anxious to see him and started fumbling, as usual to get in my car because the moment I knew I would see him, I would become a complete clumsy train wreck. I opened my car door to put down my purse and backpack and absentmindedly locked the door, leaving me outside my car without my keys, my purse and my phone. Everything was locked up. I had never done anything like this before. I was in trouble! I went into a bit of a panic and ran across the street to the coffee shop running straight to John asking for his help. Instead of John helping me, he told me to stop acting like a victim and just sit awhile and have a cup of coffee. I told John I had no money for my purse was also locked up in my car. John never offered to buy me a cup of coffee and just told me to get a cup of water from the staff inside. His buddies at the table offered to buy me coffee, but not the man I loved.

    I asked John if I could use his phone, and he grudgingly handed it to me. I knew my younger son had a key to my apartment where I kept a spare key to my car, so I called him and asked for his help. Thankfully I knew his number by memory. He offered to come and help me but needed about an hour or so to get there. I handed John back his phone. About five minutes later, John and everyone else at the table started getting up to leave. I asked John if he would wait with me, and he said, he was busy and had to leave. I waited in the hot sun next to my car for about an hour and fifteen minutes until my son showed up. I stayed close to my car because my purse was sitting right on the front seat and did not want to experience a "break and take" if someone noticed my valuable stuff sitting there. John never called during the day to make sure I was okay and got home alright. When he popped in at night after his evening at his special bar, I voiced that I was disappointed and that just out of common decency, he should have checked on me. John told me to get over it and I just dropped the subject, because if not he would just leave and that would devastate me more. We sat on the couch for the next two hours cuddling and watching a movie.

A few weeks later, the day before Thanksgiving, he invited me over to watch a documentary with him. After about an hour or so, I was getting hungry and apparently so was he. He actually asked me if I would like some Chinese Food. I was shocked that he finally offered me something to eat. I said, "Yes." And he ordered some food over the phone, but never asked me if there was something specific, I would like him to order for me. Not a shocker! When the food was delivered, we wound up sharing one small container of lo mein and a container of soup. *Thank goodness, it came with two fortune cookies,* I thought to myself. *At least I could have my own cookie!* It was a measly meal, but at least he gave me something to eat. I loved to eat. I was a body builder and needed food. This strange relationship lacked food.

I wondered if John was really that cheap or he did not want to spend any money on me. He seemed to penny pitch everything when I was around, but I also accepted everything and anything he did without ever speaking up about it. I was allowing John to dictate and control our relationship because it was more important to have him in my life then to have my pride and self-esteem. This made me just as bad as he. After we ate, we finished watching the documentary and cuddled up as always on his couch. For the first time, since I met him, he asked me to stay over. I was ecstatic, thinking maybe this relationship was taking a turn in a new direction. "Food and a stay over in one night, this was monumental!" It was different. I had nothing with me, so John gave me a brand new toothbrush and lent me one of his tee-shirts to sleep in. We got into bed, and he held me in his arms all night. He was a complete gentleman which rattled my brain.

John never seemed to want more than cuddling and kissing. At least I could not say he wasn't in anyway using me. I just couldn't figure him out, but maybe I should just enjoy the moment and let everything fall into place like it did that night. I slept soundly in his arms, and you know how much I loved those arms of his.

When I awoke in the morning, John was preparing a dish to bring to his son's house for Thanksgiving. I told John I had not been invited anywhere for the holiday because my sons were going to be with their dad this year which left me to fend for the holiday on my own. I asked John if I could join him at his son's house. I could bring a dish or two and I do not eat much. John told me to get over it, it's just another day, and that he did not want to bring anyone with him today. To me, it was not just another day. It was a time for family and friends to come together and enjoy the holiday. Tears started rolling down my eyes. What he said stung me really hard. It was like taking a bullet to the heart.

John told me to hurry up and get dressed so we could grab a coffee together at The Coffee Hut. He didn't even notice my tears, let alone care about them. He told me to drive over in my own car, which was probably because he didn't want anyone to see us get out of the same car together. When we got there and walked inside, he ordered his coffee and as always did not acknowledge me. I guess the Chinese food last night put him over the edge with his budget for the week.

We sat down with everyone and all anyone talked about were their wonderful Thanksgiving plans for the day. I tried with all my might to not look sad or cry. It was embarrassing that I had nowhere to go and even the people or person I was hanging out with would not invite me to go with them. When it was time to go, I actually begged John to let me come. He just kept saying, no! He told me he would bring me a large plate of food back and drop it off on his way home. We said goodbye to eat other and as soon as I got into my car, the tears started rolling down. I felt hopeless and helpless as I hung around my apartment all day since everything was closed on Thanksgiving. The worst part was I waited all evening for John to call or drop off my food that I was counting on for some sort of holiday meal, but he never called and never showed. I felt like a forgotten fool that no one cared about. I drank a glass of wine and ate some potato chips and just went to bed. That day for me couldn't be over quick enough.

The next night John called me telling me he would stop by on his way home from the bar. When he got to my apartment, I told him, "I waited for the dinner you promised to bring me."

He laughed and said, "I was just saying that so you would stop crying, I had no plans to bring you food from my son's house." In that moment, I knew he didn't care one iota about me. I didn't even understand why he kept stopping by. Maybe my leather couches were more comfortable than his? I couldn't think of any other reason. He really was a very narcissistic man. How self-absorbed can someone be?

John was fourteen years older than me, but quite frankly his behavior was like a twenty-year-old. I had no one but myself to blame for this behavior because I was allowing it. In my plight to have someone in my life and someone handsome and charming around, I was willing to reduce myself to the lowest form of human there was. I had no backbone or strength left to run or fight so I stayed in a relationship, if you want to call it that, that bordered almost on mental or emotional abuse. I kept feeding his ego and he kept draining mine. How sad this was, I allowed this pattern of behavior to continue for months. I was unhappy and unfulfilled but couldn't let go.

One evening when he was over, we were just lying down and chatting, I lost my mind and told him I loved him and wanted more. I felt at this point, I had absolutely nothing to lose. His response to what I said was cold and flat, "I do not love you; I have never loved you and I never will love you." The words that came out of his mouth made it feel like I just got smacked in the head with a baseball at full speed. I did not know what to say or even how to look at him. My heart was completely broken as was my ego and sense of self-worth.

I did not want to cry, but I did need to know why he was always coming over, so I asked him, "What have we been doing all these months?"

His answer was, "We are just friends hanging out, and nothing more."

I told him that I wanted to be in a relationship with him, and John looked right into my eyes, and with a lot of zest and a firm stare, he told me, "That will never happen. You are not someone I would ever want to be in a relationship with." The tears started rolling down.

At that moment, John said he had to go. He kissed me goodbye on my forehead and ran out the door. I felt so hurt and so unwanted, still with no real answer with what was wrong with me. What was I supposed to do with all this pain that was filling up my heart? I cried so hard, and eventually just cried myself to sleep right on the couch for the night.

    I hadn't heard from John over the next couple of days and then those days turned into weeks. After that whenever he saw my car pull up at The Coffee Hut, I noticed how quickly he got up and left. The pain of all this was unbearable for me. My heart was breaking apart into pieces, especially since he did not want to even be my friend anymore, let alone an acquaintance, or someone he could at least say hello to. I knew all along this was a dysfunctional relationship that would go nowhere. I hoped in the beginning, that since I met him in a natural way, not on the internet, and with how he kept pursuing me, that maybe it had a chance, but it didn't. I needed to truly let go of it all so that I would be able to move on. I tried so hard to tell myself that John was all wrong for me. He was a square peg, and I was a round hole. It would never fit. A dog just can't be with a cat. I really tried day after day to move on, but I was lonely and felt even more alone than before I met him.

    I needed to do something to relieve some of this pain, so I went back onto to Match & Catch. It had felt great all these months not having to be on those dating sites, but now I needed a distraction. I needed something or someone else to get me out of my apartment. The only way to get over John was to find someone else. I put up some new pictures, refreshed my profile, and contacted some new prospects and waited to see where it would take me. When I came back later to check my responses, I was overwhelmed by all of them. I went through each one, profile by profile, to see if any of them sparked an interest in me. I decided to be a little pickier than before, and while I wanted someone I was attracted to, I decided to not go out with any man that was too good-looking, because they turned out to be nothing but trouble. I needed to date with a different prospective. To not be so desperate and not let my obsession drive the wheel.

    Maybe John came into my life to bring me clarity on who I am. He brought me hurt and pain, but maybe enough of it so I would be forced to change who I am. While navigating through Match & Catch, I found a profile for John. He had just joined even after he told me he did not believe in on-line dating. I felt even more betrayed by his lies to me regarding these sites. He would tell me all the time; he would never join something like this. It was beneath him. All the things he wrote in his profile like going out to beautiful restaurants and moonlit walks on the beach just sickened me to read. It was just more lies and betrayals. I needed to stop looking at his profile and at his pictures if I was going to set my sight on someone else.

    Over the next few weeks when I bumped into some of John's buddies from The Coffee Hut, they informed me that John met a woman online and she was moving down to Florida to live with him. That felt like a knife being pierced through my heart. I guess when it is the right one, it works out all around. I asked them many questions especially about this woman because it seemed so quick for him. They told me that she was a wealthy woman who was moving down here to be with him but keeping her house in Ohio. Wow, a rich woman from the state of Ohio. They told me she was a year older than him. *Ouch!* He would rather have a woman fifteen years older than me, who is from another state that he barely even knows. *How can I ever win?* I felt the tears start to swell in my eyes, so I told his friends I had to go and quickly dashed back to my car. I cried so hard, I could hardly breathe, but I guess this was the closure I needed to finally move on. I must've cried for hours that day. It was finally over and done!

Chapter 25 - Bruce

That night I checked my emails and noticed there was a very long, well written note from someone I never contacted and probably never would. His note read something like this:

"I have seen you go off and on Match & Catch for months now, and since I see you are now once again on, I am guessing you have yet to find the one. You are a beautiful woman who is probably looking for a handsome man, but have those good-looking men you seek treat you right? I am not a handsome man. I am overweight, but I have been on weightwatchers and have already lost over one hundred pounds. I am hoping to lose another seventy-five and doing great on this plan. I know how to treat a woman right and take care of her and make her feel special. I make a very handsome living and I am looking for my one true love that I can adore, spoil and make feel like she is the most important thing in this world. Maybe this time you should try something different. I might just be the Mr. Right, you have been looking for. How about taking a chance on me? Sincerely yours, Bruce."

I was blown away after reading this. I give this man kudos for having the nerve and confidence to speak his heart. It took courage and tenacity to write what he did especially to someone he felt was out of his league. I thought about it, and he probably would treat me better than any of the guys I had met or will meet.

I decided to write back to him. He had a nice face and if he lost the weight, he probably would be very good looking. Everything I was doing up to now was not working. This was my chance to come off my high horse and do something totally out of the box. I wrote him back and told him I was running over to Walmart to get something I needed and that we could talk later.

He wrote back to me, "You are welcome to meet me in front of Walmart and see if you want to pursue a relationship with me, instead of spending wasted time with emails and phone calls."

I said, "Sure."

We planned to meet in thirty minutes at the main entrance of the new local Walmart. I felt for the first time like I was the one in control and I liked it. I didn't change my clothes nor do my hair. I assumed he would think I looked great no matter what. I know I was being a little presumptuous, but I had never been with a very obese man before and was not sure I could be attracted to one, but I would try. Bruce deserved that from me.

When I pulled into the parking lot and got out of my car, I saw a very large man standing and waiting by the entrance. I really knew nothing about Bruce, except that he had a weight issue he was trying to resolve. We hadn't really talked. I only knew about him, whatever was on his note. I walked over to the man and asked if he was Bruce? He said, "Yes," and thanked me for meeting him. We took a seat in the little café, and he did ask me, if I wanted anything? I told him, "No thank you."

We took this time to learn about each other. He told me he was divorced, but never had any kids. His wife had cheated on him and left him for someone else, which triggered him into depression and binge eating. He ate himself up to almost four hundred pounds. When Bruce saw he was destroying his life with this massive weight gain, he joined Weight Watchers and has lost 125 pounds so far. I congratulated him and told him how sorry I was that he had to go through all that he went through.

Bruce also told me about his job. He was a senior director of a Fortune 500 company and made a great living. He traveled quite a bit, but also got a lot of time off when he was home. When he was done telling me about himself, I then in turn told him all about my two sons and my awful dating experiences. Bruce was very easy to talk to and seemed to have a very compassionate heart. He asked me if he could take me to dinner the following night? I agreed to let him go out with me and he told me about his favorite sushi restaurant in Boca Raton. We made plans to meet there at 7:00pm and then we said goodbye.

The following day I got ready to go out with Bruce. I wanted to get to know him better and see who he really was. I met him at a quiet, quaint little sushi place in Boca Raton. He gave me a big hug hello and then we were seated. I went to order the dumplings for the appetizer when the server came over and Bruce said loudly, "Please don't, I am really trying to stay on my diet and anything other than sushi can ruin my diet. I don't want to be tempted by other foods. Sushi is great for me because it is on the Weight Watchers point system, so it is an easy food to work with."

I said, "Okay." But was he kidding? I couldn't order anything I wanted because he would be tempted? I don't like anything raw, so I was limited. I ordered the one eel roll but was still a little hungry afterwards. I didn't think dessert was something he would want me to order so I told him I was done. We had a nice conversation during dinner, but I was a little concerned about the food situation with him. He walked me to my car and kissed me goodnight. It was okay, but, in all honesty, there wasn't much of a spark, but let's be real here, what was really on my mind was who is going to really ooh and ah me after John? We made plans for the weekend to spend some time together. I was going to try to see if I could get a spark going with him, so I kept plugging along in the dating zone.

On Saturday, I was invited over to see his place. He had a beautiful, swanky apartment in a ritzy community. Bruce also had great taste in furniture, unless someone else decorated it for him, but he didn't say so. His place was as neat as a pin, and he had really impressive gaming system and an unbelievable advanced entertainment center with all the latest bells, whistles and technical advances. My sons would have had a blast hanging in this apartment all day.

We spent the next few hours watching a movie, listening to music and playing some games on his gaming devices. I told Bruce I was getting hungry. He told me it was not time for him to eat and he kept nothing in the house, but some Weight Watcher's snacks and meals. I had asked him, if I could open his refrigerator to see what he had.

And he said, "Go right ahead."

I was a little shocked to see there was basically nothing in there. No crackers, no fruit, no veggies, no drinks, no peanut butter, not even a bottle of ketchup. He had a few containers of some Weight Watcher's snacks and some frozen Weight Watcher's meals in the freezer, but nothing else. I actually asked him about this deficit in food and he just told me that he would not allow anything in the house that would tempt him or ruin his Weight Watcher's point system for the day. I thought to myself *dieting is also about learning how to deal with temptation and overcoming it.* I believed Bruce had bigger issues than he was aware of.

I asked Bruce if we could take a ride to Best Buy because I bought an iPod, and it was not working correctly, and I needed to exchange it. Bruce agreed to drive me there. They wound up exchanging the iPod for the latest version which would not fit the new case I bought so I had to exchange the case for the right one, and it was a difference of $4.00 and some change. When I reached into my wallet to take out the money, I was short $1.00. I asked Bruce if he had a dollar, he could lend me. He told me he had it but does not like to lend money to people. I said, "It is just a dollar, otherwise I have to put the dollar on my credit card." Then he actually told me "No." I used my credit card but was shocked by his lack of chivalrous behavior.

When we left the store and got outside, I told him I was going to run into the pizza place and grab a slice to go. He told me he would appreciate if I waited for dinner which was in about two hours. I didn't want to fight or argue with him, so I didn't get the pizza even though I was starving. When dinner came, we once again went to his favorite sushi restaurant where once again my only choice was an eel roll or a California roll. I asked him if we can sometimes go to a regular American restaurant to get maybe fish or chicken. Bruce explained to me that he could, but the sushi allows him more accountability with his points, and he knows exactly what he can eat and how much, so this is what he sticks to and will not change it up. I told him, "Okay," but I thought he was crazy. I really was not happy with this extreme lifestyle of his.

I scrolled down the bottom of the menu and noticed they had a small Thai section. When the server came over, I happily ordered Chicken Pad Thai, one of my favorite dishes. Once again, Bruce raised his voice and said, "Please don't order that dish. I cannot resist Chicken Pad Thai and it will make me crazy." This was the most ridiculous things I have ever witnessed; and I witnessed a lot of craziness. I said, "Fine," but with a very cranky tone, hoping he would understand that I was frustrated. Be it me to be responsible for Bruce breaking his diet. So, once again, another day and night of no lunch, no appetizer and no dessert, just another roll of sushi. Bruce wouldn't even let me order rice.

I have a fast metabolism and I was hungry and needed more food. After dinner we drove back to his place, and he wanted to know if I wanted to watch another movie. I was thinking, *"Not if there is no popcorn to munch on, which I knew there was none in the house!"* The truth was I was really hungry and wanted to go out and get something fun to eat. I was thin and it was not fair that I had to be a diet victim in his world.

I told Bruce I was not feeling all that well and told him I was going to go home. Bruce did not seem pleased but walked me to my car and kissed me goodnight. When I got into my car, I drove to my favorite pizza place and had three large slices. I was really starving. I had only had breakfast and Bruce did not do lunch or snacks, so I was existing on a smoothie from the morning and one eel roll for dinner. I was not even reaching the low point of my required calories for the day. I do not know what Bruce's definition of treating a woman right is, but he and I were reading from two very different handbooks. I didn't think this was going to work out for me. I love to eat, and I exercise every day of my life, so I *needed* to eat. I also really needed to re-think this relationship with Bruce, but for the moment, I went home and downed an entire container of Haagen-Dazs Mint Chocolate Chip ice cream and didn't think about anything else for the rest of the night.

When I woke up the next morning, I checked my emails, and saw that I received a notice from one of the women I had met at a function. She was sponsoring an upcoming singles cruise for a long weekend. That sounded like something fun and different, so I responded back asking for more information about it. A few hours later, I received an email highlighting all the details of this singles cruise. It was four-fun filled days at sea and in the Bahamas. There were already seventy-five people signed up to go, so without hesitation and without any over-thinking of it, I filled out the paperwork and gave my deposit. I was excited to be going on a grand ship with men and women that had the same interest and needs in mind. Instead of looking for my match alone in a jungle, I would be boarding a ship with new friends to hang out with and enjoy.

The next weekend, excitedly, I told Bruce about my upcoming adventure. He was not happy for me and told me he didn't think I should go. I told Bruce that I needed a vacation and was looking forward to it. Bruce traveled at least 50% of the time for his job so why shouldn't I go for a weekend. He just kept going on about it, so I let the conversation go, since I did not want to spend the time with him fighting. We spent the whole Saturday in his apartment watching movies and not eating anything. I was a little smarter this time and brought snacks with me. When I took out a small little bag of pretzels, Bruce asked me to please not eat those in front of him for he loves pretzels. I put my snacks away as I was told and went back to watching the movie and not getting to eat anything as usual with Bruce not caring one bit. It just seemed too always be about him.

A few days later, I got a call from one of the women that were signed up for the cruise. She told me that a group of her friends that were going also were chipping in for a bus to get to and from the port so they would not have to fuss over parking, tolls and dealing with their luggage and she asked me if I would like to join them on the bus. I happily agreed and told her I would put a check in the mail the same day. I then went online and paid the balance remaining for my cruise and I was rearing to go, plus I could eat off the buffets all day without Bruce telling me not to.

A few days later Bruce called me and out of the blue, he told me that he forbids me to go on the cruise.

I told him I had already paid for it in full.

He told me he would give me the money back for it.

I told him, I was going and that is that!

Bruce then abruptly replied, if you go, then this relationship is over!

I was telling myself in my head, *Oh happy day!* I told him, "I guess it's over." He then really harshly, slammed the phone on me, and I felt relieved like a giant weight came off my shoulder. He was definitely not for me. He had so many issues, that he was reflecting onto me and trust me, I had enough of my own and did not need his. I now felt free since Bruce was out of my life and ready to set sail on the ocean sea.

A few days later, I received a horrible email from Bruce telling me I am a spoiled, *jappy* princess who is always looking for more. He when on to say that I will never find a man that treats me the way he did. I wanted to answer him and truly tell him how horrible of a boyfriend he was, but decided Bruce thinks he is perfect so why have an email battle with him, that I would not win. And Bruce was correct, I would never find anyone who would treat me the way he did because he treated me so badly that I couldn't wait to run home every time I was with him. Most men value a woman who wants to eat, not make them starve and live on a daily fix of water and sushi. His email was two pages long, but not even worth reading to anyone. I felt bad for Bruce. He was a very insecure man who needed counseling in order to function in the real world and be able to deal with food in a good way and not deprive himself of life's special pleasures, in order to keep the weight off. I let Bruce vent through his emails, never responding until they finally stopped. I was free of him and knew I would not be eating sushi again for a long time.

Chapter 26 - Justin

Now that things were over with Bruce, I decide to contact a few people from Match & Catch. I made sure to block Bruce from seeing my profile and sent some messages to several men I was interested in. A few hours later a man named Justin responded to me. He was a sergeant in the police force and extremely very good looking and well-built. His profile had him listed as being 6'5". He was divorced with two grown sons and looking for that special one, so his profile said.

I emailed him back letting him know I would like to meet him. He then responded back, telling me that he would like to meet me also and asked for my phone number. A few days later he called, and we hit it off immediately on the phone. He had a beautiful speaking voice that was very charming, and he was very easy to talk to. Justin told me that he would call me back with a plan to meet once he got his schedule at the station worked out for there have been a lot of changes going on there. This strange pattern went on with him for a week or two. He would call me out of the blue to chat and then tell me, he would call back to make plans when he was able to meet me. Justin was giving me whiplash with his indecisiveness to make a decision and just meet me for an hour.

When we spoke over the phone, Justin told me that he owned a boat and his passion was fishing, which aside from his job took up most of his time. I told him to just get home early from a fishing outing and meet me quickly for a cup of coffee. He liked my sense of humor and promised me we would meet, and it would be for dinner, not just coffee. A few days later when his calling pattern changed, and I had not heard from him, I decided to call him. The call went straight to voicemail. I did not want to leave a message, but when I tried it later in the day, it once again went to voicemail.

A day later Justin called to tell me he just came back from fishing. He told me all about the fish he caught and how he has to pack everything on ice on the boat, so it doesn't spoil. It sounded like the movie I once saw, called *The Perfect Storm*. He also went on to explain how he cuts everything, cleans it, stores it, and gives a lot away to family and friends once he brings it home. I wasn't sure about Justin. I had just got over existing on sushi and really wanted to rest from the whole fish-eating venue for a while.

I asked Justin, at that exact moment, as he was telling me his woes and tales of the fish world; I asked him if we could just meet that night, maybe just for an hour. He told me it was a bad night because he had to maintenance the boat, especially when it was out on the ocean all day and that takes a few hours. But he promised me, we would meet real soon. I told Justin, "This is your last chance, and if you let me down, I will move on and meet someone else." He agreed and told me he would call me this week to make definite plans.

A few days later while I was shopping in the supermarket, Justin called. We chatted on the phone a bit while I shopped and then boldly, I asked him if we could meet that night. He said he really had a lot of things he needed to get done. I decided to stick to my word, and I told him, "I am done, and it is a shame we never got to meet."

Then Justin said hurriedly, "Wait, how about tomorrow night? I would love to take you to dinner."

I told him, "Great! That's more like it!" The next day, which was a Thursday, we met at a Mexican restaurant. He was very tall and handsome, just like his profile said he was. He had a beautiful smile that could light up the room. I was a little smitten with him. We had a wonderful dinner, and the conversation was flawless. Afterwards he walked me to my car, kissed me and told me, "I was worth waiting for."

The next day was Friday and I asked him if we could go to a movie together? He said, "Absolutely, I will call you tomorrow." When I got home, I felt good. I was happy with myself that I was bold with him and told him over the phone exactly what I wanted. I was hoping that I was becoming from all these horrible experiences, a stronger person, someone who did not play the victim all the time but took matters into their own hands. Justin was definitely worth waiting for, but needed a little push along the way, when it came to this dating game.

On Friday, by the time Justin called me, it was too late for a movie. He told me that he went out with his buddies on his boat, and they got home later then they planned for, but he would call me in a few days to make plans to see that movie we talked about. When I hung up with him, I was really pissed. My rival in this scenario was a fishing boat and it was starting to get on my nerves. Justin did not call me again until the following week. He once again threw at me his lame excuses of working, fishing and having to spend time cleaning his boat. That boat was having more fun than me and I was jealous of it. He told me we could catch a movie the next night, which would be Thursday and I foolishly agreed.

When Justin picked me up the next day, I couldn't be upset with him because he would just smile that enchanting smile of his and I was hooked, just like a fish. We had a great evening together and before he spilt, I told him, "Saturday night is for me, so don't make any plans."

He said, "Okay." And then he kissed me. I couldn't wait for Saturday night. I had not had a Saturday date yet with him, so I was excited. I loved going out on Saturday night. We had plans to go to a beautiful restaurant on the beach. I spent the afternoon getting ready to look great for him. If there was one thing I could do, it would be to look better than a fish.

I was busy touching up my make-up when at about 5:00pm the phone rang, and it was Justin. To my surprise, or was it? Justin was explaining that he had been out on the boat all day and he was exhausted and wiped out. He went on to tell me that he would have to clean the fish, cut them, pack them up, store them and clean down his boat which would probably take about three hours or more. This was making me fume. That damned boat again! I decided to try a different approach. I asked him if I could come over that evening and help him clean the fish and cook him a nice fish dinner? I figured if I can't beat them, I better join them.

Justin's response to that which did not surprise me was, "My place is a complete mess tonight and I rather you come another night when I have the chance to clean it." I tried so hard to persuade him by telling him I didn't care, I could help clean his place with him, but he did not budge on his decision. He seemed in a rush to get off the phone with me and proceeded to tell me his fish were going to spoil if he did not tend to them and take them off the boat. He told me he would call me in a day or two. I started thinking that how could his fish spoil, if they were packed on ice? I was livid. He needed to tend to his fish. What about tending to me, his girlfriend, or something in that category.

All these men write in their profiles that they are looking for a true, romantic, impossible love, but when they find someone, they refuse to put any effort into it or try for that matter to make anything work. I was so baffled by all of this, that I wasn't even sure if I wanted a husband anymore. These men were immovable objects that just gave me heartache and uneasiness.

A few days later, Justin called me to see if we could go out on Thursday. I was starting to take note and notice that Thursday was the only day we ever go out on. I was wondering if there was something else going on in his life, he had not been up front with. I once again asked Justin and tried very hard to talk him into letting me come over to his place to cook him dinner, especially that I now had new insight into his strange dating pattern with me and a very large red flag that was swaying over my head. When I suggested it, he would just tell me what a wreck his place was and did not have any time to clean it. I really needed to find out who he was and what skeletons were in his closet, so I asked him to take me out on his boat. He actually told me he doesn't go out fishing with women because for him, it is a guy thing. The red flags were not only there, but they were doing sidekicks all around. I started wondering if maybe he was married. How would I be able to find out? He was a police officer so he would be more street wise than me. I had to be careful. I tried to do a search on him, but nothing came up and if he was truly a police officer, his privacy would be much protected. If Justin was not a police officer, which I had no proof of that either, then he was probably going under a different name, because I could find nothing on this man. I decide to wait for our date on Thursday to interrogate him with questions. It was best in person, then over the phone.

On Thursday Justin came to my place to pick me up. We drove to a very nice restaurant for dinner together. We had a lovely meal, and it was during dessert that I asked him, "Why do we only go out on Thursdays? And why can't I ever see where you live or go out on your boat?" He told me nothing more than what he said before: That he was busy with his boat, his job and had no time to clean his house and until it was clean, he would not have me come over. I then proceeded to ask him what his address was, but he ignored me, paid the bill and we walked back to his car. While we were driving back to my apartment, I sort of asked him a question which implied that he could be married.

Again, Justin just darted my questions like a bullet and quietly walked me upstairs to my apartment. He said he couldn't come in because he had a lot of things to take care of at home, but he would call me in a few days. Well, you can only imagine what I was thinking.

A few days passed and then a week and still no call from Justin. I called him but his phone was now saying it was disconnected or maybe he set it up to just give me that message. Whatever it was, I knew I would never hear from Justin again, and I knew I would never find out what it was he was hiding or who he really was. I went back onto Match & Catch to send a message to Justin one more time, but his profile was totally removed, or he blocked me. I would never know. I wasn't as upset as I normally get when men do these things to me. I guess I was expecting Justin to do something as ludicrous as this or I was starting to get skilled at not letting my heart fall and break so quickly. Justin played a charade with me, but the truth eventually always comes out. The longer you lie and spin your web, the sooner you get caught up in it. I was okay because whatever he was hiding, I wanted no part of.

My membership on Match & Catch was ending and I decided I needed something new to join that maybe could inadvertently change my luck, well at least I hoped it would.

Chapter 27 - A Bucket of Fish

I navigated through the internet and found a free dating site called A Bucket of Fish. I wasn't thrilled that the word fish was in the title, but at least I didn't have to eat it. It appeared to be a cute site and a little different than the others, plus I needed a change. I was tired of looking through the profiles on Match & Catch and seeing many of the same men that were there for a life-sentence because the perfect, gorgeous, model they were waiting for had not joined the site yet. I didn't want those men to view me with the same thoughts, so it was time for something new.

I uploaded new pictures, put up a new, dynamic, but honest profile and started to fish. I decided to choose men who had a different agenda this time. I did a search for widowers. I figured men who had children and lost their wives would be more inclined to want the same thing again unlike the men who went through divorces and had all kinds of issues stemming from the calamity of it. So, I set my parameters for my search. I looked for widowers who wrote in their profile that they had been happily married. I found two men who had nice profiles and appeared successful and had nice pictures, not that it was written in stone which I learned from experience that profiles and pictures can sometimes be nothing more than a facade. I sent beautiful messages to them telling them I want love, romance and marriage, and if they are not looking for these things to please not respond.

A few hours later, I received responses from both of them. The first man was James. He was tall, handsome and the same age as me. He lost his wife suddenly and was looking for someone to fall in love with and eventually get married again. He lived in Pembroke Pines and had children that were involved in sports; he sounded like a real family man.

The second man was Alan. He also had lost his wife and had twin daughters getting ready to go off to college. Alan was an accountant and lived in Boca Raton. I wrote back to both of them to see who a better fit for me would be and who would be the one I had chemistry with and felt a spark.

Alan was the first one to ask me out. We were going to meet at an Italian restaurant across the street from where I worked. When I arrived at the restaurant, Alan was exactly on time and looked like his picture. We had a very nice lunch and he told me all about his daughters and the loss of his wife two years ago. He told me, "It has been hard finding someone again." I was thinking to myself, "You got that right."

It's hard to find anyone that was real and wanted the same things you do. Alan seemed real, sincere, and different than other men I had dated. Maybe there was something to this widower thing and I was just finding out. After lunch, Alan walked me to my car and we made plans to go to dinner the following Friday night, since he would be away on business this week. He told me he would confirm this with me the next week before we when out and he couldn't wait to see me again. He said it was going to be a very long weekend without seeing me.

When I got home that night there was an email from James. I decided to cut to the chase and ask him if we could talk on the phone instead of sending emails. James responded to me, telling me that he was so busy running his party rental business and helping out with his son's baseball league a few evenings a week that he does not have too much time for too much else, but would like to speak to me over the phone. He gave me his phone number and asked me to please call him tonight after 9:00pm. I decided to wait for 9:30pm to call so I wouldn't appear desperate and obsessive, which of course I was. When I called him, we chatted for about twenty minutes or so. He seemed very nice, intelligent and very easy to speak with. We made plans to meet the following night in front of the bookstore near my home. This was good! I had two men at the same time that appeared to be sweet and very responsive to me. This doubled my odds in this dating game, and we all know at this point, I needed those odds in my favor.

The following night I met James. He was actually better looking in person than he was in pictures; much better looking! He was also very nice and extremely bubbly. He had five children which were more than I could imagine, but he told me two of them were grown up and on their own, while the other three were just becoming teenagers. He was a lot of fun to be with and he seemed really into me.

We walked up and down the street on University Drive in Coral Springs. It was a beautiful night with the stars shining brightly in the moonlight. He asked me if I wanted anything to eat or drink, but I was content to just walk and talk with him. I told him all about my horrid adventures with the men I met on my dating journey. This was James first encounter from a dating site, and he seemed happy, so he probably thought I was crazy, but I shared with him my experiences, good or bad anyway. It was also important to me to know that he was someone I could talk to about anything that was on my mind or meant a lot to me. I was tired of walking on eggshells with these men I was meeting so it needed to be different going forward.

    Even though I had become a desperate woman looking for love, I still wanted a best friend, someone who would listen to everything I had to say and not just a fair-weather friend who only wanted to hear things that made him feel good. Even though it was our first meet, James appeared to be that man I could talk to about anything and everything with and I savored that during this time together. We had a great evening together talking and laughing and as it was getting very late, he walked me to my car, kissed me goodnight and asked me out to dinner for Saturday night. I drove home thinking about the night and thinking about how this new dating site I was trying, A Bucket of Fish, was so far a charm. Between James and Alan, I felt like I was in the driver's seat for a change.

    When Saturday night came, I had James pick me up at my apartment. He was punctual, gracious and very charming, and looked extremely happy to see me. He took me out to a beautiful restaurant and insisted I get whatever I wanted, including dessert and we sat in the restaurant talking for over two hours until we got the look from the staff that since we were done eating, they needed the table for other guests.

James and I really seemed to click. We didn't want the night to end so we drove to my favorite coffee shop and sat outside and talked until 1:00am in the morning. We had so much to say to each other. We could have talked all night long if we let ourselves. James drove me home, walked me upstairs, and kissed me gently goodnight. Everything was so perfect. I really had that feeling in my gut that James could be someone special. He asked me if he could see me during this upcoming week, and I told him, that would be great.

The following Friday I met Alan for dinner at a seafood restaurant just as he planned. He handed me a box with a corsage in it. What a strange gift! Was he re-gifting this or was he really behind the times, and I mean way behind. I hadn't seen these types of corsages since junior high. I told him thank you and it's beautiful, but I did not put it on. The corsage just made this evening feel like a bad prom date. I would have been too embarrassed wearing it.

We had a nice dinner and afterwards he walked me to my car and kissed me goodnight. His kiss was missing the *Va-Va-Voom* I was searching for. Alan was a very nice guy, but I really did not feel anything with him. "There was no spark!" And you need a spark, at least in the beginning. I wasn't ready to end the relationship yet because I was still searching it out and getting to know Alan but had a feeling the spark would not show up. I told him I would see him in a few days and drove home.

This routine with of dating both Alan and James went on for another week until it was time for my cruise. I went out with James the night before my cruise. It was a Halloween cruise, and I was over the top, excited to be going and be part of a large group who all, both men and women were looking for a mate. James and I had a great dinner and afterwards went back to my apartment where we talked, cuddled and kissed. He was a great kisser and there was a spark, but for right now, my mind was centered on this upcoming cruise.

James might have been anxious or jealous of me going on a single cruise, but he never showed it or let it affect our night together. He wished me well and also told me, he would not stand in the way of me having a wonderful time and a great vacation. James was a real gem. He was amazing and knew how to say all the right things, the right way, at the right time. I really liked him, but I vowed to myself, I was going to take it slow with him and not let my heart drive in too quickly like I had done with other men before. I was looking for real love, not the crazy, mindless, one way only love which broke my heart over and over again in my past relationships. I had a habit of falling, hook, line and sinker all by myself, and then having to pick up the pieces when they did not feel the same. I told James I would call him as soon as I docked on Monday to let him know I got home alright.

After James left my apartment that night, I called Alan to let him know I was leaving tomorrow and would call him when I returned. He also appeared very cool with me going on this singles cruise for the weekend, which also made me think; maybe he could wasn't that into me as I assumed. *Who knows?* I was so excited about the next day and also getting away to sea and hopefully meeting a lot of special people, both men and some special ladies who would become my friends. I also decided that if I did not meet anyone special on this cruise, I would then have to make a decision on who I wanted to continue building a relationship with, James or Alan. I couldn't continue to date them both but decided to let it go and not think about until I was back home. I just wanted to focus on my upcoming adventure. There were seventy people signed up and forty of them were men which put the odds in my favor. I made sure I had everything I needed, finished packing and picked out my outfit for tomorrow. I was rearing to go and ready for a weekend at sea.

Chapter 28 - A Weekend at Sea

I woke up the next day to a beautiful morning and so much hope in my heart. I got dressed and made sure to look great. I packed very carefully the night before, making sure I had the perfect clothes for this trip. This was my last hoo-rah and I was determined to meet my soul mate even if it killed me. I was very fond of Alan and James but did not know if either man was *the one* at this point and the obsessive, compulsive voice in my head was telling me to keep looking until I know for sure.

I got in my car and drove to Barbara's house where the group of us women were picking up the bus we rented there. I knocked on the door and Barbara answered. I introduced myself to her and she told me to come in with the strangest look on her face. When I walked into the living room, the other women were already there. If looks could kill, I would be lying on the floor dead at this moment. They seemed annoyed by my presence, and it was until I overheard one woman making a very loud comment to another, did I understand why I was getting ready to be stoned. One woman said to the other, "Well, look at her! She is going to take all our men." These women appeared to be about ten years older or more and they were all dressed like my great grandmother. Even the women who were slim were dressed like the little old lady who was living in her shoe. One of the women was even wearing a moo-moo. I guess she never received the memo that we don't wear those anymore in this time and era.

Most men, even older ones are generally turned off by that kind of dress ware. I walked in with my well fitted designer jeans, a frilly blouse and a pair of new, sexy, ankle strap sandals, in the color red, no less, that I bought for this trip, so these women must have thought that I was their Harlot ruination for this cruise. I tried to be sweet and cordial to all of them, but I was not going to win any popularity contests with any of them. I grabbed my bags and got on the bus with everyone and of course sat by myself. I decided not to let it bother me. Their insecurity was their problem, not mine and besides, I honestly was here for the men, not these older, bitter women who wouldn't give me a chance and get to know me. I felt confident that when I got onto the ship, there would also be other women my age who dressed like me and enjoyed shopping. They would be the ones who welcomed me and greeted me with open arms.

We made it to the port, got off the bus and went through the onboarding process. Everything went smoothly and then of course, by myself, I set out to take a look at my cabin, I was really hoping the woman that I would be sharing my cabin with would be nice and happy to spend the next three days sharing a space with me. Maybe we would have a lot more in common than the women I rode the bus with. I was excited to meet her and find out.

I waited an hour for my roommate to show up, but then decided maybe she was upstairs mingling with the others, so I left my cabin and went upstairs to meet the group and see the group of people I was tied to the hip to for the next three days. The group of women I came with was together at the amazing buffet having lunch and sitting with others from our group I had not met yet. There were six more women who looked just like them, also dressed like they walked out of a 50's daytime sitcom, and three men who looked worse than the women. What was going on here? The age group on the cruise notice flyer said the age group for this trip was forty-five to sixty-five, but so far everyone was in the sixty-five plus group, except me, no wonder I stuck out like a sore thumb.

As of this morning, there were one hundred people signed up in this group. Maybe the younger ones were off somewhere else on the ship having a good time. I went and got lunch and sat with a smaller group of people on this cruise with us. The men started small talk with me, while the women continued to eyeball me like a plague.

We all received a memo that the entire group would be meeting in one of the large conference rooms after the ship's safety rules, drills and the bon voyage of our ship out to sea. I couldn't wait. I would get to meet everyone, including the younger folks and finally my roommate. I ate a quick lunch because I have never been one to gorge at a buffet, no matter how grand it was, and I just wanted to see if my roommate was there or if at least her bags were.

When I got back to my room, there was no sign of anyone else so far showing up. We had not shipped off yet, so maybe she would be arriving late. I decided before I had to go back up to meet everyone in the conference room to unpack and get settled in. Since I there was no trace as of yet of my roommate, I decided to take the bed by the window and took the dresser space closet to me. I did leave her equal drawer space and one half of the closet. I was just about done when I heard the signal to come up on the check for our set sail procedures. At this point I had gotten separated from the group I was part of, so I just stayed with the regular passengers until this part of our day was completed, and then I would be able to reunite with my group in the conference room. I felt excited to meet everyone and I knew just sharing a room with someone gives you an automatic friendship that I was thirsting for.

After we finally set sail, I went to the meeting room and as I walked in, there was a woman standing at the doorway holding a clipboard. I had to sign my name to some papers and initial everywhere next to my name. She then gave me a red bracelet to wear at all times, so we would always know who belongs to this group through the remainder of the cruise. After I was signed in, I walked into the attached lounge and for the moment, I thought I made a wrong turn and entered a nursing home. I looked around. Everyone was looking at me as I entered, like I did not belong here. I would've felt like Cinderella, but the only prince in this room was in the over seventy group and they were incapable of bending down and picking up my glass slipper, if it was to fall off. I thought to myself, "Maybe this was the wrong group," but then I saw the grumpy faces of the women I rode in with and knew there was no possibility I took a wrong turn on the way to this room.

I seemed to be the golden goose in this group because all the men were coming over to me to introduce themselves to me. They were very nice, but this is not what I signed up for, nor the age group on this cruise. I thought about asking the head and coordinator of this group for my money back, but then had visions of them throwing me overboard, suitcases and all so I said nothing. Maybe I signed up for the wrong group because there was absolutely nobody in this room that was under sixty-five. Some of the people even had walkers and canes. I felt like I joined the geriatric cruising club and was stuck in it for three days with no escape hatch.

    I went over to our group director and asked her who my cabinmate was. He told me the woman I was supposed to share my cabin with decided at the last minute not to come and there was no one else to put in there so I would have it to myself this weekend. I thought to myself, "Did one of the women I shared the bus with, call her and tell her about me?" I decided not to get upset. Maybe it was for the best. Sharing a cabin in such close quarters with a stranger who resents you would be like being locked up in jail with a cellmate with no chance for a pardon.

    The director gave us an agenda for the weekend with all our special group activities and excursions listed on it. The Halloween party was tonight and I wondered if the men would look more appealing with masks on? I had bought a very cute, alluring witch costume for the party, and now had second thoughts about wearing it. I was sure this costume was going to be a big hit with the women in this group, to say the least. We were meeting back in the meeting room for the Halloween cocktail party at 6:00pm. There would be hors d'oeuvres and a buffet dinner so we would not be eating in the dining hall with the regular passenger aboard.

I was leaving the conference room when one of the older gents cornered me and asked me if he could be my date for the evening. His name was Leonard and while he was slightly distinguished looking, he had to be at least seventy-two. I thanked him for asking me, but told him I was flying solo that night, little did he know, I had to keep what little options I had open this weekend. He put his hand on my shoulder and asked me to reconsider. I pushed his hand away and told him, I will see him later at the party. I took off on my own down the hallway like a freight train and knew if he tried to follow me, he would never catch up. The last thing I needed was for Leonard to know where my cabin was.

I got back to my cabin and only had about forty minutes to get my costume on. I freshened up my make-up and re-did my hair for the costume. I had no idea why I was even making a fuss, since I would be wearing a mask and looking at the age of the general population of the men in our group, I would look young and refreshed next to them no matter what I did or didn't do. My costume was very cutesy and very short. It came with fish net stockings and gloves, a very adorable mask, and I had chosen very high, black stiletto heels that went perfectly with it. I also was carrying a broom to compliment the costume which could double as a weapon if any of the older gents did not behave. I was hoping with the very large mask that covered most of the top of my face, the women would not recognize me and let me hang out with them, otherwise it was going to be a long, lonely night which up to now in my life, I was no stranger to.

I walked into the meeting room and this conference room looked amazing. It had been transformed into a haunted mansion with all the bells and whistles. They had dimmed lights that had that purple and orange glow to it which made it a little hard to truly see each other very clearly. For me that was a plus since between the costumes, masks, Halloween paraphernalia everywhere and the dim, dark type lighting, I was hoping no one would be able to find me out or pay much attention to me.

Some of the people came out in some amazing costumes. I underestimated them. I walked through the dark glowing room and worked my way over to the buffet. I felt eyes on me. The men glared at me like a swarm of bats waiting to attack their prey. I took my delicious food and sat down to eat. It was not too soon before; the herd of older men were all gathering around me. The women did not smile or come over to say hello. It was at this moment that I started re-thinking my Halloween costume, which of course was too late to do anything about it. I wanted to borrow one of the women's moo moos and pair it with a straw hat, and some falling down hosiery just to be liked and to fit in.

Leonard came over and sat down without asking and put his arm around me. I started eyeballing my broom in case I needed it. I pushed his arm away. He was dressed like Dracula and looked like the real deal. He looked better with all the theatrical make-up then without it. He once again put his hand on my shoulder and whispered in my ear, "I want to suck your blood."

I now had my hand on my broom. I asked Leonard, "What is up with the hands on me?" I continued to tell him that "The only blood you are going to suck is your own after I take this broom and break your nose with it." He only laughed at me and continued to put his hands on me. I wondered what gave these older men the right to think they could just touch a woman whenever they wanted without her permission. I guess chivalry went out with their youth because some of them were far from gentleman.

There were a lot of activities going on including a costume contest. I just sat and watched everything since none of the women included me in their group and the men were getting on my nerves. Another man named Marvin kept coming over to me and sitting down next to me without any acknowledgement of approval. Marvin would just talk to me, even though I was not listening and at the same time, place his hand either on my leg or arm. This was also making it look bad for me as the women eyeballed the men interacting with me in this impolite way, not fully knowing how annoyed and disrespected I felt. The women were probably thinking I was enjoying it, but I was not in the least. I wish I could have shared with these women the perils of being touched by such childish behavior, but they would never believe anything I had to say.

I was contemplating going back to my lonely, cabin because I was having a very bad time. The women were looking at me in my cutesy costume like I was a dime store floozy, and all the old geezers surrounding me were making me feel like one. Marvin was following me around all night like a puppy asking me over and over again what I thought of his costume. He was dressed like a baby wearing a big diaper, a baby bonnet that he put together and carrying a baby bottle which I was hoping he would just keep in his mouth. It was creative, but honestly, he looked like an overgrown idiot. I just couldn't lose this man, and I was embarrassed by his costume and his behavior.

This singles cruise group made internet dating seem like a dream. Only I could go from bad to worse in such a short time. I decide to leave this party and venture out onto the ship by myself. It was Halloween so everything was themed oriented and everyone in costumes scurrying around and having a good time. I walked around looking for all the dance clubs on board. I certainly was dressed for it tonight. As I wandered through the ship to find the dancing, I kept looking back to make sure Mutt and Jeff had not followed me out of the party.

I loved the decorations all over the ship. They had taken Halloween to a whole new level. It was like walking through a haunted mansion from a Hollywood movie. As I went up a level and found one of the nightclubs, I was drawn in by the sound of the Monster Mash song that was playing loudly while everyone was dancing and acting like monsters stomping on the ground. Everyone here had a costume, so I just fit it perfectly.

In this club, where no one knew me, I could be anyone I wanted to be without ridicule or nasty looks. I took a seat at one of the nightclub tables and was just enjoying watching all the fun and listening to all the oldie type Halloween music. Out of nowhere a man dressed like a pirate came up to me and asked me if I would like to dance. His name was Mike, and he was fifty-one. I was overjoyed to finally meet someone close to my age range. He might have not been part of my group, but here was here on the ship with some friends and I loved dancing. While we were dancing, he told me he was an investment banker, divorced with two grown daughters and he loved cruising. We must have stayed on the dance floor for almost two hours.

The music was fun, motivating and a blast from the past, and we knew it all. Afterwards we sat down, got a drink and talked about everything. It started getting very late and the music had died down. It actually looked like they were getting ready to clean this nightclub from the big spooky night it just had. I was starting to get tired myself.

Mike offered to walk me to my cabin. He was 6'1" and very good looking even with all the pirate gear and make-up on. When we got to my cabin, he kissed me at my door and asked me if my roommate was sleeping? I made the big mistake of telling him that I was not sharing a cabin with anyone. He wanted to come in and just cuddle with me all night but told him I was exhausted, and it is not a good night for that. Mike seemed like the kind of guy that gets what he wants, so he actually began pushing his way into my room without my permission. He then had the audacity to ask me if he could sleep in my extra bed because his roommate snores. I told Mike, it was out of the question, and I really need to go. He then grabbed me to try to kiss me again, and this time I picked up my broom and threatened to hit him with it. *I knew that broom would somehow come in handy tonight.*

He tried to grab the broom from me, while he laughed at me, and told him for the last time as I held the broom above his head, "Walk away and forget what cabin I am staying in, or I will call security and you will be removed from the ship, hopefully thrown over." He walked away while cursing at me under his breath, with words that as a lady, I would not repeat. I ran into my room, locked it with both security locks, took off my five pounds of Halloween make-up, got undressed and laid down on my bed staring up at the ceiling in pure limbo.

I truly believed after this night, that there were no decent men left in the world. I pondered this notion, I wondered why? What entitled men these days to think that they could just you inappropriately or have sex with you just because they danced with you or knew you more than an hour? Everything on this ship was free, even the drink, so it was not like I owed anyone anything. He was just another jerk I could add to my list. I seem to attract them like magnets. I got into bed and eventually went to sleep. Two more days and counting down, until I could jump ship safely and go home.

The next morning, I got up, did my three-mile run on the upper deck which was beautiful in the morning and then met my cruise group in the dining room for breakfast. Of course, once I sat down, Marvin and Leonard were the first to pounce down on the seats on each side of me. Leonard was wearing white socks with sandals…I am not even going to say, how I feel about that; he just looked ridiculous. And Marvin was wearing pants that were all the way up to his chest. Didn't

Marvin get the memo that pants couldn't be used as a shirt? The baby costume from last night was an improvement from this.

These men were the typical stereotyped old guys, but didn't they see it? Do they look in the mirror? Do they own mirrors? If they were young, good-looking men and they dressed like this, I would still run. The director was handing out the excursion agenda. I waited until all the men picked their excursion for the day and then chose another one. I chose the party boat excursion. It was a boat with a Reggae band, dancing and unlimited Mai-Tai drinks. There would be a stop-over at a secluded beach in the Bahamas. It sounded fun and easy, and I would dance, drink and party until I forgot where I was and the group I signed up with for the weekend.

We were leaving for our excursions at 1:00pm, right after lunch, so I ate something at the buffet quickly, and packed a small bag with beach stuff, suntan lotion, and a change of clothing. I jotted quickly to the boat ramp before Mutt and Jeff spotted me. I didn't tell Leonard and Marvin which excursion I was taking, even though they had been asking me since last night. They were doing the sightseeing tour of the island we were docked at, and I planned on keeping it that way.

When I hopped on the boat, there were a lot of people there already. Our group director was standing there talking to some good looking man, who looked about my age. I put my bag down, grabbed a Mai-Tai, and listened to the music playing while I waited for our boat to leave the port, we were docked in. I just wanted to go already so those who I did not want to come on this excursion would have no chance of going.

They did an attendance check to match those on the boat with those who signed up and when it was completed and all was good, a loud horn was blown, and we started to go. It was a nice size boat with an upper deck that had more seating. I assessed everyone onboard, and it was a younger crowd mixed also with many my age. I felt relieved that the older men who had been bothering me non-stop were not aboard, and Mike from last night was not part of this excursion either. I took a deep breath, able to really relax and breathe in the beautiful aroma of the ocean air. Life was good for the moment.

A nice looking woman about my age sat down next to me and we talked for a while. It was nice and she personable and happy to chat with me, while we were both enjoying the sun and the great music and the free drinks. While getting off the ship, my director's friend that he had come on with, helped me climb down. He smiled at me, and I decided I would try to find out a little bit more about him. He was the only good looking, charming man I had seen so far on this excursion, and I was not going to let him get away so fast. My obsessive, compulsive ego was in conquering mode today, so I would try to stimulate his attention even if it killed me.

The island had a small pool club located directly over the ocean. It was beautiful! I followed all the other women that came off the boat and we all went as a group to find lounge chairs by the pool. I sat next to the woman I was talking with on the boat. Her name was

Janet. We sat with all the other women and just enjoyed the timeless day while listening to the ocean wave's break and the seagulls flying above us, flapping their wings and sounding their wails in the baby blue cloudless sky. We were all laying on the beautiful, floral, tropical lounge chairs taking in all the wonderful sights and deep breezing blowing over us.

We had two hours on this island before the horn would sound alerting us to get back onto our boat for a return to the cruise ship. After the two hours were up, and I came back to life from my relaxing coma, I started feeling a little itchy. I felt like I was bit and I jumped into thin air off my chair. I wiped off my hands and feet and ran to the pool to wash off whatever decided to have me for a meal. The other ladies had the same reaction at the same time and were all running into the pool thinking if this was in our minds because none of saw anything or could connect the itching to any visual bites on our body.

At once, the horn sounded, and we all packed our gear and retreated quickly to the boat for roll call. When we got on, the Reggae music was loud and had seemed to take on a new life of its own. The boat pulled away from shore and everyone was in line for their Mai Tai drinks and dancing to the party beat had begun. As the boat was moving up and down through the steady waves of the ocean, everyone was really rocking it out, including myself. I was having a blast.

The director announced that they were going to be having a dance contest in a few minutes and before I could think about anything, I was grabbed and pulled in for what appeared to be the start of a conga line. This line made it all around the boat, and we were on a nice sized boat. Everyone was laughing and having a blast. Some appeared to have had too many drinks already, but what happens at sea, stays at sea.

After the conga line dispersed, they announced again the dance contest. We had to find a partner and you would receive a number. I saw the good looking man standing alone and drinking a Mai-tai. This was my chance. *Should I ask him to dance, or not*, I thought to myself I shyly went over to him and just stood staring at him. He smiled and said, "Hi." I timidly asked him if he would be my dance partner for the contest, and he gracefully accepted. We introduced ourselves to each other. His name was Marc, and he was here on the cruise helping out the director of my group. I hadn't noticed him last nice because he was all over the ship getting things copied and together for our director, and a full costume on, so I couldn't see his face. When I told him my name, he seemed surprised that I was in this group. He said I seemed too young to be in it.

No kidding, I thought to myself.

We both grabbed our numbers and another Mai-Tai, thinking another drink might help us dance better. Everyone participating got on the floor and the band played different types of music. We had to change the way we danced to be compatible with each different song and rhythm played. Marc was a really good dancer, and I was having a blast following all his moves, until we eventually got voted off.

We wound up talking for the next fifteen minutes and he gave me a hug to thank me for the dance. He was so nice and so much fun to be with. For the next dance activity, they took out a large bamboo stick and started to play limbo rock music. I used to be great as this, so I participated. I threw off my flip flops and three Mai-Tai's later, I was going underneath the limbo stick. Marc started out with me, but he was 6'3" and by the time the limbo stick was down really low, he just couldn't get down under it without touching it, so he was eliminated. When the stick was less than three feet from the ground, there were only three of us left. Everyone was cheering us on and whistling. People were shaking their toy maracas that had been given out earlier. What an explosion and celebration we were all having.

I wanted so badly to win, but I was competing with two other girls that looked half my age. The stick was just about as low as it could go before you couldn't do it anymore. The first girl went slowly, and I mean slowly. She was almost through it when her legs gave out and she fell. I was next. I tried to concentrate willing my back and legs to stay strong. I went slowly and I mean really slowly, but my legs started to shake a bit. Everyone was screaming and cheering me on. It was hard to keep your mind on what you were doing with all the noise. I was almost through it when suddenly, I started to lose my balance, and just when I thought it was over, I caught myself and made it through.

The last girl went and with her amazing twenty-year-old, double jointed body, she went under it in a minute. They made it a pinch lower and it was so hard this time, especially with my legs shaking severely. I was much older than the other girl, so my limbo days were numbered anyway. This could be my last hoo-rah. I tried so hard to get under it, and when just about through it, my legs collapsed. Of course, the other girl made it through with no effort and won a gift card. I received a consolation prize of an oversized party boat t-shirt.

Marc came over to me and hugged me. We laughed. He was very impressed with my dancing and limbo abilities. As the boat docked where our cruise ship was, Marc walked off the boat with me and asked me if I wanted to join him that evening for the Captain's cocktail hour and dinner? I said, "Absolutely!" We agreed to meet in front of the main ballroom at 7:00pm.

I spent the next two hours getting ready so I could dazzle Marc. He had only seen me in a pair of shorts, an old shirt, without make-up and my hair up. I wanted to look great, plus it was Captain's night so everyone dressed up. I did my hair and make-up and picked out one of my formal gowns that I was saving for a special occasion aboard ship. I took one last look in the mirror, felt satisfied and went off to meet Marc. I wondered how he would look with a suit on. Marc looked pretty good today all sandy and beach ridden.

I got down to the ballroom and there he was in a nice black suit and royal blue shirt. He looked amazing and I felt amazing being with him. We told each other how wonderful we both looked, and he held out his arm for me to take as we entered the exquisite ballroom together. We lined up to have our pictures taken with the Captain, and then went and got some of those amazing hors d'oeuvres and champagne they were passing around. Marc was quite the gentleman and treated me just like a lady.

When the band started playing and he asked me to dance, he held out his hand and led me onto the floor just like a man should. He knew all the classic and ballroom dances, so I just followed his every lead. I could feel all eyes on us as we were dancing. We surely did look together like queen and king at a prom. We danced until the Captain's cocktail hour was up, and he escorted me off the dance floor and into the dining hall for dinner. We sat with our cruise group, and he even pulled out my chair to seat me. I was in total awe, and it was the first time, none of the older gents came over and bothered me, including Leonard and Marvin who by the way were both wearing colored velvet suits. They looked like a circus act, but for tonight, I could care less because my eyes were on Marc.

Marc was a massage therapist and lived in Naples. When his buddy ran these group cruises, Marc would help him out because while he did not get paid for his time, he would get to enjoy a free cruise with all its amenities, so it was worth it. After dinner, Marc and I went to the show. I was so ecstatic to meet a nice man on board who wasn't old enough to be my great grandfather.

We both enjoyed the show and then wandered outside on the deck to enjoy some moonlight, stargazing and each other. The stars were shining so brightly as they glistened upon the sea. I asked Marc a lot of questions about his life in Naples and his massage career. Marc told me he was never married and had no children. He had lived for a while with a woman, but that relationship eventually ended. He went on to tell me that he lived in a room in a boarding type of house and could not afford much else. He told me that the massage industry does not pay well, unless you are an owner of a massage company or work for famous people, but he loves what he does, and money was not that important to him. He was very content with his life.

    I asked him if he ever gets out of Naples, not counting the cruises. Marc explained that he doesn't really go anywhere because he cannot afford to own a car and does not make enough for traveling expenses. *Wow*! I looked around thinking I must be on some type of reality show or maybe *Candid Camera* is back on the air because this stuff only happens to me. I finally meet a beautiful, charming man who is a complete gentleman and everything I am looking for and then KABOOM, the floor falls out from under me. It is always something, and I don't feel like I ask for too much!

    We strolled the deck some more and out of the blue, Marc, said, "You can come out to Naples and visit me. I have a pull-out couch in the room I rent that could sleep two." I thought to myself, "Like that is going to happen, and where will this relationship go?" I in no way wanted to hurt Marc or insult him, but it was a real turn off to know this man had so little in life or did not have the motivation to do more with it. I am not a fancy person, but there were times in my life, I worked two and three jobs to keep my car running and to support an apartment that at least allowed me a bed to sleep on. I also felt in this young stage of the relationship, we need to get to know one another, and I could not be the one traveling two hours back and forth every weekend, covering all my gas and paying for our dinners out just so we could court each other and see if something is worth moving forward with. Marc surely was not the one for me and I felt so bad for him and for me. He was the sweetest guy I met in a long time. It was just my luck!

I was in deep melancholy thought when Marc reached over in the moonlight and gently kissed me. I felt nothing with that kiss. The chemistry we shared earlier was gone, probably due to the fact that there was a lack of normality going on in Marc's life and it was too much for me to bear. It was late and Marc asked if he could walk me to my cabin? I nodded my head in approval.

We quietly walked to my cabin, and he kissed me goodnight at the door. He asked me if he could spend the day tomorrow with me? I told him, I was not sure and since it was a day at sea, I reminded him about all the activities planned with the group that I wanted to partake in. I just was no longer feeling it with Marc and did not want to lead him on and then he might think, I would be visiting him every weekend. I just thought it was for the best if I limited my time with him, while we were still on board the ship, so this way he might not have too many expectations when we got home Monday morning. He told me, "Okay," and then he gave me a hug. I yelled out as he was walking away, that we can hopefully catch up tomorrow. This was the weekend of me dodging bullets. Instead of trying to build relationships with them, I seemed to be put in a position to try to avoid them.

In fairytales, every time she finds her prince, he really turns out to be a prince, but in my life, every time I find one, he turns into a frog. I just can't seem to win no matter what I try. I went into my lonely cabin, got ready for bed and then stared out at the stars in the night looking down at me. I realized I had to stop forcing relationships to happen and to stop dreaming about the things in life I desired so much that may never be. I thought about God as I looked at the stars. Maybe I needed to have faith in God in order to find the right man. Maybe God was sending me messages that I refused so many times to see. I was probably blinded by my obsession to find and have what I wanted without thinking about anyone other than myself. Maybe God had not brought me the right guy because I never had time for God and had put other things like finding "the one" before him. I had made finding a husband and my soul mate a full time job and that had taken over everything in my life no matter what the cost. I continued to stare at the stars hoping and praying God was not too upset with me. I yawned, rolled over and fell fast asleep. It had been a very long day.

I was awakened early in the morning by a beautiful sunrise glaring into my window. Still feeling depressed, I got up, got dressed, grabbed my music and made my way to the upmost deck where all the exercisers walked and ran. It was the most amazing sight to be on the highest deck of the ship walking or running while the sun was coming up upon the horizon and all you can see on all sides was the magnificent ocean. After I was done walking, I dodged the dining room in lieu of the buffet in another area of the ship. I did really like eating at the buffet, but I didn't want to see Marc, and have to hang with Leonard and Marvin. I was in a just want to be left alone mode and a buffet to pig out on was the answer.

I was still itchy from whatever I couldn't see that bit me or I was allergic to yesterday. I ignored the itchiness and grabbed a big plate of food at the buffet and went back to my room to eat without anyone annoying me. I spent the next part of my day perched in my window seat looking out at the vast ocean as I listened to the music on my iPod. I actually felt settled and content. I loved the massive ocean I was engulfed in, and it brought me peace and tranquility for the day. The buffet ran most of the day so whenever I felt hungry, I would sneak quietly out of my room, quickly grab some food from the buffet and go back to my seat in the window. I was like a bird perched on a tree branch only popping off to snatch a worm. In my alone and strange weekend, I was actually enjoying my day at sea with just me. *Now that was different.*

When it was almost time for dinner, I felt compelled to join the group I signed up with for dinner. I got showered, put on make-up and did my hair and put on a simple, but dainty sundress with some casual strappy sandals. I entered the dining room where I spotted Marc sitting with the director and some of the other people he came with. He waved at me and I waved back at him. I think he got the hint that he and I were not going to work out because he did not save a seat for me next to him at his table. Marc was a very nice man, just not the man for me.

I sat down at the table with the group of women, I rode the bus with, and they were actually cordial to me. I guess they figured out that I was not around much and did not take any of the men in the group from them, so I was no longer a threat to anyone. I didn't see any of them with any of the men in the group either, so it probably was slim pickings for all of us. We were all meeting in one of the conference rooms after dinner to wrap up our weekend and say goodbye.

As soon as I walked into the conference room, I got charged by Leonard and Marvin. These two just did not get the hint. They probably did not even know what a hint was. They actually handed me their business cards so that I could give them a call sometime in the future. If I didn't want to hang with them on the ship, what would ever make them think I would go out with them when we got home? These two were beyond clueless, and I turned down their business cards, but did thank them in a cordial way. I also told them I felt they were a bit too old for me. They both just rationalized that they were young for their age. Leonard told me he was a young 74. I always wondered why people use that phrase. Your age involves so much more than what you can do or can't do. I just do not like that line and they were not going to win any brownie points with me using it. I told them both that I had someone special I was seeing at home and excused myself to find a seat at another table.

After the goodbye meeting, I went to the nightly show by myself and then wandered into a comedy club to see if it was funny. I kept myself busy just to make time fly. I wanted the night to end. This cruise did not turn out to be what I expected. Finally, around midnight, after they brought out the buffet, I started to finally feel tired. I went back to my cabin, got ready for bed, pulled out what I needed for the next day and then packed and left my suitcase outside my door like you're supposed to.

This disappointing weekend was finally over. The bug bites that I got at the island were getting worse, not better. You were no able to see the bright red dots all over my feet and legs. They were driving me crazy. I had been putting Benadryl on, but it was not helping. The other ladies I sat with had the same thing, so it probably was some sort of bug that lived on that little island we went to. I applied more of the Benadryl, slipped under the covers and looked forward to going home.

When I awoke the next morning, the first thing I did was look out the window. We were home! Like the movie said, "There is no place like home." The engines had seized, and we were docked at the port in Fort Lauderdale. The first thing I did was turn on my phone. There was a text message from James. It said, *"Welcome home and I really missed you. If you need a ride home from the port, I cleared my schedule for you for the entire day. I can pick you up anytime you need me to. Let me know."* I read the message and it sounded like heaven. I quickly called him, and he answered. I told him how wonderful it was to wake up to his message, and "while I do have a ride home, I would love to spend the rest of the day with you". We agreed to meet at my apartment at 1:00pm. I hung up with James and for the first time since this cruise began, I felt happy and content.

Chapter 29 - My Happy Ending

I drove home from the port with the women, and they were semi-cordial to me. I think they knew for sure by now that I was not out to get their men, and let the truth be told, there were no quality men worth getting. When I arrived back at Barbara's house, everyone was saying their goodbyes and exchanging numbers. I was a little shocked when some of the women asked for my phone number. I gave it to them, but I didn't see a big future in going out anywhere with them. I quickly grabbed my bags and hopped into my car so that I could go home and freshen up for my day with James. I felt so grateful to have him this interested in me, even after I was gone for a few days, no less on a single's cruise.

When I got home, I quickly got showered, dressed and sure enough, there he was at my door at exactly 1:00pm. He gave me a big hug and a long kiss. I really liked being with James. It made me feel like I was home with him all the time. He took me out for a beautiful lunch and then we went to get a cup of coffee and sat there talking for over three hours. I told him all about the cruise and the men. He listened to my every word with great interest and understanding like I was everything to him. As I spoke, he watched me with great admiration and held me in such high esteem. I had never had any man show that kind of care and approval for me.

We had a perfect day and then he took me out to dinner at night. We ate at a sidewalk café and talked again for hours. I really loved being with him, but I refused to get my heart broken again, so I did everything I could to control my heart and my feelings, until I had proof this time that he was a keeper. I showed James my legs bites and told him it was getting worse each day, so this caring man drove to a pharmacy and showed the bites to a pharmacist who asked me if I had an idea where I could have gotten bit? I told the pharmacist; I just came back from being in the Bahamas and the pharmacist knew immediately what it was. He told me it was a bug mite, called Chiggers. He gave me a special topical ointment for it, which James insisted on paying for, and once I put it on, I felt almost instant relief from that horrific itching. James was my hero.

James then drove me home, walked me upstairs and kissed me. I could have stayed in his arms all night. As he left, he told me, "We will go out again before the weekend comes, since it is only Monday and I cannot wait so long to see you." My cup overflowed at his statement. James left and it was a wonderful day, better than any of the time I had on the entire cruise. I just really enjoyed being with him. We clicked! I still wanted to take it slow with James and I mean very slow. My track record with men has been disastrous. A real train wreck most of the time, and I really needed to do everything I could to prevent another one.

James took me out to dinner on Wednesday. As always, we had a wonderful meal filled with an overflow of great conversation and a good time. We called it an early night because we both had to be up early in the morning, but when he hugged me goodbye, he didn't want to let me go. It felt great! On Thursday, I received a call from Alan. He wanted to take me out for dinner on Friday night. I decided to go even though my heart was with James, because things were moving a long so quickly with James that I feared the ceiling would drop down on me, as it always has in the past. My thought process or my fear factor was keeping Alan in the loop in case James did not want to see me anymore.

Alan and I met at the same Japanese restaurant in Boca Raton that we met at the last time. He hugged me hello and handed me another strange gift. Last time he gave me a corsage to wear and today he gave me an old fashion trinket that looked very old and felt like it came out of someone's garage sale or something like that. I hope he wasn't expecting me to wear this gift either. I still did not know Alan very well, but I can tell you right off the bat that gift-giving wasn't his strength. We sat down and ordered, and I started telling him all about my cruise. Unlike James, he had no interest in anything I told him about it.

After dinner, he asked if I wanted to go down to the beach with him, but I was not feeling him and I missed James. I told Alan I was exhausted, and he walked me to my car. He went to give me a kiss goodbye and it was pure torture for me. He couldn't kiss and after James, Alan would never be able to measure up. I drove home knowing I would never see Alan again and the good news was it was my choice this time.

The following day was Saturday, and I was going out with James in the evening. I waited all day for him to finally get here. Finally, at 6:30pm the bell rang, and it was him. I ran into his arms like a foolish schoolgirl, but I couldn't resist. He reciprocated the feelings back, which for me was unfamiliar territory. *See this is how it feels to really care about someone and have them like you back*, I thought to myself. I cautiously looked up at the ceiling to see if it was shaking, but so far, so good.

We had a great evening. We went out to a Japanese Hibachi and when we were done, there was a ton of food left. I told James, "My younger son was working tonight, and I wish I could bring him over some of this food."

James said, "Let's go, I would love to meet him." James was such a gem.

We drove all the way up to Boca Raton just to bring him some dinner. When we got to his retail store where he was working, I hugged my son and introduced him to James. I could tell my son liked him and the feeling with James regarding him was mutual. I handed my son his twenty pounds of leftover food, and he was beyond excited to eat it on his break. My son spoke with James for a few more minutes and I could see an instant bond forming between them. We left the store shortly after, but I was pleased that they both had hit it off and that James was willing and excited to drive up this way to meet my son and to please me. No one had ever cared about pleasing me until now. Is it possible that James might be the right guy for me?

A week later, James and I went back to the same Japanese Hibachi. But this time it was meet all his children, including his older son's wife and my two sons. We thought the hibachi was a good place to break the ice with everyone. We had seven children between us. A lot more baggage than I had hoped for, but you can't put stipulations on love, which I felt could be growing between James and I.

Dinner was okay, but we were able to feel the slight confrontation from his children. They had lost their mom this year and they were still having a hard time coping with it. It was going to be a difficult task to win them over, but James and I made a pact to never let anyone, or anything come between us no matter how difficult it was.

Over the next couple of weeks our relationship grew stronger, and we were both falling in love with each other. I had actually found a nice guy. Isn't that something? We loved being together and never argued or fought over anything. We had a great relationship, but it was not without its trials and tribulations. Everyone in James family, including all his children, his mom and sister felt he was moving too fast, since his wife died less than a year ago. We had no support from his side, but James held strong to our pact, and expected me to do the same.

He had loved his wife and her unexpected death left him lonely, on his own and having to raise three children by himself. When he joined the dating site, it was just to get out of the house and maybe go out to dinner with this one and that one, but he found me, and love just happened. He wasn't going to walk away from our relationship because of a timeline of his wife's passing, but no one understood which caused much pressure, and push and pull in our relationship. Love is unpredictable and doesn't wait for the right time. You either have to accept it and grab onto it, or you lose it. James and I decided to hold on tight with both hands, and everyone else around us would have to accept it and be happy for us. We knew in time, it would all work out.

The holidays were quickly approaching, and I offered to make the entire Thanksgiving dinner for his kids and mine at his home. James and I shopped together for everything I would need and on Thanksgiving Day, I made a beautiful dinner with all the trimmings. James was so grateful that I was there to help him for his first holiday without his wife. His children had an attitude all day that I wasn't cooking things the way their mom did and one of his children wouldn't even try my turkey, but James assured me like he always does that his family would come around.

A week later when he came over for our usual Saturday date night, he handed me a gift. It was a set of new windshield wipers for my car tied with a red bow around it. I asked him, "What is this for?"

He told me "I noticed last week that your windshield wipers needed replacing, so I bought you new ones that I will put on for you when we get downstairs."

Wow! I was overwhelmed with such joy and love. No one had ever cared about something like that. That is true love. This was the best gift; I have ever gotten from a man. I actually had found someone who truly loved me, unconditionally, unequivocally, and completely. I wanted to sing, dance and send an email to the entire world. I stared back up at my ceiling. It appeared solid and I truly believed it would stay that way. James and I went downstairs, and he installed my new windshield wipers. I truly loved him.

As Christmas approached, James said he does Christmas big and would like me to give him a list of things I wanted for myself and my sons. I told him it wasn't necessary to spend so much money on us, but he insisted and wouldn't have it any other way. If I didn't give him a list, then he would just buy stuff and he rather buy gifts we would all really enjoy. I didn't really know what to ask him for, because he already gave me all I needed, but I gave him a list for my sons so they would have presents under the tree and I just felt James could figure out on his own gifts that I would love because they were from him.

On Christmas Eve, I drove to his house with my sons. James had set up the dining room table beautifully. Everything was in the true meaning of Christmas, and we were all so excited to have the delicious, traditional seafood night dinner. We sat down to a feast of unlimited crab, shrimp and lobster tails. *Yum*!

Afterwards we all talked a little and went into the living room to watch a movie. Everyone fell asleep everywhere and when we awoke in the morning, it was Christmas. We ate pancakes and opened presents around the tree. James over did it and everyone including my children, his and me received more than anyone needed. James was a real gem. I had bought James a lot of gifts also and he loved everything I got him. I also bought his kids gifts. There was so much, no one felt slighted. It was a terrific Christmas with everyone getting along and new hope for a great future.

On Valentine's Day, I wanted to do something special for James since he was so good to me, always so I set up my apartment like a little Italian restaurant and made him an amazing meal, hopefully one he would never forget. I set everything up on my patio with special candles burning and even creating a menu to highlight all his Italian dishes that he loved. I created the illusion and ambiance of a real Italian restaurant. I wanted so much to please him.

I served him an appetizer of shrimp cocktail which he loves, a pasta dish with homemade sauce, served with all his favorite seafood combos and even had a special dessert of cannoli and his favorite pot of coffee for after his meal. I wanted James to feel special and I believe I made that happen. James was so pleased and loved that I didn't make this holiday all about me. He loved these little things about me. James walked in holding beautiful long stem roses, a beautiful box of chocolate, and had a gift bag with a beautiful piece of Jewelry in it. We both felt so blessed on this day with each other.

We enjoyed the delicious dinner and dessert and then opened our gifts. I gave James a nice shirt and he loved it. James loved clothing and loved shopping, so we were a good fit. This was the first gift, let alone jewelry; I had received in a while. We took our coffee into the living room and talked, cuddled and kissed on the couch. The three things we enjoyed doing best. It was a perfect night and a perfect Valentine's Day.

The next few months quickly flew by. Things were moving along nicely between James and I. Even though his kids were not by biggest fans, I believe they were starting to get used to me being around. When my birthday came around in May, James planned a little surprise birthday party for me at one of my favorite restaurants in Boca Raton. He invited a few of my best friends, my younger son and his girlfriend and had the table decorated with balloons and other party paraphernalia. I was surprised when I walked in and overwhelmed with joy knowing in my heart that James was the real deal. I had to finally stop waiting for something bad to happen or for the ceiling to finally fall down on me and just enjoy and accept the fact that James loved me and would not hurt me. It was a great party and a great night, and I was happy.

Our first year together came and went so quickly. I was in a secure, committed relationship and I was finally beyond happy. We had a beautiful relationship with no fighting, and we had a lot of respect for each other. Every Sunday, if there were no family events, James and I would set out in the car and take a long road trip for the day. We covered different cities in different parts of Florida and experienced new restaurants, different beaches and coffee houses along the way. It was our special day together and I looked forward to it every week when possible.

On my following birthday when we were together almost two years, we made plans that night to have dinner and see a movie at our favorite premier dinner theater in Boca Raton. We loved this place because you would eat dinner, get your free popcorn and be escorted right into the balcony to sit in your own comfy style love seats.

We were seeing a real chick flick that was coming out this weekend. James would go to any movie I wanted and never complain about it. You know you have a real keeper when your partner will always sit through a chick flick or any romantic comedy, as long as he is with you. Since it was my birthday, James insisted on buying me a new dress and new shoes for our night out. James loved buying me clothes and enjoyed shopping with me and helping me pick nice outfits out.

We arrived early at the theater and went straight up to the restaurant. James looked amazing. He bought a brand new sports jacket with a beautiful shirt just for my birthday occasion. We both looked great and were so happy to be with each other. The host escorted us into our own room and when she opened the doors, I had friends and family that popped up and shouted "Surprise!" I couldn't believe it. Another year and another surprise party just for me. I had never in my life had anyone do for me what James does. There were balloons and decorations everywhere. I felt so special. There was a big chocolate birthday cake sitting on another table for me. I couldn't even imagine the time, work and money he put into this night to make it all happen. I was so beyond happy that I didn't know if I was going to cry, laugh or just jump out of my chair. I couldn't stop hugging and kissing James. He was the best!

We all had an amazing dinner and then they brought over this gorgeous cake, and everyone sang 'Happy Birthday' to me and then I got to open all the gifts that were brought for me. What a night! James gave me a beautiful necklace that had little pink pearls all over it. What a beautiful gift.

When I was done opening all the gifts and everyone was finishing up their cake, James turned toward me and got down on one knee. He held open a little black velvet box with a diamond ring in it. He asked me if I would marry him? I was stunned beyond belief. I would get to spend the rest of my life with this wonderful man. While everyone, including James was waiting for my answer, the tears were rolling down my cheeks from sheer happiness. Cinderella really found her prince this time. I told him, "Yes."

The ring was breath-taking. It was one carat with cornerstone diamonds on each side of it sitting on a very high white gold setting. I couldn't stop gazing at my hand. Even though the ring was beautiful, it was not the diamond that excited me. It was for me what the diamond represented. This ring was a symbol that I would never have to date again or go back on those internet dating sites. It was also a token of James love and devotion for me. My days of heartache, loneliness and despair were finally over. I found the one. I found my true heart's desire, my soul mate that would go through great lengths just for me so he could see me smile and be happy.

After I said yes, we all got up and headed for the theater. James had even paid for everyone with us to see the movie. It was a night of happiness and pure celebration. I couldn't stop looking at my hand and my man. I didn't want to ever wake up from this wonderful dream I was engaged to be married. *Finally*! All my dreams were coming true. James really loved me and wanted me forever.

I had found my happily ever after.

Epilogue

As of today, I am no longer in a relationship with James. There were many issues that arose in our years together with our children and between us that just couldn't be resolved. These issues left us unyoked and we grew apart. We remain good friends and talk on the phone each week; we even grab a meal together from time to time.

Along the way in my relationship with James, I found my one and true forever relationship, which is with Jesus Christ. I was stumbling and falling most of my life, always going in the wrong direction, because my eyes were continuously fixed on the wrong things. Even after meeting James and becoming engaged to be married to him, there still existed an emptiness, a longing and a deep void that could not be explained.

One night while James and I were at The Coffee Hut, just sitting enjoying our coffee and the beautiful night air, I got up to throw my cup in the trash. As I stood over the garbage can, taking my last sip, I spotted out of one eye, a dog sitting with a couple, also having coffee. The dog stared at me with the most unusual gaze and eyes I have ever seen. The dog's eyes locked mine, and as I threw my cup out, that gaze led right to their table. To this day, I cannot explain exactly how this happened, but I can tell you that God was in the midst of this, and He always has a plan.

The moment that the dog broke his gaze with me, I realized that I was standing by the couple's table looking at them. I told them, "I am not crazy, but your dog's eyes have somehow led me to your table, and I have no idea why." They had very kind faces and immediately introduced themselves to me. They told me their names were Dennis and Kate, and they were happy to meet me. They even asked me to take a seat. I told them my name was Sharon.

I sat down and just started talking, forgetting that I left James alone with his coffee at our table. James had gotten up to look for me when I did not return, and he found me sitting with this gracious couple who I introduced him to. James had happily joined me at their table, and we just talked. We were talking about many subjects, but at some point, in our conversation, I brought up the subject of God. I always knew God the Father but being raised in a Jewish family and living in a Jewish neighborhood, I never knew anything about Jesus, except that He always appeared hanging on a cross, whenever I saw Him. Dennis and Kate explained to me who Jesus was, what He did, and why He was on the cross. I sat and listened attentively wanting to know more.

The idea of dying and being able to go to heaven one day excited me and made me thirsty to find out everything I could about Jesus and this grand design they explained to me. We talked about God and the Bible, which I had many of, but never read any of them. We talked for hours and when we checked the time, it was close to 2:00 in the morning. We made plans to go to dinner the following week, which I couldn't wait for. Before we parted for the night, or morning for that matter, Dennis told me to read from the New Testament in the Bible, the Book of John. I left feeling exhilarated and different, like something big and out of the ordinary was coming my way. I couldn't wait for tomorrow to open my Bible. I had never had that longing before. It felt great!

The next day, I sat alone in my room and opened the Bible. I turned to the Book of John, just like Dennis told me to. I had received many Bibles throughout the years, so I chose one of the new ones that I never opened before. There on the first page of John was a yellow post-it. I found that strangely odd. I wondered if the person who gave me this Bible as a gift, intended for me to start with the Book of John as well.

I sat down and started to read. My excitement turned to burdensome as I struggled to comprehend what I was reading. I kept reading, but my ability to process everything in this book was wearing at me, however, I needed to get through it. I somehow felt Dennis had a message in this book; he needed me to find out about and I really wanted to please Dennis and Kate, so I was determined to read through it no matter how long it took. I needed to see if what they told me about heaven was real. I had a severe fear of death and dying and if the answers in this book could liberate me or release from me those fears, I would read and learn everything I could about Jesus and what He came and did for all of us on earth who believed and had faith in Him. I didn't know then, while reading that one of my favorite Bible verses would be: *2 Corinthians 5:7(KJV) "For we walk by faith, not by sight:"*

It took me an entire week to get through the twenty-one chapters of the Book of John, but I did it and gained a small understanding of it. When we met up with Dennis and Kate the next week, I had so many questions for them and was excited to get answers. I was on fire. With every question they answered, I had another one to ask. I couldn't stop. I was like a runner in a race trying to make it to the finish line. I just kept asking. I had a deep need to know everything about God the Father, His Son Jesus, and the Holy Spirit. It was all so amazing!

Over the next couple of months, they mentored James and I. They brought us to their church every Sunday, introduced us to other folks who followed Jesus and over the next few years, my entire life that I was meant to have and live unraveled and unfolded before my very eyes. I had found Jesus, or to say it correctly, Jesus found me! *Luke 19:10 (NIV) "For the Son of Man came to seek and to save the lost."* All the things in my entire life I thought mattered, did not anymore. Jesus filled in the missing gaps in my life. He sealed the voids with His love and gave me for the first time in my entire existence, hope and a brighter future. Jesus gave me the gift of salvation and eternity. *Jeremiah 29:11 (NIV) "For I know the plans I have for you, declares the Lord, plans to prosper you and not to harm you, plans to give you a hope and a future."*

I look back on my dating journey now with a different prospective. I was lost, lonely and vulnerable. I wanted to be rescued by a man so I could feel whole. God created mankind for His glory. We were created for relationship with God. *1 Corinthians 1:9 (NLT)*

"God will do this, for He is faithful to do what He says, and He has invited you into partnership with His Son, Jesus Christ our Lord." We were created to be with Jesus so the loneliness and emptiness I had felt all those years was for a relationship with my Creator. I just was so blinded by the world around me that I was not able to see God drawing me near and reaching His hand out to me. *Hebrews 4:16 (NKJV) "Let us therefore come boldly to the throne of grace, that we may obtain mercy and find grace to help in time of need."*

A relationship with God was the only relationship that could close my wounds and bind up the loose pieces of my heart. It is a wonderful thing to find a partner to share your life with, but a husband will not fully fill you like God does. Even if we never find that husband, wife, or friend we so long for here on earth, it is a gift from God that we can find and have the love and trust we need in our Lord and Savior Jesus Christ. Jesus will never leave me or forsake me. He loves me unconditionally and that love fills me up each day like no human being can. *Jeremiah 29:12-13 (NKJV) "Then you will call upon Me and go and pray to Me, and I will listen to you. And you will seek Me and find Me, when you search for Me with all your heart."*

I no longer am afraid of spending my life alone or not being able to sustain myself financially. I never again have to prove to anyone my value or worth. I belong to God. *Galatians 3:26 (NIV) "So in Christ Jesus you are all children of God through faith."* I now have a God who loves me just the way I am, unconditionally. I wake up each day knowing I belong to Jesus. He will never leave me and will always take care of me. I no longer am afraid of the world and its circumstances. **_Deuteronomy 31:6 (NIV) "Be strong and courageous. Do not be afraid or terrified because of them, for the Lord your God goes with you; He will never leave you nor forsake you."_**

When you feel lost, unwanted and cannot find your way, do not turn to anyone in this world, turn to Jesus, He is your only way. **_John 14:6 (NKJV) Jesus said to him, "I am the way, the truth, and the life. No one comes to the Father except through Me."_**

I am presently living on my own and dating no one. I feel content and joyful in a way I have always longed for, but before Jesus came into my life, I had no idea what joy was. These days I am richly blessed with the love of God always by my side directing my steps each day and shining His light on my path, even on days when I feel lost. I wish all those times when God was calling me near, I would have listened, but I am grateful that even when I ignored His calling, God never let go of my hand, even when I did not want to hold His. **_Psalm 119:105 (NKJV) "Your word is a lamp to my feet and a light to my path."_**

I am still open to meeting someone, but the difference is, I will wait for God this time to bring someone into my life. The person will be someone who God chooses for me. However, if God decides I should live out my life without a special someone, then I am content and know that God has equipped me to do just that each day. **_Philippians 4:12-13 (NIV) "I know what it is to be in need, and I know what it is to have plenty. I have learned the secret of being_** *content in any and every situation, whether well fed or hungry, whether living in plenty or in want. I can do all this through Him who gives me strength."*

I thank God every day for what he has done for me. When I think back on all those years of how warped my thoughts were. I was never able back then to see beyond what I thought I needed to be happy, but now I know the lessons God was teaching me so that when God came knocking again on my door, which He did, I would be more than ready and able to open the door and let Him in. I am so in love with the Lord, more so that I could ever be with anyone else here on earth, and if falling off a cliff over and over is what I needed to find my Lord and Savior Jesus, I would do it over and over again.

Reach out to Jesus and get to know Him. He gave up His life for you and that is proof of how much He loves you. He died on the cross for all our sins and three days later, as it is written in God's Word, Jesus was resurrected by the Father, and is now seated on the right-hand side of the throne of God. *John 3:16 (NIV) "For God so loved the world that He gave His one and only Son, that whoever believes in Him shall not perish, but have eternal life."* All you need to do is believe and have faith that Jesus died for you, and one day, you too will spend eternity with Him in heaven. All the other things of this world, you think you need to make you happy will eventually fade away. I can vouch for that. Just run into the arms of your Savior and salvation and heaven will be waiting for you for the rest of eternity. *Psalm 23:6 (NIV) "Surely your goodness and mercy will follow me all the days of my life and I will dwell in the house of the Lord forever."* If you trust and believe in Jesus's name, just hold on tight and watch your whole life change.

God bless you!

Author Bio

Sharon Dawn Feingold grew up in Howard Beach, New York which is located in the borough of Queens where she attended Queens College and received her BA in Sociology. Sharon was raised in a Jewish traditional home and transitioned to a Messianic relationship with Christ in 2013. Sharon is presently working for a non-profit organization as a manager leading a fundraising team that helps the poor in the Caribbean and Latin America. She has always enjoyed writing and working with children. She created and ran a children's entertainment storytelling business from 1997-2015.

Sharon lives alone in Florida and has two grown-up sons and one beautiful grandson who she continues to share her storytelling with and the love of God.

For any inquiries, please contact Sharon at sdfhelovesme@gmail.com

www.ingramcontent.com/pod-product-compliance
Lightning Source LLC
LaVergne TN
LVHW021758060526
838201LV00058B/3149